BISON
BOOKS

OUTDOOR LIVES

BENEATH BLOSSOM RAIN

DISCOVERING BHUTAN ON THE TOUGHEST TREK IN THE WORLD

Kevin Grange

UNIVERSITY OF NEBRASKA PRESS | LINCOLN AND LONDON

∞

Library of Congress
Cataloging-in-Publication Data
Grange, Kevin.
Beneath blossom rain: discovering
Bhutan on the toughest trek in the
world / Kevin Grange.
p. cm. — (Outdoor lives)
Includes bibliographical references.
ISBN 978-0-8032-3433-8
(pbk.: alk. paper)
1. Mountaineering — Bhutan.
2. Bhutan — Description and travel.
3. Grange, Kevin — Travel — Bhutan.
I. Title.
GV199.44.B48G73 2011
915.498 — dc22
2010028970

Set in Arno by Bob Reitz.
Designed by Nathan Putens.

DISCLAIMER This book describes my experiences while hiking and yes, sometimes crawling, the Snowman Trek in Bhutan and reflects my opinions and memories relating to those experiences. Some names and identifying details of people have been changed to protect their privacy, and since the book concerns the trek, I have condensed the pre- and post-trekking days in Bhutan.

For my parents,

Steve and Barb Grange,

who taught me to love the outdoors

Spring up from the risk of sinking and be heroic.
It's time to flee to the white snow peaks.
It's not just time, it's rather late.
MASTER NAMKHAI NYINGPO

"Walk on! Walk down the Path of Release!"
DRUKPA KUNLEY

CHINA-TIBET
GASA
PUNAKHA
JAKAR
PARO
THIMPHU
WANGDUE
TRONGSA
HA
BHUT
ZHEMGANG
CHUKHA
DAGA
DAMPHU
SAMTSE
PHUNTSHOLING
SARPANG
GELEPHU
INDIA

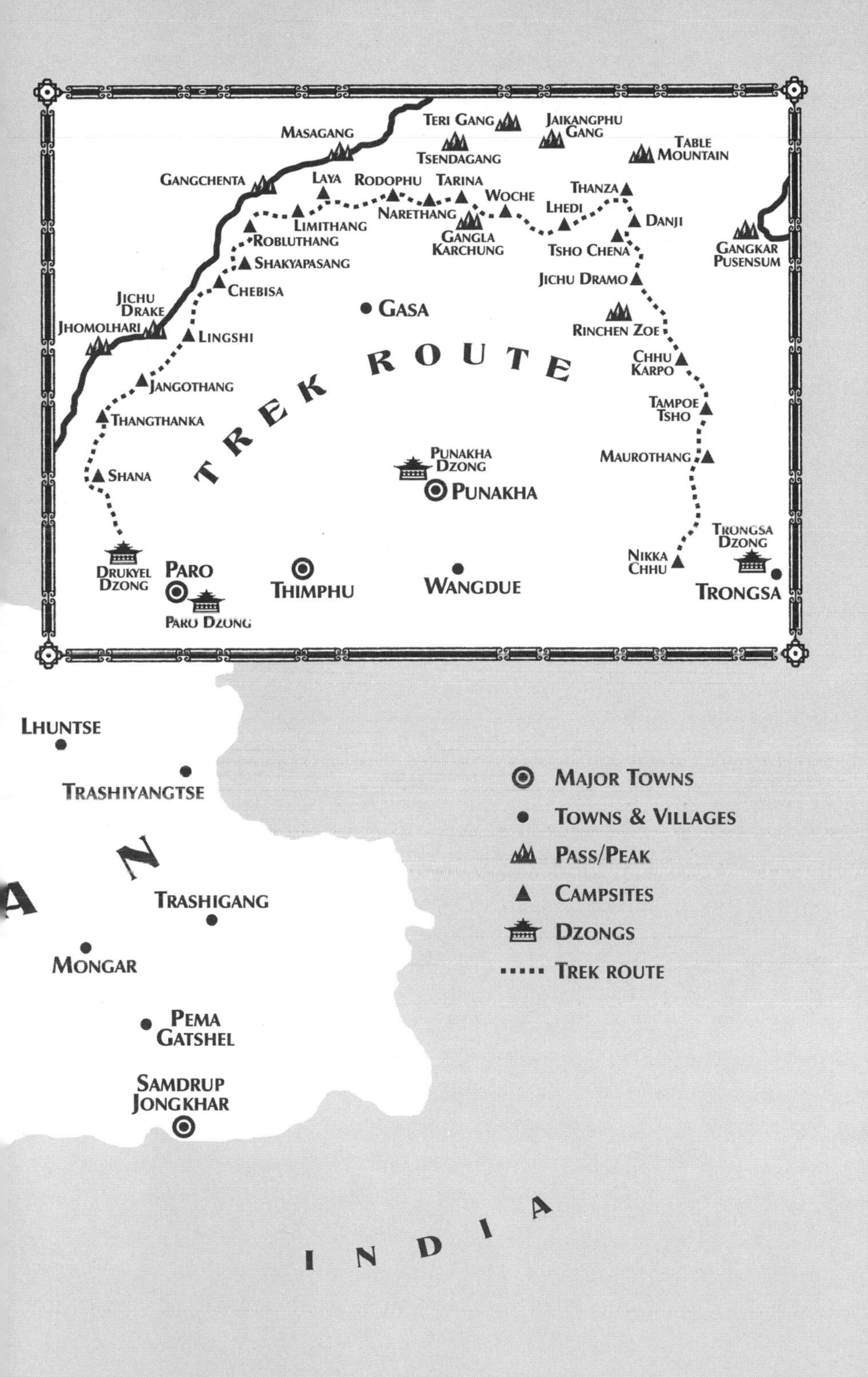
TERI GANG
JAIKANGPHU GANG
MASAGANG
TSENDAGANG
TABLE MOUNTAIN
GANGCHENTA
LAYA
RODOPHU
TARINA
THANZA
WOCHE
LHEDI
NARETHANG
DANJI
LIMITHANG
GANGLA KARCHUNG
TSHO CHENA
GANGKAR PUSENSUM
ROBLUTHANG
SHAKYAPASANG
CHEBISA
JICHU DRAMO
GASA
JICHU DRAKE
JHOMOLHARI
LINGSHI
RINCHEN ZOE
TREK ROUTE
CHHU KARPO
JANGOTHANG
TAMPOE TSHO
THANGTHANKA
MAUROTHANG
PUNAKHA DZONG
SHANA
PUNAKHA
TRONGSA DZONG
NIKKA CHHU
DRUKYEL DZONG
PARO
THIMPHU
WANGDUE
TRONGSA
PARO DZONG
LHUNTSE
TRASHIYANGTSE
MAJOR TOWNS
TOWNS & VILLAGES
PASS/PEAK
CAMPSITES
DZONGS
TREK ROUTE
A N
TRASHIGANG
MONGAR
PEMA GATSHEL
SAMDRUP JONGKHAR
INDIA

BENEATH BLOSSOM RAIN

I

STEPPING UP TO THE FIRST PASS OF THE SNOWMAN TREK IN the Land of the Thunder Dragon, my heart pounding, I removed each arm from my shoulder straps, set my backpack down, and stood tall to have a look around. The pass was totally socked in, but with short fitful bursts, the highest mountain range on earth slowly revealed itself. A vast expanse of snowy peaks, rocky spires, and immense glaciers flashed through brief openings in the dark clouds.

Remembering my vow to put up a string of prayer flags for the peace and happiness of all sentient beings at the first and last pass of the trek, I knelt down on one knee, removed my gloves, and unzipped my backpack. I'd bought the prayer flags a week prior in Paro, a small Bhutanese town nestled in the mountainous folds of a river valley. When I'd entered a shop and told the kind-faced woman at the counter I was doing the Snowman Trek, she nodded, set aside the vegetables she was washing, and immediately disappeared into the back room. She returned moments later, beaming with magnificent pride and cradling a set of fresh-pressed prayer flags in her arms. When she gently handed me the flags, she gazed deep into my eyes, and it was then that I truly realized prayer flags weren't simply colorful fabric squares but were something breathing and alive, something sacred. Thus, I'd placed the flags at the top of my backpack, delicately and devoutly folded, that September morning. As I took them out, the flags smelled of incense and trembled with a strange kind of electricity in the gusting wind.

The pass was marked by two mounds of rocks shaped like small, thigh-high pyramids and set ten feet apart. Weather-beaten branches, wedged between the rocks, stuck up like bony fingers and anchored numerous strings of prayer flags, flapping and fraying in the whipping wind. With fast-numbing hands, I quickly wrapped my string of flags around a barkless tree branch and tied a knot. But before I could hurry to the second rock pile to tie the other end of my rope, the wind kicked up and the cold cut my fingers. Shivering uncontrollably, I thrust my hands into my pockets. When the wind died moments later, I saw my opportunity. I grabbed my string of prayer flags, shuffled to the other side, and set about tying the second knot. But by then, my fingers were painfully slow and bone cold. Before I could secure the knot, I rushed them back into my pockets a second time.

"Come on," I muttered, my teeth chattering.

Over the next few moments, the wind picked up and moody clouds massed overhead. A storm was blowing in. As I sunk deep into my jacket and drew my hands high into my coat sleeves, I realized the wind wasn't going to let up. If I was planning to tie my prayer flags, I had to do it then. And fast. I took a deep breath, gathered my energy, and leapt to my feet. But as I did, a great gust of wind tore the string of prayer flags out of my hand and tossed them into the sky like a kite.

Norbu, my Bhutanese guide, hurried over. "I will help you."

"Please," I managed. "I'm freezing!"

Like a cowboy about to tame a colt, Norbu stood back a moment, watching the flags bucking wildly. It was this loose end of the rope I had come to Bhutan to contemplate, for it seemed to represent

Prayer flags whip in the wind. Photo by Ryan Goebel.

all the loose ends in my life that were, at once, alluring and elusive — all the dreams that invited my reach but then retreated the moment I did.

The moment the wind died, Norbu pounced, and as he wrestled with the prayer flags, I sat back and watched. "Why couldn't I do that?" I lamented softly to myself. As Norbu tied the second end of my rope, I couldn't help but feel frustrated. But in my defense, I hadn't yet hiked 216 miles of the most beautiful and challenging trail on earth or visited time-lost villages and hidden valleys. I hadn't yet sat with a spell-spitting shaman or truly understood the Divine Madman's precept that "whatever happens is the path of release." Despite the glory of my surroundings, I was in exile that morning, for I hadn't yet stood beneath blossom rain and discovered its secret of lasting grace. But little did I know as I grabbed my backpack and started down the trail . . . I was about to.

2

BHUTAN IS A SMALL COUNTRY, ROUGHLY HALF THE SIZE OF Indiana, squeezed between Tibet and India. The first thing to understand about Bhutan is that nothing is black and white — there are varying names, meanings, measurements, and explanations for everything, beginning with the name "Bhutan" itself. Some scholars suggest the name Bhutan is derived from the Sanskrit term Bhots-anta, which translates to the "end of the land of the Bhots" (Bhots being Tibetans); others believe the name came from the phrase, *bhu-uttan*, which is Sanskrit for "highlands." The Bhutanese call themselves Drukpas (Dragon People) and their country Druk Yul, or "Land of the Thunder Dragon," named after the loud thunder "dragon" that routinely shakes Bhutan's skies and protects its people. Historically, Bhutan has also been known by the names of Lhomen Khazi (Southern Land of Four Approaches), Lho Men Jonh (Southern Land of Medicinal Herbs), and most ominously, as Lho Mon (Southern Land of Darkness).

Based upon ancient Buddhist statues, weapons, and tools, scholars believe Bhutan may have been populated as early as 2000 BC, although the first written records of the country begin with the spontaneous appearance of the Buddhist saint Guru Rinpoche in AD 746. Until 1960, Bhutan had few roads and no schools, hospitals, telephones, postal system, or national currency, and it followed a strict policy of isolationism until 1974. Now Bhutan has the distinctions of governing by a policy of Gross National Happiness, not having a single traffic light in the entire country, being the last Buddhist Kingdom in the Himalayas, and having one of the scariest airport landings in the world.

My adventure began when I was checking in for my flight to Bhutan from Bangkok. Bhutan's only airport, in Paro, is serviced by Druk Air, Bhutan's national airline, which has a very strict weight policy of forty-four pounds of checked luggage per person. I thought the weight restriction was due to the fact that an airplane loses engine power when landing at a high altitude, but as I stood in the check-in line, I realized it was so the many well-dressed men with moustaches getting off in Kolkata, India, could transport all their recent, Bangkok-bought goods. From the number of flatscreen TVs, stereos, and DVD players teetering on luggage carts, I realized I wouldn't be flying in an airplane so much as an appliance store with wings.

To be honest, I never would have passed the weight restriction if Joe Pilaar, the forty-six-year-old owner of Canadian Himalayan Expeditions — the company I was traveling with — hadn't told me a clever way to beat the system before I left. "The weight limit only concerns checked luggage," he'd said over the phone with a Canadian accent that seemed to add a soft "eh?" at the end of every sentence. "So, if you wear as much weight as you can, eh? You'll be fine, eh?" It was an ingenious idea. That is, until I stood in the sweltering Bangkok airport wearing a heavy sweater, hooded jacket, fleece pants, and hiking boots. Not only was I sweating like hell, but as the evil-eyed Thai security guard asked me to step out of line for additional screening, I realized I also looked exactly like the Unabomber.

"Empty your pockets," he said, handing me a plastic basket.

"No problem," I said, cheerfully.

My pockets were stuffed with duct tape, chewing gum, Power Bars, and energy gels. These were trekking items to be sure, but in the security basket, they look strangely like the tools of a terrorist.

"Those are sticky bars," I told the man, stressing the word "bar" so he didn't think they were sticky bombs.

"Give me your hat!" he said.

"My what?"

He motioned to my head. "Hat!"

I'd almost forgotten I was wearing my favorite hat, a black baseball cap I'd gotten in Lake Tahoe years ago. That baseball cap was my pride and joy. I'd spent years molding the shape of its bill to just the correct curve. That hat had been everywhere with me and had hidden more days of bed head in college than I cared to count. As I handed it over, the guard began inspecting it, flipping it over, peering at the tag, and giving it a good sniff. I was calm and composed, but when he started bending the bill, I got anxious. One careless move on his part and he could mess up the bill and kill my beloved hat forever, destroying years of my hard and devoted labor. I raised a hand. "Can you be gentle —,"

"Quiet!"

"Sorry."

"Where are you going?" the guard asked, gesturing for my air ticket.

"Bhutan."

"For what?"

"The twenty-four-day Snowman Trek," I said.

Suddenly the security guard burst into laughter. "Yah, enjoy your trip, buddy!" he said, handing me back all my stuff.

I thanked him and hurried to the terminal to catch a bus that would take me to my flight. As the bus navigated through the predawn darkness, in the window I saw my own sleep-deprived, bloodshot eyes, and the face was barely recognizable. When the bus finally stopped and I hopped out to see the airplane waiting alone on the tarmac, I nearly had a panic attack. As I pondered the grim statistics of the Snowman, I almost turned around and quit the trek before I'd begun. But then I thought of Sean, my older brother, and how, on the morning I left for my trip, he'd called a "board meeting" which, in Huntington Beach, California, meant surfing at sunrise. Sean hadn't been to Bhutan, but he always preached the life-changing potential of a good trip. In between wave sets, as a red sun rose over the Santa Ana Mountains, Sean told me the Snowman Trek would challenge me on every level. "But you have to go for it," he instructed. "Forget about the cost, forget about fear or how tired you are, and just go for it. Live it all, my man, live it all!"

As the airplane's engine woke up in great exhaustive gasps, I watched the plane fill with tourists. Torn between staying or going, between my old life and the new one waiting for me, I decided not to focus on my worry. Instead, I thought of Sean and every other traveler who had stood on the threshold of a new adventure with apprehension and yet still somehow found the courage to move forward. "If they can do it, I can do it," I thought to myself. "Let me embrace the unknown journey the way countless travelers have before me." Then, as a gentle wind rose off the tarmac and the sky began to lighten in the east, I smiled, boarded the plane, and found my seat.

Nonetheless, flying Druk Airlines to Bhutan was still scary. As I boarded the plane, the words "Druk Air" written on the airplane looked strangely like "Drunk Air." I imagined the pilots stumbling, blurry eyed, into the cockpit from Bangkok's Khao San Road, mumbling, "We'll just put her on autopilot!"

I was also scared because part of my airline ticket was handwritten. Living in the digital age, I certainly missed heartfelt, handwritten notes, but in birthday cards, not on my boarding passes. The handwriting was very nice and neat, mind you, but it was still handwritten.

Lastly, I was scared because the landing in Bhutan is one of the toughest landings on the planet. Paro International Airport sits in a bowl-shaped valley at 7,300 feet, surrounded by 16,000-foot saw-toothed mountains, and landing there requires the plane to make all kinds of sharp twists, plunges, and turns. Then there's the matter of the wind, specifically high jet stream currents, which have a nasty tendency to bounce off the surrounding peaks, creating a bubble effect that could, at any time, swat the plane out of the sky like an annoying insect. Making matters worse, the runway is significantly narrower than other international runways and feels a lot shorter. In fact, landing on this STOL (short take-off and landing) runway is so dangerous that Druk Air must follow VFR (visual flight rules) and not fly at night or in unruly weather, which means if there's any problem, you are SOL (shit outta luck). I was comforted knowing the Druk Air pilots were among the best trained in the world. And I was relieved knowing this Boeing Airbus-319, purchased in 2004, had extra engine power and had been blessed by Buddhist monks. But those facts did little to lessen my fear. Of course, the Druk Air flight didn't scare me when I visited Bhutan for the first time in 2004, but I was more certain back then — about faith, hope, love — and the success of everything, including airplane landings. Thus, as our plane approached Bhutan, I looked fearfully out the window and clung to both armrests with white knuckles.

Most mountain ranges follow a similar pattern of plate tectonic behavior — they start as rolling hills, gradually rise to forested mountains, and then pierce the clouds as sharp, storm-beaten peaks. Traveling into those mountain ranges, you are eased into the experience of elevation and slowly initiated into the prospect of inclement weather; you can prepare yourself mentally, physically, and spiritually for the adventure.

Bhutan didn't get that mountain memo.

Rather than slowly rising, the eastern Himalayas of Bhutan explode from the earth in a jagged series of rows, like shark teeth. When I saw Bhutan's mountain range — sliced by raging rivers — rise up from the flat, fertile tea plantations of West Bengal that morning, I didn't have any deep spiritual thoughts. I thought, "I'm screwed!"

"Is this your first time to Bhutan?" asked a Bhutanese man with dark, short hair in his mid-forties sitting next to me. "My name is Tenzin."

"It's my second," I replied, tightening my seatbelt, "but I slept most of the flight last time."

The pilot came over the loudspeaker. "Flight attendants, secure the cabin for crashing."

I turned to Tenzin. "He just said crashing?"

"No, my friend," replied Tenzin, patting my knee. "The pilot said landing."

The management at Druk Air knows the landing is scary, which is why they try to distract you by hiring the world's prettiest flight attendants and playing soothing music. Ever had the experience of watching a horror movie where there's really scary music playing but nothing is happening? Well, the landing in Paro was the exact opposite: Druk Air plays soft, classical music — as if all is well with the world — while the plane is slaloming around snowy peaks and high-fiving the forest.

The plane turned left, aiming directly at a home on the hillside and then turned hard. As the plane veered right, all the passengers leaned their heads to the left, as if their collective craniums could counterbalance the aircraft. Far below, Paro Valley appeared — a thin, flat patch of farm fields squeezed between thick mountain folds.

"There is the runway!" said Tenzin, pointing to a narrow asphalt strip.

"Runway?" I gasped. "That's a driveway!"

Suddenly it felt as if the floor dropped out of the plane, and when the wheels lowered, I swore the engine fell out with them. As the plane snaked through the mountains, everything was whirling and the cabin bounced as if going over speed bumps. I held my breath, shut my eyes, and apologized to God for having impure thoughts of Anne Fowler in seventh grade, taking an extra swill of communion wine at church, and illegally downloading the collected works of Bruce Springsteen. I should tell you now I am a child of the '80s and place *Born in the USA* on the same spiritual shelf as the book of Psalms. But that morning, as the ground fast approached and the trees whipped by, I couldn't remember the words to the Bible or the Boss. It was the end. I knew it. My life was over. Done. Finished.

Suddenly Tenzin nudged me. "Sir," he said, "we are in Bhutan."

I blinked my eyes open, certain I had died and gone to heaven. I wasn't dead, but when I looked out the window and saw mountains, monasteries, and a river shining in the morning sun, I realized I just might be in heaven.

3

FORTY-EIGHT HOURS LATER I WAS SEATED WITH MY TREKKING companions at a Buddhist puja ceremony to bless our trip. The second bedroom in the single-story home behind our hotel had been converted into a *choesum*, or "prayer room." Since 4:00 a.m., two young monks, with shaved heads and happy smiles and wearing burgundy robes, had been seated before silver offering bowls, candles, incense sticks, and Buddhist statues, chanting *Sutras*, or "scriptures," for the benefit of all beings, namely the nine members of our trekking party. Once we were all seated before the elaborate altar, the monks showered us with sacred rice to rid us of all our toxins and impurities, which, for me, meant there was a high likelihood there'd be nothing left. When I didn't disappear, I rose and went to the altar where one monk poured holy water into my cupped hands. I made a gesture of drinking (to bless the inner spirit) and then poured the water on top of my head (to bless the physical body). After this, the monk placed a white silk scarf around my neck, and I sat back down. Once we were all seated, the monks continued with their Sutras and then, suddenly, someone's cell phone rang. It caught the monk right in the middle of reciting "Om Mani Padme Hum," the most sacred mantra in all of Buddhism:

"Om — *ring!* — Mani — *ring!* — Padme — *ring!* — Hum — *ring!*"

Everyone immediately started glancing around anxiously. I expected the monk to halt his prayers, but he continued: "Om — *ring!* — Mani — *ring!* — Padme — *ring!* — Hum — *ring!*"

That's when I realized a horrible truth — the cell phone sounded exactly like mine. "Oh no," I thought, shifting in my seat. My cell phone had a history of going off in college lectures, at the movies, and during final relaxation at yoga class. As I discreetly patted my pockets, I was certain that once found out, I'd be kicked off the trek and be reborn as a cockroach or some other dark-dwelling creature. But then an amazing thing happened — the young monk on the left side of the altar pulled a cell phone out from under his robe. Not only did he pull the phone out, but he also checked the caller ID! He stopped his prayers, answered the call, and proceeded to have a short conversation in Dzongkha, Bhutan's national language. I didn't know whether it was funny, insulting, horrifying, or all three. Moments later, the monk hung up and, as if nothing out of the ordinary had happened, continued with his prayers. "Om mani padme hum . . . "

As my trekking companions and I exchanged quizzical glances, Norbu, our twenty-six-year-old Bhutanese guide, motioned for us to leave. We all stood, nodded thanks to the monks, and were silently ushered out the door.

As we walked to the bus under moody clouds, I struggled to make sense of what I'd just witnessed — a monk stopping his prayers to answer his cell phone. I couldn't help but feel a bit cheated. But as I stepped on the bus, I realized that within the last few moments, I'd experienced many of what Buddhism calls the afflictive emotions: doubt, anger, resentment, and non-faith. It dawned on me that the monk was using the phone to teach us a lesson, as a way to hold up a mirror to our minds and challenge our expectations. And who was to say it wasn't the Buddha calling? Maybe the lesson was that in Vajrayana Buddhism, everything is holy — the mantra, the call, the act of calling, and the caller. I wasn't sure, but as I took my seat, I was certain my life was about to be turned upside down.

As the bus crawled down the dirt road, riddled with yawning holes and muddy puddles, I hollered up to Norbu, "This road is terrible! Why don't they pave it?"

"That is a good question," said Norbu, grabbing the bus microphone.

Norbu was a dark-skinned Bhutanese man with brown eyes and short-cropped black hair. When he met us at the airport a few days earlier, he wore a gray *gho*, a traditional Bhutanese knee-length robe, along with argyle socks and black dress shoes, which curved up at the toes like question marks. That morning he wore hiking boots, blue nylon trekking pants, a yellow rain jacket, and a red baseball cap. "They don't pave the road," he said into the microphone, "because then people will just speed."

His answer was frustratingly simple and yet seemed to speak to Bhutan's overall development policy — the country could speed from the Middle Ages into the twenty-first century, but something special would be lost along the way. I wanted to pass off this practice of methodical modernization as archaic, but as we bounced down the dirt road, I noticed things I would have missed had we sped — stalks of red rice gently swaying in the morning breeze, village children singing their way to school, and cicadas whistling from willow trees.

The bus turned left on the main road leading up the Paro valley, where it would end abruptly at the ruins of Drukyel Dzong, the fortress that serves as the starting point of the Snowman Trek. As we drove up the valley, rain fell in heavy gray sheets and a gloomy fog draped the mountains. While the weather was wet and somber, my trekking companions were a spirited bunch.

"Anyone up for a short meander?" joked Peter, a thirty-six-year-old rugby-tough photojournalist from Colorado.

"A Sunday stroll perhaps?" added Paul, a handsome and debonair fifty-two-year-old landscape architect from London.

"Perfect day for a lil' walkabout," declared Rob, a red-haired Australian with merry cheeks, also in his early fifties.

As for me, it seemed only like a perfect day for a hot coffee, a cozy couch, and a movie.

Norbu directed our attention to the right side of the bus. "If it was sunny today, you could see Taktsang Monastery, or Tigers Nest, perched on the side of a cliff 2,500 feet above the valley floor," he said, turning up the volume on the bus microphone. "Guru Rinpoche, also known as Padmasambhava, was the Lotus-born Tantric master and second Buddha, who brought Buddhism to the Himalayas. He flew to Taktsang on the back of a winged tigress to subdue evil spirits and convert them to protectors of the Dharma. Taktsang burned down in 1998, but an exact replica was rebuilt in 2000. It is one of the most famous Buddhist pilgrimage sites in the world."

I leaned in close to the window, hoping my steady gaze could magically part the clouds, but the rain increased, rattling the bus roof like nails. As I watched raindrops slide down the window, I decided there was something terribly disheartening about starting a trek on a rainy day. Indeed, it was the trekking equivalent of having a fight on your honeymoon. Hoping for some optimism, I yelled up to Norbu. "Hey Norbu, think the weather will improve?"

"There are two types of weather in Bhutan," he said somberly. "Either it is raining in the mountains — or about to rain."

"Funny joke," said Peter.

The truth was that Norbu may not have been joking. Bhutan is first in line for the Indian monsoon, and each year from June through August, rainstorms drench the country. As low pressure systems loiter over the Tibetan Plateau, warm, moist air is swept up from the Bay of Bengal, cools when it hits the Himalayas, and condenses into rain. It's not uncommon for parts of Bhutan to receive more than sixteen feet of rain a year, and during the three months of the

Taktsang Monastery clings to a granite cliff high above the valley floor. Photo by Peter McBride.

monsoon, it swells rivers, floods farm fields, and washes bridges and campsites away. It's also not uncommon for the monsoon to, like a rude party guest, arrive late and stay late, falling as snow in the mountains, sealing up the passes, and stranding trekkers. Disheartened, I tried to cheer myself up by reminding myself of why I'd come to Bhutan in the first place.

On the outside, the answers are easy: I wanted to experience the unique culture of Bhutan, which lists Drukpa Kagyu, or Red Hat Tantric Buddhism, as the official state religion. I also wanted to hike through some of the most pristine and well-protected wilderness on earth and experience twenty-four days of living in a tent, without any access to the outside world. Lastly, I wanted the physical challenge of doing "the world's toughest trek" and had an obsession to see Thanza — a rarely visited hidden valley that many people considered to be a Shangri-La. While these "external" answers sufficed for the casual chat of cocktail parties, inside I needed to know the real motivation behind my desire to do the trek. In the months preceding my trip, I had felt unsettled and had no clue why. I knew there was a shadow side to my wanting to do the Snowman Trek — my life wasn't as fulfilling as I thought it could be and I'd decided to seek something else — what that was, I wasn't exactly sure.

THE SNOWMAN TREK BEGINS BESIDE THE RUINS OF DRUKYEL Dzong, known as the fortress of the victorious Drukpas. A *dzong* is the Bhutanese equivalent of a castle, and there is one in almost every one of the twenty *dzongkhags*, or "districts," of Bhutan. Dzongs serve as the religious and administrative headquarters of each district, and their construction resembles some of my college term papers — they were created without written plans and the builders relied entirely on a mental image of what was to be created. But while my term papers occasionally received low marks and teacher comments like, "Mr. Grange, I suggest reading the book and spell-checking your name," Bhutan's dzongs get the highest marks. Massive white stone structures, each has a red band of paint called a *khemar* running beneath their red roofs. The imposing white walls enclose an elaborate flagstone courtyard, at the center of which stands an *utse*, or "central tower." Throughout history, in times of war and strife, whole villages sought refuge inside the dzongs, fetching water from underground tunnels and shooting marauding invaders through tiny holes in the walls. The dzongs were virtually impenetrable from the outside, but their one weakness was to be found within — they were lit by butter lamps, which often started raging fires. One such fire destroyed Drukyel Dzong in 1951, and though it is but a wood-and-beam skeleton of its former self, it still retains an impressive and imposing presence.

As we hopped off the bus, Norbu told us some of the history of Drukyel Dzong. "The dzong was built in 1649 by the Shabdrung Nagawang Namgyel to celebrate Bhutan's repeated victories over the Tibetans. The Shabdrung was born in 1594, and after being persecuted at Tibet's Ralung Monastery as a young man, he fled to the promised land of the Dragon Kingdom by following Bhutan's protective deity, which appeared to him in the form of a raven. Once in Bhutan, the Shabdrung became the spiritual leader of its people and began unifying the country by building dzongs and creating taxes and laws. He also instituted a policy of national dress and celebrated the rich history of Buddhism through colorful *tsechu* dance festivals."

"Who ruled Bhutan before the Shabdrung?" asked Larry, a jovial sixty-six-year-old from New Jersey.

Norbu told us that before the Shabdrung there was a lot of infighting between rival tribes in scattered valleys.

"And who ruled after he died?" asked Tom, a retired teacher in his late fifties from upstate New York.

"For two hundred years after the Shabdrung's death, there were civil wars and rebellions," explained Norbu. "But in 1907, after he'd shown true leadership in mediating a dispute between Tibet and the British, as well as military prowess in defeating local uprisings, Ugyen Wangchuk was elected our first king."

As the rain continued, we hauled our duffel bags from the back of the bus, and it dawned on me that we weren't so much going to hike in the elements as going to war with them. Over the next twenty-four days, wind, rain, sleet, and snow would launch a massive assault, which we'd counterattack with down jackets, gloves, and Gore-Tex boots. As for the rest of our gear, the term "ultralight" didn't apply. The scope of our expedition was huge. A trekking staff of seven was busy loading gear onto thirty horses who, let it be known, didn't look too happy. There were stoves, gas tanks, big tents, small tents, toilet tents, camp chairs, folding tables, pots, pans, silverware, lanterns, canned goods, boxed goods, fresh vegetables, dozens of boxes of cookies, hundreds of eggs, and enough rice bags to fill several army bunkers. I realized that like the wagon trains of the American frontier, we'd be transporting an entire village across the wild country.

"Huddle up, everyone," hollered Joe, our athletic guide who, despite the rain, was full of boundless energy.

All packing immediately stopped, and we shuffled over to him.

"I'd like to introduce you to our trekking staff," Joe said, gesturing to a group of rag-tag Bhutanese men who smiled back at us with red-stained mouths.

Rob leaned over to Kira, a thirty-eight-year-old journalist with shoulder-length blond hair and cobalt blue eyes. "Say, Kee-ra, are their mouths bleeding?"

"It's doma," Norbu replied. "Roll an areca nut and lime paste in a betel leaf, chew it, and you get a little buzz."

"Ah ha," said Larry. "Now the red, polka-dotted sidewalks in Paro make sense!"

When Joe continued with his introductions, we learned our head chef was a forty-six-year-old Tibetan named Achula.

"Yes, yes!" said Achula, stepping forth, nodding, and waving to us.

Helping out Achula in the kitchen tent and serving meals would be Sonam and Sangey, both eager young men in their early twenties. Dressed in a red, short-sleeved golf shirt and blue jeans, Sangey looked like he just wandered over from prep school. Sonam, on the other hand, wearing a sweat suit, black boots, and paperboy cap, looked like he was heading to a hip nightclub.

When Joe introduced the horsemen who'd be helping transport all our gear, their names blurred together in the windy drizzle, and it sounded to me like all five of them were named either Chencho or Doji.

There are only about fifty personal names in existence in Bhutan. While southern Bhutan is more traditional, in the north, there are no family names. A name can be used for both men and women and can appear as either a first or last name. Complicating matters, a woman doesn't take her husband's name when they get married, and the kids don't take the last names of their parents, nor of each other. Instead of parents naming the child, babies are often named by an astrologer or monk, who picks a name with religious meaning.

The horsemen were a bunch of guys of varying age who wore a mish-mash collection of clothes they'd inherited from past expeditions — jeans, sweatpants, wickable trekking pants, sweaters, fleece jackets, wool caps, and baseball caps. "*Kuzuzangbo la*," they said, nodding to us, Dzongkha for "hello."

When I asked if there was any significance to the names, Norbu told me indeed there was. "My name means *valuable treasure*," he replied, laughing.

Suddenly, a loud rhythmic whirling sounded from the clouds above.

"A helicopter?" gasped Larry, turning to Norbu.

"Yes," said Norbu with a worried frown. "But I'm not sure why it's here."

As Norbu hurried over to consult with a pair of guides who were at Drukyel with another group, Rob, Paul, and I exchanged anxious glances. Moments later, Norbu thanked the other guides and returned to us. "The helicopter is going to the Lunana District, a fourteen-day hike from here."

"Someone injured?" asked Tom, his eyebrows arching over his wire-rimmed glasses.

Norbu told us someone had altitude sickness on the Snowman Trek and needed to be evacuated.

I swallowed hard. I didn't need to hear that. Not then, not any time. With the rain, the helicopter, and the daunting mileage and elevation of the Snowman Trek, I didn't have a good feeling in my stomach. The helicopter receded into the cloudy distance and left us standing in a damp silence. We exchanged worried glances, and then Paul answered a question none of us had asked but were all, no doubt, thinking.

"Well, I'm still going," he said, marching down a dirt road, leading away from Drukyel Dzong.

"Me too," proclaimed Ryan, a bright man in his early thirties from Illinois with short curly brown hair and glasses.

"Slowly but surely," added Larry, grabbing his trekking poles.

I watched them go and then walked to the line where the asphalt ended and let the toes of my boots dangle over the dirt, as if standing on the high dive, my mouth full with the acid reflux of uncertainty.

"Aw come on, Kev," said Rob, slapping me on the back. "Nothin' like a good ol' advencha!"

The force of Rob's encouraging slap sent me over the threshold and shuffling off down the trail. As I walked forward, I found myself glancing back to the road with a strange kind of longing. It didn't feel like I was simply waving good-bye to the Bhutanese villagers, who had assembled to see us off, but to everything I had ever known: civilization, security, and safety.

As I continued down the dirt road, the rain increased and a group of stray dogs — barking and yipping wildly — ran down from the dzong. They were a ragged bunch; some had open wounds, others were missing tails, and all had the visible ribs of malnourishment. In Bhutanese lore, a dog chasing a trekking group was reported to be the soul of a dead trekker. If so, from the number of dogs, it appeared we were not only about to trek to a land of towering crags and glaciers but also graves.

4

SPANNING TWENTY-FOUR DAYS AND TRAVELING 216 MILES over eleven high-mountain passes — including seven over 16,000 feet — the Snowman Trek is not only the ultimate high-altitude traverse of the Himalayas but the toughest trek in the world. In mountaineering terms, the Snowman Trek is the Mount Everest of commercial treks, and in fact, more people have scaled the world's tallest peak than have finished the Snowman. Historically, fewer than 120 people attempt the trek each year, and of those, less than 50 percent finish. If climbing Everest is primarily about acclimatization, finishing the Snowman Trek is about endurance and the ability to hike nearly ten miles a day for twenty-four days on precarious, exposed trails well above 13,000 feet. A sampling of the obstacles faced on the Snowman Trek includes weather, duration, remoteness, high mileage, high camps, and high elevation — all of which means there is a high likelihood something will go wrong.

On the Snowman Trek, you will find none of the luxuries that exist at Everest Base Camp. There are no cappuccino machines, massage tents, movie tents, or, most important, a medical tent staffed with on-site specialists. Break a leg or have a severe case of altitude sickness in the remote district of Lunana and the only way to receive medical care is to call for a helicopter evacuation. That is, if a helicopter is available. The government of Bhutan doesn't actually own a helicopter, so in the event of an emergency, your trekking guide would call his tour company on a satellite phone; the tour company, in turn, calls the Tourism Council of Bhutan, who then calls the Royal Bhutanese Army, which calls the Indian Army, who sends a helicopter, if one is available and if weather permits a safe landing. Is it me, or does that seem like a long game of telephone to play when someone's life is at stake?

The Snowman Trek, named after Bhutan's notorious Yeti, passes six mountains over 23,000 feet — Jhomolhari, Masa Gang, Teri Gang, Jaikangphu Gang, Table Mountain, and Gangkhar Puensum — and, over the course of the twenty-four days, forms a great horseshoe across northwestern Bhutan. The trail, which travels through multiple climate zones — bamboo forests, temperate broadleaf forests, alpine meadows, and glaciated peaks — is really a combination of three treks: the Jhomolhari, Laya, and Lunana. Connect these three adventures, add two rest days, and you have a recipe for one amazing expedition. The trek travels north for the first three days to the base of Mount Jhomolhari, Bhutan's most sacred peak, and spends the next eight days in a northeastern traverse of the rocky vertebrae separating Bhutan and Tibet, ending in the village of Laya. After a rest day in Laya, the trail travels east for the next week, hiking to and through the luminous valleys of Lunana. Naturally, I was very excited to visit this paradisal valley, but according to Himalayan folklore, people either died trying to reach Shangri-La or, once there, were so enamored with it, they never left. Either way, if I made it to the remote village of Thanza, there was a good chance I wasn't coming back.

Despite the grim truths regarding the mileage and remoteness, the Snowman Trek started out like a Sunday stroll. From Drukyel Dzong, we followed a winding dirt road down to the Paro Chhu (*chhu* is "river") and started up a wide, green farming valley, dotted with traditional Bhutanese homes. The trail continued up the valley for an hour, passing a small village and a single-story white stone schoolhouse with a red corrugated metal roof. The dirt playground was empty that morning, and the Bhutanese flag flapped forlornly on a nearby pole. Even on a dreary day such as that, the Bhutanese flag was striking and well representative of the country's priorities. The flag is divided diagonally. The yellow upper part of the flag represents the secular authority and mindful action of the king, and the lower orange section represents Buddhism and the monastic community. A white thunder dragon roars at the center of the flag and in its mighty claws holds a collection of jewels representing Bhutan's spiritual, cultural, and environmental wealth.

After the school, we crossed a suspension bridge teeming with colorful prayer flags that led us to the east side of the river and through more fields of barley, mustard, and red, meaty potatoes. As I glanced down, I noticed the dirt road had disappeared, and I was now walking on a thin, muddy trail. There was only one direction then — forward.

WE WERE STARTING THE TREK ON THE TWENTY-FOURTH DAY of the ninth month in the year of the Fire Pig, or September 24, 2007. Bhutan's calendar was inspired by the Tibetan calendar in which five elements and twelve animals are paired together to name each year, creating a sixty-year cycle, and here's the great thing — the calendar can change from year to year based upon the guidance of astrologers. Days and months can be added, subtracted, or repeated based upon their merit, or lack thereof. I immediately fell in love with the idea of this calendar and thought the United States should adopt it. Think about it, we could double up on Fridays and get rid of Mondays. We could have two Thanksgivings, repeat the whole festive month of December and make the fifth of July a national holiday because you really need that day to recover.

HIKING ALONG THE TRAIL, I HAD A WONDERFUL SENSE OF surrendering to the adventure, of looking resolutely forward, and feeling ready for what may come. As I walked past vast timbered hills, I felt giddy and happy. Sure, it was drizzly and the mountaintops were shrouded in clouds, but it was Bhutanese rain and, therefore, seemed to glitter in the gray light. As I looked up the rolling green valley, I was seized with *It's Happening!* excitement and reminded of the miracle of travel. How amazing is it that you can leap time zones in a single airplane bound and step off into a new country, humming with a completely different culture and customs? Indeed, time travel is possible! In Bhutan, there was a palpable sense of going back in time or of tossing the time away altogether and venturing forth into an enchanting kingdom.

Day one of the Snowman Trek consisted of an 11.2-mile hike with 1,020 feet of elevation gain to a campsite called Shana. As I hiked, glancing to my left and right with a crossing-the-street curiosity, I was reminded that walking really is the best way to explore a place. Yes, the trail was wet and muddy, but it was absolutely wonderful. Despite its difficulty, distance, and duration, the great thing about the Snowman Trek is that you are incredibly pampered. Your alarm clock each morning is a hot cup of tea brought to you in your tent; warm washing water arrives fifteen minutes later for you to take a bird bath. And a hearty breakfast of oatmeal, eggs, sausage, or pancakes awaits you in the dining tent. Lunch is a hot meal consisting of a meat dish, rice, and vegetables. At the end of the day, your tent, cookies, and hot tea greet you as you enter camp and a multicourse dinner and tasty dessert follow a few hours later. Camp is packed up after you start your hike each morning and — in some feat that nearly defies logic — is routinely waiting for you when you stop hiking in the afternoon. Since horses and yaks haul all your gear, you carry only a modest daypack. Thus, someone doing the Snowman Trek is, at once, afforded the experience of a monthlong expedition with the ease of a day hike. Best of all, since less than 120 people attempt the trek each year, it is rare to see another group of trekkers on the trail, which means, you'll have a half million steps of scenery and sweet interaction with the Bhutanse villagers virtually all to yourself.

As I trod past perfect yellow blossoms of mustard plants and over red doma-stained rocks, I fell in line with Joe, our fit and knowledgeable guide, who was the kind of guy you'd book a trip to the grocery store with because he made every experience so fun. Joe had been guiding treks in the Himalayas for more than twenty years. Despite being a full-blooded Canadian — right down to his love of hockey — Joe spent five years of his childhood in India and spoke Hindi and Urdu fluently. He has traveled extensively throughout the world and has led more than fifty expeditions in Nepal, India, Pakistan, Bhutan, Tibet, Kenya, Tanzania, Argentina, Chile, and Peru.

As we walked, Joe told me about the first trek he ever lead, "I was nineteen and in college and put together a trek to a holy Hindu pilgrimage spot in the high Himalaya in northern India. When one woman saw me, she gasped, 'You're the guide?' and promptly burst into tears.

"Did she end up going?"

"She did," Joe said with a laugh. "And she had a great time."

I chose Canadian Himalayan Expeditions (CHE) because it was one of the few companies with a guaranteed departure for the Snowman Trek in September 2007, but I also liked CHE's founding principles of: Invest in your life experience. Collect memories, not material. Expand your global perspective. In addition, to Joe's goal of taking people to exotic parts of the planet, he also had a personal goal: "To spend as little time in an office as possible," he said, chuckling.

Just before entering the woods, we passed a Bhutanese home, and I stopped to take a picture. Like the dress, the homes in Bhutan adhere to a traditional design. They are two-story, wood-framed structures with wood-shingled roofs. The window frames are intricately carved, and often decorating the whitewashed, pounded-mud walls are Buddhism's eight auspicious symbols: white conch, lotus

A traditional Bhutanese home decorates Paro Valley. Photo by Peter McBride.

flower, golden wheel, precious umbrella, endless knot, golden fish, victory banner, and treasure vase. The ground level of the home is used to store farm equipment and serves as a barn for farm animals, whose warm body temperatures act as a kind of natural heater for the family living above. The second floor contains sleeping and cooking quarters, and an open-air attic sits just above the second floor roof to dry freshly harvested crops and hay. Last and most important, a single white prayer flag, with colorful ribbons on each of its four corners, decorates the rooftop — the Bhutanese answer to the TV antenna.

As we approached a house, I saw a local man coming down the trail in the opposite direction. His face was wrinkled with age, his head closely shaved, and he wore green canvas sneakers and navy blue long underwear under his gray gho.

"Hola," I said as he shuffled up.

"*Kuzuzangbo la*!" the man said, flashing a missing-tooth smile.

After he passed, I turned to Joe excitedly. "Did I say hello right?"

"You did," Joe replied, "if you were in Mexico."

I felt more than stupid.

"Hey, you tried," said Joe. "And you have twenty-three more days to perfect it."

"Kuzuzangbo la!" I repeated to myself, drilling it back into memory.

Kuzuzangbo la could be the longest word for "hello" in the world. But perhaps, like the rocky road leading out of our hotel, it wasn't about speed and saying it quickly but slowing down and connecting. As we plodded on, I decided to consciously slow everything down on this trek — my walking, my talking, and if I could, my thinking. Most of the time, my thoughts are like a radio, set to speed-scan and perpetually switching from station to station.

OUR FIRST LUNCH SPOT WAS BESIDE A *CHORTEN*, OR A BUDDHIST "spiritual monument." Chortens, which dot hillsides all over the Himalayas, have three distinct styles — Nepali, Tibetan, and Bhutanese. In Bhutan, they are rectangular white stone structures with a red band of paint running just below the wood shingle roof like the dzongs.

I found the others seated around the chorten, eating crustless cheese sandwiches, hard boiled eggs, and boiled potatoes. As Sonam handed me my lunch, Ryan immediately made room for me to sit beside him on the modest shelf of the chorten.

"How's the hiking, Ryan?"

"Not bad," he said, "considering I've been on an oil platform for most of the past three months."

Ryan was currently stationed on an oil rig in Indonesia, where he worked as an engineer. The flipside of spending weeks at a time on an oil platform was that Ryan got loads of free time to travel. Prior to the Snowman Trek, Ryan had backpacked throughout Europe and ventured to Russia, Chile, Easter Island, Egypt, Cambodia, Malaysia, Thailand, and Bali; he had come to Bhutan in 2005 to do the Jhomolhari Trek. However, along with sites such as Angkor Wat and the Rapa Nui, he also had a keen interest in another kind of cultural attraction — parties.

"If we finish the Snowman Trek in exactly twenty-four days and if we don't get snowbound and no one gets lost or dies," Ryan said very seriously, as if explaining how to itemize taxes, "we'll be back in Thimphu, the capital of Bhutan, on Saturday night — just in time to hit Space 34!"

"Space 34?" I asked.

"Oh, yes," declared Ryan. "Space 34 is a great disco, right down the hall from this cool lounge called the Om Bar. I hit it on my first visit to Bhutan in 2005 and it was amazing!"

I never would have guessed that hidden behind his genteel, studious demeanor, a party provocateur lurked in Ryan.

"Twenty-four days," I declared. "We're there!"

Paul, Joe, Peter, Rob, and all the others quickly signed up. Thus it was decided that we'd do our best to stick to our trekking schedule — not so much so we can beat the winter snows and stay healthy — but for the sole purpose of arriving back in Thimphu on Saturday night to party at Space 34. When I asked Ryan why he travels, his answer was simple. "The world is bigger than the small town in which I grew up, and I want to experience all of it."

As I ate, I admired the chorten: each side had a small prayer wheel built into it, under which sat a tiny ledge where offerings had been placed — juniper branches and clay figures that looked like large Hershey's kisses. "What are these?" I asked Norbu, holding one up.

"Poor man's stupas," he said. "Instead of offering animals as sacrifices, people now offer these little mud statues to bring good luck."

"Looks like they even offer beer," said Ryan, picking up an empty bottle of beer, ominously called Hit.

"That beer bottle is an offering?" gasped Tom, taking a sip of his apple cider box drink.

"Yup," said Norbu. "As a wise man once said, 'If there is reverence, even a dog's tooth emits light.'"

Sonam and Sangey smiled as they made the rounds, serving tea from tall, colorfully painted thermoses. As I cracked my hardboiled egg against the stone chorten and began peeling, I pondered the empty bottle of beer. Was it litter? Or was it an offering? Surprisingly, it didn't seem out of place alongside a small collection of clay figures and finger-like juniper branches.

I turned to Ryan. "What do you think, is a bottle of beer holy?"

"Do you know who you're asking," asked Ryan, laughing. "Of course!" Then he grew serious. "Truthfully, I think it comes down to the intention behind what's being offered. If the intention is pure, the offering is pure."

As Ryan said this, I remembered a birthday card my four-year-old niece Lauren gave me just before I left. "Kavin Happy You Birthday," she'd scrawled almost illegibly in red pen "I Love Lauren Kavin I love I love." Alongside the letters were colorful etchings and her first attempts at drawing flowers. Recalling that, the beer bottle seemed to sparkle with a glassy radiance.

Norbu sauntered over. "You boys know what chortens are used for?"

I told him it was a receptacle for offering.

"Yes," said Norbu, "but chortens are also used to pin down demons."

"Demons?" I said, tentatively.

"Oh-h-h-h yes," he said with wide, ghost-story eyes. "Guru Rinpoche vanquished demons all across the Himalayas and converted them to Buddhism. He used chortens to pin them down and trap them."

The Bhutanese are very superstitious. Many Bhutanese believe deities live in rocks, rivers, trees, and mountains. These were beliefs inherited from Bon, the animistic and shamanistic religion that predated Buddhism in the Himalayas. As a result, Bhutanese farmers plow around large rocks in their farm fields (lest they disturb the resident deity), prohibit mountain climbing, and will even go so far as to hold off having a celebration. According to the calendar, we were doing the majority of the Snowman Trek during an inauspicious month — October — in one of the most inauspicious years ever. In fact, the year 2007 was so inauspicious that the hundred-year anniversary of Bhutan's monarchy had been postponed until 2008.

"Wow," said Ryan, "Postponing a party is never a good sign."

FOLLOWING LUNCH, THE TRAIL CROSSED THE PARO CHHU again on a wooden cantilever bridge and ascended through the forest. The elevation gain began to reveal itself as my breath became visible, hail pellets replaced rain, and the river quickened, slamming into rocks with cymbal-like cadences.

As I rounded a corner, I discovered Kira, resting on a rock and admiring the foggy splendor of the scenery.

"Mind if I walk with you?" I asked.

"Sure thing," she said standing and threading her arms through her backpack straps. "Let's do it."

While I'd only been on the trail a few hours, already I was enjoying the way in which visits arose spontaneously, fortuitously, and were full of substance.

Kira had been called "the gutsiest woman — and some say craziest — adventurer of our day," by *Book Magazine* and had been dubbed a "real-life Lara Croft" by the *New York Times*. She had written two successful memoirs and numerous travel articles and traveled to most everyplace that began with a *D* as in Dangerous: Mozambique, Rwanda, Madagascar, Borneo, Burma, the Congo, Papua New Guinea, Iran, and Libya. She'd also done a six hundred–mile solo kayak expedition on the Niger River from Mali to Timbuktu, and dodged grizzly bears on an eight hundred–mile bike ride through Alaska to the Arctic Ocean. Given the nature of her trips and the descriptions I'd read of her in the media, I expected Kira to be loud, rough, and tough, but when I first met her in Bhutan, she was sitting shyly on the couch in the hotel lobby with her hands politely folded across her lap. I thought to myself, "That can't be her!" But then I looked into her eyes and saw something immovable and courageous. They were the seasoned eyes of a tough traveler who had seen both the best and worst of humanity. The chance to travel with Kira was part of the reason I booked my trip with CHE; I thought it'd be fun to meet her, hear firsthand about her adventures, and if we encountered any trouble, I could hide behind her and say, "Get 'em, Kira! I'm right behind you!"

As the trail entered the forest and we walked beside large, rain-wet ferns and over mossy rocks, I asked her why she travels.

"Traveling makes me feel alive," she replied. "It's the best feeling in the world."

"And why the crazy trips?"

Kira told me she likes to challenge preconceived notions of what's possible for herself and other women travelers.

"Why did you pick the Snowman Trek?"

"Oh this," replied Kira, laughing. "This trek is just for fun."

"For fun!" I repeated. "You say that as if it's a game of mini-golf!"

Kira also said, as a practicing Buddhist, she'd always wanted to visit this tiny kingdom hidden in the Himalayas and couldn't pass up a chance to write a story about it. While I liked the sound of traveling with Kira before the trek, that day it dawned on me the Snowman Trek must be on par with all her other extreme adventures. It was a worrisome thought, so when Kira asked me about my life, I was happy to change the subject.

I grew up in a happy household in New Hampshire, the youngest of three kids, graduated with a degree in creative writing, and since then had been struggling to make it as a screenwriter. A screenplay is like a poem or a great puzzle, and I love the challenge of putting the pieces together. I fell in love with movies when I was eight and watched E.T. and Elliot soar across the moon on a bicycle in Steven Spielberg's classic film. After that movie, I thought anything was possible.

Kira smiled and then asked the natural question, "Have you sold anything?"

I hadn't. "But when I get back home, I should hear about a Disney Writing Fellowship I applied for. They've turned me down before, but I've got a good feeling about it this year." In fact, I had it all planned out: I would finish the Snowman Trek in October, win the Disney Fellowship in early November, and then move to Los Angeles in January to begin my new life.

"That's great!" Kira replied. "I'm sure you'll get it!"

I told Kira more about my favorite movies, but what I didn't tell her was how, after eight years of sending out screenplays and constant rejections, I was thinking about giving up my dream. I didn't tell her that if Disney rejected me, I was done with screenwriting forever. Nor did I tell her that over the past year, I'd had the unsettling feeling that what I wanted from the universe wasn't what the universe wanted for me — not in screenwriting, love or, most important, faith. I didn't tell Kira that grace had been playing a game of hide-and-seek with me lately and that every time I thought I'd found lasting contentment, it evaporated in my embrace. I didn't tell her I'd begun to lose faith in faith — I didn't tell her it was make or break time for me.

HALF AN HOUR UP THE TRAIL, THE VALLEY WIDENED AND WE passed a sign for the entrance to Jigme Dorji National Park — "Take Nothing But Memories, Leave Nothing But Footprints" — and arrived at the army checkpoint of Gunitsawa. There, two broad-shouldered soldiers, dressed in camouflage from the Royal Bhutanese Army, checked our trekking permits.

As opposed to other trekking destinations in Asia, in Bhutan you must be part of a prepaid package. You must always be in the company of a local Bhutanese guide and pay a daily tariff that covers your food, lodging, driver, guide, and entrance fees to dzongs, museums, or monuments. The kings of Bhutan, having watched the Buddhist kingdoms of Ladakh, Tibet, and Sikkim get swallowed up, realized that preserving Bhutan's culture was mandatory for its survival and thus instituted a tourism policy of "high value, low numbers." Certainly, it is an unusual system, but it is not without its rewards — Bhutan has kept its culture and environment intact.

A few feet from the soldiers, Rob, Tom, Ryan, and Larry were loitering around a large water-powered prayer wheel, which looked like a concrete roller turned on its side. With each revolution, a small bell rang, and written in gold Sanskrit letters over a green backdrop was the prayer we heard that morning at our puja ceremony: *Om Mani Padme Hum* or "Hail the Jewel in the Lotus." The lotus is a sacred and symbolic flower for both Buddhists and Hindus. The Easter pink petals of the lotus, which floats and blooms above dirty water, is a metaphor for the human soul's ability to flower above earthly ignorance and attachment. "The mantra originated in India," Norbu explained, "and whether seen or spoken invokes the blessing of Avalokiteshvara, the Buddha of compassion who is also known in Bhutan and Tibet as Chenrezig."

"How does the whole process work?" I asked.

"The idea of the prayer wheel is that, as it turns, Buddhist prayers are released to the universe," said Norbu. "One spin can release over a hundred thousand prayers."

"Spiritual multitasking," I said. "I like it."

OUR CAMP FOR THE FIRST NIGHT WAS A GRASSY CLEARING next to the Paro Chhu called Shana. Sonam, Sangey, Achula, and the horsemen had overtaken us soon after lunch, so we arrived to find camp set up and hot tea and cookies waiting. Spread out over the small grassy clearing were two large family-style tents for dining and cooking, as well as nine dome-style tents and a blue canvas toilet tent, whose size and shape resembled a telephone booth. After a brief tour of the camp, I wandered over to the kitchen tent where I found Achula, hunched over two gas burners, stirring chicken noodle soup. Next to him, spread out on an orange tarp, carrots, onions, and lettuce leaves awaited washing.

"Say, Achula!" I said, snapping a picture. "How many times have you done the Snowman?"

"Yes," he said. "Eleven."

"Eleven times!" I gasped, pulling the camera from my eyes.

"Yes-Yes."

"And you're still smiling?"

"Yes!" replied Achula, his eyes twinkling like a merry sage.

I quickly did the math of hiking eleven Snowman Treks — 264 days, 2,376 miles, and 121 mountain passes, including 77 over 16,000 feet! Not only that but since he's part of the crew, he'd probably run the trek each and every time. There was no doubt, the support staff of Bhutan and the Sherpas of Nepal were the true heroes of any expedition in the Himalayas.

"Are those chilies?" I asked pointing to some green and red vegetables.

"Yes, sir."

Chilies are huge in Bhutan, and you're apt to see them drying in the sun on most every rooftop. The chili isn't native to the Himalayas, it arrived about four hundred to five hundred years ago and has been prized in Bhutan ever since. In Bhutan, chilies are used as a vegetable, a spice, and are occasionally burned to ward off evil spirits. Chilies, vegetables, and cheese are often mixed together to create *ema datsi*, the national dish of Bhutan.

"Are those hot?" I asked.

"Yes, sir." Achula said.

"How often do you eat them?"

Achula shook his head, not understanding. Since English is taught along with Dzongkha in Bhutanese schools, you can roughly guess

With two sticks and a tarp for their tent, the horsemen hunker down. Photo by Peter McBride.

someone's formal schooling by their command of it. "Yes, sir" might have been the only English words Achula knew.

The sun dropped behind the forested ridges, bathing our camp in shadows. The temperature fell swiftly and ghostly mists rose from the meadow like tiny tornado tails. I found my duffel bag on a blue tarp with all the others, a colorful collection of fancy brand names and one green army bag. My bag was heavy — I had every imaginable piece of high-tech camping gear, plus a medicine cabinet worth of pills and potions for every ailment and a pocket-size backcountry first-aid guide I hoped would explain just when and how the heck to use everything. When I lifted it, the bag's weight sent me staggering back a few feet and Sonam ran over to rescue me.

"No, sir," said Sonam. "I carry."

"Let's compromise," I said. "We'll each take a strap."

As I settled into my two-person dome tent that would be mine for the duration of the trek, I saw a horseman peeking out from his modest tent — a green tarp hung over two Y-shaped branches, spaced five feet apart. He hunkered with his fellow horsemen under a stack of yak-hair blankets, while I huddled in my warm, down jacket in my four-season sleeping bag. Embarrassed by my extravagance, I quickly zipped up my tent door.

AROUND SEVEN, SONAM AND SANGEY CALLED US TO DINNER. The dining tent truly felt five-star: nine folding chairs surrounded two metal folding tables that had been joined to make one long table. A red-and-white checkered tablecloth decorated our table, and at the center, a gas lantern broadcast bright white light. Rob, Ryan, and Tom sat on one side of the table, Kira, Paul, Peter, and I sat on the other side, and Joe and Larry occupied each end.

Dinner started with chicken noodle soup served with Japanese-style miso spoons and bowls, followed by potatoes, red rice, green beans, mushrooms, curry peas, and sliced apples for dessert. The conversation veered from today's hike — considered easy by all — to our favorite Monty Python skits, and we also joked that Joe should advertise a GUARANTEED WEIGHT LOSS PROGRAM* in a magazine in large bold letters to get everyone to sign up and, at the very bottom of the page, include a disclaimer in the finest and smallest print: *the snowman trek.

"I'm sure everyone would sign up," chuckled Peter. "But then they'd realize nothing in life comes without effort!"

We laughed, but there was a lot of truth to this weight-loss forecast: many people initially lose their appetite at high altitude and simply have to wait for their body to produce more red blood cells before it returns. From the people I spoke with before my trip, it didn't sound uncommon to lose five to fifteen pounds over the course of the trek. That night, I was not terribly hungry, but I was also not nauseous from the altitude, so I took that to be a good sign.

Larry raised his hand to speak. "May I have your attention," he said, formally, "I'd like to know what everyone has heard about the Snowman Trek?"

Larry was a man of immense good cheer with a loud laugh, Santa Claus belly, and a pair of glasses with adjusting lenses. He was proof that it's never too late to go after your dreams. He'd spent the past twenty-five years working as a chemical engineer. When he retired at fifty-five, he decided to start his adventure travel career. "If I didn't start then," he told me, "I'd just be one year older when I did." He quickly fell in love with the Himalayas, visited the Everest and Langtang regions of Nepal, and also trekked the Manaslu and Annapurna circuits. He'd traveled extensively throughout New Zealand, but when he read Barbara Crossette's book, *So Close to Heaven,* about the vanishing Buddhist kingdoms in the Himalayas, he knew he had to get to Bhutan. "Since I was going," he said, "I reasoned I might as well try the hardest trek."

In the dim candlelight, Ryan told us he heard the Snowman Trek described as a death march.

"I've heard it's the ultimate high-altitude traverse of the Himalayas," said Tom.

"I did an Internet search on the 'toughest trek in the world,'" added Paul, "and this trek came up!"

Kira told us she read it should be called the "Mudman Trek," because the trail was horrendous in parts.

"I'll tell you what I heard about the Snowman Trek," said Peter, suddenly serious.

"What's that?" asked Joe, turning to face him.

Peter looked around the table at all of us individually, and the message was clear—we should listen up. "Well," he began, "I've heard that everyone cries at some point on the Snowman Trek."

"What do you mean cries?" I asked, setting down my cup of tea.

"Tears," said Tom. "Ever heard of them?"

"Do they have something to do with eyes?" I joked.

Larry said he didn't believe it. "You're lying to us, Pete."

By then, everyone had set their tea down and all the air felt as if it had been squeezed out of the tent. The only noise was the gas lantern that sounded like it was hissing a warning.

"That's what my friend told me," said Peter in a near whisper. "Everybody cries at some point on the Snowman Trek."

"Because of what?" asked Paul. "The difficulty, the weather . . . the stench of the toilet tent?"

"I don't know," Peter said, standing and slowly making his way to the door, "but we'll find out!"

Larry protested. "You can't just throw that on us and then say goodnight!"

"Oh yeah?" said Peter, unzipping the tent door, "watch me!"

"Watch me too!" said Tom, standing and politely folding his paper napkin.

Rob slugged the last of his tea. "Me too!"

I followed them out into the misting blackness of the Himalayan night. With their headlamps, everyone looked like miners in some foggy underworld.

IT WAS A BITE OF A MADELEINE COOKIE THAT BROUGHT THE French writer Marcel Proust back to the thoughts of his childhood, but evidently for me, it was the sound and sight of a sleeping bag zipper. As I zipped myself up in my sleeping bag that night, suddenly I was six years old again in our New Hampshire home with my older brother and sister, Sean and Kristine. We used to make elaborate forts out of sofa cushions and bed blankets and then grab our sleeping bags and flashlights to spend the night sleeping in the living room. Despite being indoors, sleeping in our living room was really my first camping experience, and it was magical. My dad would stoke a fire in the fireplace, and McGee, our black lab, would sleep next to us, keeping an eye out for the bears and mountain lions that lingered in the imagination of our young innocent minds. We'd tell jokes and ghost stories (with the flashlight held up to our faces for dramatic effect) then fall swiftly into a sweet and silent sleep, dreaming of the wonderful pancake breakfast mom would have waiting for us when we woke.

Well, I had no such luck getting to sleep the first night of the Snowman. As I clicked off my headlamp and stretched out, sharp rocks stabbed at my back, as if urging me to get up and go home. The only difference between sleeping with a pad and sleeping without is that with a sleeping pad, the sharp rocks causing immense discomfort become dull rocks causing immense discomfort. In either case, you're uncomfortable and terribly aware you're miles away from the nearest mattress. Hoping to fix the situation, I slid to the right where a rock dug into my right shoulder blade. I slid to the left and another rock dug into my left hip. I tried sliding diagonally, but a rock dug into my rear end. Then I stopped sliding altogether because I realized I was doing something very similar to the break-dancing move called "the worm." I clicked on my headlamp, spun around to my original position, and shoved my sleeping pad aside to feel for a flat spot with my hand. There wasn't one, and the green nylon floor of my tent looked like it had been spread over a pool table, littered with balls. Of course, I could have moved the rocks but that might have disrupted the resident diety, and I knew I needed all the help I could get to finish the Snowman Trek. So I decided to take the lesser of rock evils and positioned myself in such a way that where the rocks rose my body did too — the small of my back, the bend of my knees, and the curve of my neck. And I positioned myself around the rocks — bending a leg here and an arm there — which worked until I realized I was horribly uncomfortable and resembled one of those convoluted white chalk body drawings at crime scenes. There was nothing to do but let the rocks push up where they may and attempt to sleep. I grabbed my fleece, bunched it up, and lay back down. But as I closed my eyes, I realized a second truth about sleeping in the woods: along with not being soft, it's also not quiet.

While the woods may not have airplanes flying immediately

overhead, barking dogs, or your neighbor's car alarm going off at 3:00 a.m., it was definitely not quiet. Instead of city noises, there were the insistent sound of the rainfly whipping against the tent pole, swaying trees, someone snoring in the next tent over, rustling leaves, and horses with harness bells clomping around inches from my cranium. But loudest and worst of all was the voice inside my head — my inner critic — that old familiar foe. *You have insomnia,* it said. No I don't, I replied. *It's the first sign of altitude sickness.* I'm just adjusting. *You never should've come.* Yes I should have. *You're going to quit, waste all your money, and look stupid.* No, I won't. *Yes, you will.* No! *Yes!* No!

I rolled over, not only wanting sleep but also desperately needing to because I was still horribly jet-lagged. Over the last week, I'd flown across more time zones than I could count, went to bed late, and had to rise at 2:00 a.m. for my Druk Air flight to Bhutan. I eased myself onto my back and took a deep breath, imagining I was at the end of a yoga class in corpse pose. "Breathe," I told myself. "Just relax." I started to settle in, but as a wave of relaxation dropped over me like a warm, wonderful blanket, my inner critic reminded me that doing corpse pose on the Snowman Trek may not be an auspicious omen. I was quickly learning the toughest part of the toughest trek in the world may not be the trail but rather the mind games I would play with myself. I rolled over, attempting to sleep again, but like home, sleep felt far away.

5

A JOURNEY DOESN'T BEGIN WITH YOUR DEPARTURE FLIGHT but rather months before, when you're inspired to travel. I have often thought at such a moment, part of you departs for that distant destination, never to return and as a traveler you have two choices: you can refuse your own invitation for adventure or you can book your ticket. If you refuse the adventure, your departed self will — depending on your dream — either become shipwrecked or snowbound, and if you don't launch a search-and rescue mission, that self will soon starve.

The idea of tackling the Snowman Trek first popped into my head when I was in Bhutan in 2004. During that trip, my plan was to do the Jhomolhari Trek, which follows the Snowman route for the first five days then veers off after the first high pass in the Lingshi District and returns to Thimphu. That was the idea and inspiration, but by the time I reached Jhomolhari base camp, I felt terrible. My head pounded, my breath came in fitful wheezes, and I wanted to throw up. It was altitude sickness. Needless to say, there was no question of following the original itinerary, which involved crossing the 16,000-foot pass. Instead, my guide, Khandu, and I decided to return to Paro, which not only meant retracing our steps and seeing the same scenery but also meant cutting my trek short a day. On the drizzly morning we were to leave, as the kitchen staff generously rolled up my sleeping bag and packed up my duffel bag for me, I stood shivering outside my tent with such regret. When I looked up the valley, I saw a trail blazing up through the rocks and autumn bushes. I was seized with a terrible longing, for there is nothing more alluring to a hiker than the thin ribbon of boot-wide trail disappearing into the mountains. Who knew what adventures awaited? What elevations, epiphanies, and exultations?

I asked Khandu where the trail led.

"The village of Lingshi," he said, looking up the valley. "And then Laya."

"And then?"

Khandu suddenly smiled. "The village of Thanza, sir."

"Where's that?"

When Khandu told me Thanza was in the wild and remote Lunana District, his face glowed, as if he were standing near a warm fire or over a heap of shining jewels. "Thanza is the most beautiful place on earth. The Shangri-la, sir."

"Does a trek go there?"

Khandu nodded. "Snowman Trek, sir."

"The Snowman Trek," I repeated, gazing up at the trail winding up through the radiant rocks. I loved the way the words "Snowman Trek" swirled honey-sweet in my mouth.

Khandu explained that the Snowman Trek skirted the border between Bhutan and Tibet, passing never-to-be-named mountains and plunged into a region beyond the mapped world. Then he picked up my backpack. "We go now."

I looked at the trail again. "Let's go to Thanza instead!"

"Sir, you are very sick," Khandu said, with a hand on my shoulder. "Next time."

"Next time," I said in a broken-hearted murmur.

While I followed Khandu as he started down the valley, part of me left for Thanza that day. I knew this because over the next few years, I was reminded of my departed self—I'd see mountains or hear an inspiring song on the radio and the words "Snowman Trek" would ring through my mind and I'd see that trail leading up through the rocks. I started having dreams too—of tying prayer flags at the mountain passes and laughing with friends whose faces I couldn't discern in the dreamlike haze. But after another year of inaction, my dreams became less frequent and began to dim and fade like a flashlight short on batteries. I realized the most dangerous part of a dream isn't what it asks of you, but rather, the life of regret you'll have to endure if the dream is allowed to die. I knew there would never be a perfect time to attempt the Snowman Trek, but I had to make time. I had to get back to Bhutan.

Thus, I resolved to do the Snowman Trek in the fall of 2007. The prime trekking season for the Snowman Trek is autumn, taking advantage of a thin window of good weather after the summer monsoon leaves in mid-September and before the winter snows arrive in November. Spring is also a great trekking season in Bhutan, but with the Snowman, it's always a gamble whether the high passes will be snow-free or if the swollen rivers will have left any bridges intact. Swaying on the side of rain instead of snow, I decided to go in September 2007 and began working seven days a week to save up money. The truth was, I wasn't certain I could finish the Snowman, which was probably part of the allure, but what was certain was that day two of the Snowman Trek was going to be hard—13.6 miles with a 2,250-foot elevation gain, nearly twice the suggested rate for proper acclimatization.

AFTER A NIGHT OF FITFUL SLEEP, I AWOKE AT 6:00 A.M. TO the sound of my neighbor neighing precariously near my ear.

I sat up, feeling tired, groggy, and apprehensive about altitude

Rise and shine! Photo by Peter McBride.

sickness. Altitude sickness affects about one in four people who travel high and can occur as low as seven thousand feet above sea level. It's an elusive ailment — its symptoms are often hard to read and appear in various manifestations; there is little way to predict when someone will get sick. Descending, the only tried and true cure, can be difficult since altitude sickness routinely appears hours after arrival at your camping site and often at night. You never know who it's going to affect or when, where, or how it will happen. Someone's past experience at high altitude or fitness level guarantees nothing. In fact, professional mountaineers get altitude sickness all the time. There is no way to foresee it; you simply never know.

Acute Mountain Sickness (AMS) is generally the first sign of altitude sickness, and the symptoms range from headache, insomnia, fatigue, nausea, and lack of appetite. If left untreated, AMS can quickly worsen into either High Altitude Cerebral Edema (HACE) or High Altitude Pulmonary Edema (HAPE). As AMS progresses into HACE, fluid leaks into the brain, there is a loss of coordination and balance (a condition known as ataxia) and, if untreated, the patient will slip into a coma and die. With HAPE, fluid leaks into the lungs, producing a frothy cough, sometimes pink in color, which will eventually accumulate and drown the person if they don't receive urgent medical care. I found the information on altitude sickness that I read before the trek hopelessly confusing, and everyone I talked to had their own trail-tested advice: drink a lot of water, don't drink water, take sleeping pills, take Diamox, or if you can believe it, take the erectile dysfunction medication, Viagra, to dilate your blood vessels and allow blood to flow more freely through the body. One guy I talked to who was trying to put a group together to do the Snowman preached excessive bleeding right before going to high altitude with the idea that it would kick-start your system into producing mass quantities of red blood cells. Needless to say, I had no further e-mail correspondence with this man because, call me conservative, but I try not to venture into the backcountry with anyone who believes in bloodletting.

After bed tea and breakfast, we started up the trail. It was another dreary day of gray skies, light rain, and wispy clouds, which led me to conclude that it must be easy being a weatherman in a place like Bhutan, Seattle, or London — no one holds you accountable and all you have to do is say, "partly cloudy with a chance of rain" every day. When you want to switch it up, you say, "partly sunny with a chance of rain," and if you really want to surprise viewers, you say, "partly rainy with a chance of sun."

As I marched over soggy grass and around horse patties, I found my mood matched the day — lethargic and damp. Norbu, Tom, and Ryan led the pack, followed by me, Rob, Kira, Peter, Paul, Larry, and Joe. The trail continued up the valley, following the river through lush forests of oak, maple, alder, pine, and birch. Despite the rain, birds chirped on branches and the forest felt alive. The trail was immediately steeper and a lot rockier than the first day, and it felt like the trekking equivalent of pedaling a bike in a much higher gear. Within minutes I was soaked with sweat and struggling to breathe. I pulled off the trail, yanked off the cap to my canteen, and took a swig. As I did my throat went into spasm, and I immediately spat my mouthful back out. My body needed air before water. As I took off my raincoat and waited for my breath to slow down, there was no doubt — it would be a hard day.

THERE'S A DIFFERENCE BETWEEN HIKING AND TREKKING, mainly that the word *trekking* sounds a lot more impressive. Modern trekking in the Himalayas was the inspired idea of Col. James Owen Merion Roberts, a British Army officer who spent much of his adult life working in the Himalayas, serving in such positions as a military attaché to the British Embassy in Kathmandu and as a transport officer for the 1963 mountaineering expedition to Mount Everest. In 1965 when Colonel Roberts had the idea that tourists would pay good money to hike through the highest mountains on the planet and not have to worry about any of the logistics, he placed an ad in *Holiday Magazine* and three middle-aged women from the Midwest signed up. That year, Colonel Roberts and his Sherpa support team led the women from Kathmandu to Namche Bazaar and trekking and tourism in Nepal soon boomed in popularity.

Despite their close proximity, trekking in Bhutan is different than trekking in Nepal. From speaking with a few people who'd traveled to both countries, the consensus was that Bhutan was like Nepal was forty years ago. The obvious difference is the number of trekkers. In 2007, Bhutan welcomed 21,094 tourists, with only 903 arriving specifically to trek. According to the Nepalese Ministry of Tourism's Web site, that same year Nepal hosted 526,705 tourists, with 60,273 trekkers traveling to the Annapurna region alone. There's also the price difference between the two countries: Bhutan charges more than two hundred dollars a day, and trekking in Nepal costs less than a hundred dollars a day. Bhutan uses horses and yaks to haul trekking gear, and the Nepalese generally use Sherpas. Teahouses are a common sight along Nepal's trekking trails, but all of Bhutan's treks are strictly camping-based treks. Lunch is also different: lunch in Bhutan is precooked and prepacked in stainless steel pots that are stacked vertically in a large, columnar thermos to keep warm. In Nepal, lunch is cooked on the trail, often requiring an extended stop. Lastly, the mileage and number of trekking hours each day tend to be longer in Bhutan, and the trails, which often seem like footprints on slippery rocks, are a lot tougher to navigate than Nepal.

Although *National Geographic* writer Desmond Doig trekked through Bhutan on assignment in 1961, followed a few years later by geologist Augusto Gansser in 1963 and British physicians Michael Ward, Frederic Jackson and R. Turner visited the Lunana District in 1964, tourism in Bhutan wasn't permitted until the coronation of the Fourth King in 1974. Trekking in Bhutan began four years later when Lars-Eric Lindblad, a Swedish American adventurer and entrepreneur — and the father of ecotourism — began bringing tourists into the country. It was his suggestion to the Fourth King that Bhutan institute a "high value, low numbers" tourism policy to preserve Bhutan's unique culture and pristine wild areas. Initially, there was a quota of two hundred tourists a year, who were charged a daily tariff of $130. The only entrance into the country at the time was through the border town of Pheuntsholing, and arranging a visa to enter could take six weeks of tough negotiations in India. Once in Bhutan tourists were only allowed to visit select areas: Pheuntsholing, Paro, and Thimphu. Central Bhutan was opened to tourists in 1982, and Druk Air began operations in Paro in 1983 with an eighteen-seat Dornier airplane. Bhutan Tourism Corporation, a government agency, handled all tourist arrangements until 1991 when tourism was privatized. Today, there are more than 220 tour operators working within Bhutan; many international companies also book tours but only in conjunction with one of the local companies. Since 1991 tourism in Bhutan has grown steadily from 7,557 visitors in 2000 to 17,365 in 2006 to 21,094 in 2007. While Bhutan no longer officially limits the numbers of tourists, nor do you need a special "in" to get into the country, the limited availability on Druk Air flights during the busy season, as well as the daily tariff and lack of significant transportation infrastructure, naturally limit the number of visitors.

"Who did you book your trip to Bhutan with in 2004?" Joe asked me as we stepped carefully through a muddy section of trail.

"Through Marie Brown and Bhutan Travel," I replied and then proceeded to tell Joe about a woman who had a huge impact, not only on my first visit, but also on tourism in Bhutan.

Marie Brown first heard about Bhutan in 1977 when she was on a Lars-Eric Lindblad trip for travel agents in India. One night Lars-Eric showed a movie on Bhutan at one of the hotels and a Bhutanese representative spoke to the group. As she saw imposing white dzongs and scenic mountains, Marie immediately fell in love with Bhutan, thinking it must be the most beautiful, remote place on earth. Needless to say, when Lars-Eric offered a travel agent familiarization trip to Bhutan the following year, Marie immediately signed up. Following her trip, Marie wrote an award-winning story on Bhutan for *Travelscene Magazine*, a publication geared specifically toward travel agents. As a result of her article, she was invited to Bhutan as a guest in 1979 and offered the opportunity to help set up, and single-handedly run, the first — and so far, the only — Bhutanese government–based tourism office outside Bhutan. Bhutan Travel (formerly Bhutan Travel Service) opened in 1980, and for nine years, arranged most all American travel to Bhutan until the tourism industry was privatized. Since then it has continued to send hundreds of tourists to the Dragon Kingdom. Marie Brown also happened to be a member of the first tourist group to complete the Snowman Trek. Although her first attempt in 1983 was turned around due to snow, Marie finished the Snowman Trek in 1985 with Christy Tews, a mountaineering guide from California's Adventure Travel Center (and a member of the first Himalayan expedition led by women to climb 26,504-foot Annapurna) as well as a guitar-toting man from the Midwest named Gary Reeder. Two other trekkers, both women, had also signed up for the trek but neither made it — one woman had a panic attack en route to Bhutan and the other dropped out at Laya due to a strange skin irritation on her hands.

I'd planned on booking my Snowman Trek with Marie, but we ran into a problem often faced when attempting to do the Snowman Trek — we couldn't find enough people to form a group. However, when I found Joe and CHE with a guaranteed departure, Marie still made time to generously answer my many questions and showed a sincere and devoted interest in my returning. Marie described her Snowman Trek as "peaceful and happy" and spoke honestly of her pre-trek training ("jogging an hour every day before work"), her struggles with altitude ("I lost my appetite for the first ten days"), the companionship with her fellow trekkers ("most times we were filled with side-splitting laughter"), the friendship with her guides ("we played a card game called ponku-donkey together"), of sharing butter tea with nomadic yak herders in yak wool tents, and of taking hundreds of pictures.

But what Marie talked about most was the village of Thanza in Lunana. "It's the most beautiful, most mysterious, most otherworldly place I've ever been," she said to me before I left. "Even among the Bhutanese, Lunana has an aura. One of the eeriest places was the dzong in Chozo, just before Thanza Village. Our guides told us that no one may ride into the dzong courtyard, no matter how high their rank. There were broken windows, ravens, and a very strange atmosphere about the place."

"Oh," I said, making a mental note to stay away from Chozo Dzong. "If you could pick one thing that you remember most," I asked, "What would it be?"

I assumed Marie would mention the towering mountains or lush forests of Bhutan but she didn't. "We had two porters in the

Lunana area," she said, "a young girl and an older female relative. Christy and I made friends with them and on the day they left us to go back home, they stood by the side of the path as we started the long descent from the Lunana District and they sang to us. It was a Bhutanese song, something like "good-bye" and "have a safe journey" and "hope to see you again." These two voices singing this haunting melody against a backdrop of towering snow peaks is something I'll always remember. A Bhutanese friend told me I should be proud to have done the Snowman Trek, but I felt blessed to have been given the gift and the ability to do it. It was a great gift."

I asked what it was like to re-enter civilization after such an experience.

"On the last day we could see the road from the lunch spot, and we knew it would be just a few hours before we were back. I don't think any of us were really ready for it. I know I felt as if I could have gone on walking forever. By the time we got back, we felt as though we had been in another world, which we had."

WHILE I KNEW FROM MOVIES AND MYTHS THAT SUCH "otherworldly places" were hard to reach, nothing prepared me for day two. As we trudged up the Paro River valley, the trail was awful — wet, muddy, and filled with ankle-breaking rocks. In fact, I struggled to find the adjectives to describe the trail, but as a rock rolled and I twisted my ankle, expletives poured out of me in an angry torrent. Making matters worse, the trail couldn't seem to make up its mind about what direction it wanted to go. It was like the stock market on a day of panicked trading — up one moment, down the next, up, down, up, down — and my heart was a roller coaster in my ribs.

I didn't fully appreciate the privilege of hiking on maintained trails until I hiked in Bhutan. In America, there are hard-working men and women with the National Park Service and U.S. Forest Service who spend summers clearing trails, moving rocks, cutting back brush, felling trees, and making stone staircases over muddy and steep sections. Few such luxuries existed on the Snowman Trek. I had to not only battle the challenge of the elevation gain and mileage but also the trails themselves. Hiking in Bhutan was a full body workout — I was constantly stepping around rotting tree trunks, ducking under low-hanging branches, leaping over mud patches, plowing through wet fern sections, balancing precariously on slippery stones, and saying to myself, "This too shall pass." With the mud, moss, and slippery rocks, the slightest misstep could've resulted in a broken ankle. Thus each step had to be planned, prepared for, and executed with utmost care, requiring intense concentration. I often had the feeling the trail was working against me, and the worst part of all that downward gazing was that I'd miss looking around at sections of the trail that I'm sure were beautiful.

"Hey, Kev," Peter yelled to me as I descended a steep section of trail lined with wet ferns licking my legs. "Can you hike back up the hill and come down a little slower?"

Peter stood at the bottom of the hill with his video camera in his hand. In addition to shooting the pictures that would accompany Kira's article, Peter was making a short documentary about the trek. Peter and Kira had both arrived in Bhutan a few days before us to catch the *tsechu* ("religious") festival, a series of colorful courtyard dances celebrating Buddhism's victory over evil. I had the sense that within the adventure travel community, Peter and Kira were revered with awe — they took the assignments no one else wanted, or dared to take. However, regardless of whatever war-torn world or famine-stricken area they visited, I found their work always ended with some hopeful affirmation of the human spirit.

Peter studied English and environmental studies at Dartmouth, and upon graduation became a self-taught photographer, later winning awards for his work. His travel resume was just as impressive as Kira's; he's visited more than fifty countries, covering a diverse array of subjects, from the narcotic trade in Africa to "honor" crimes in Jordan. He spent a month documenting the Sherpas who set ropes through Everest's dangerous Khumbu icefall, swam with three hundred sharks in Tuamoto, hiked across the vast salt mines of Bolivia, and hung in midair beside Yosemite Falls to shoot the Bandaloop Dance Troupe.

While I didn't think we were making history by attempting the Snowman Trek — for the Bhutanese had been using the trails for centuries — there was a feeling that history was being made all around us. In 2008 Bhutan hosted their first elections and transitioned from a hereditary monarchy to a constitutional democratic monarchy with the king, a prime minister, and House of Parliment. Although Jigme Singye Wangchuk, the Fourth King, had transferred power to the Crown Prince of Bhutan, Jigme Khesar Namgyel Wangchuk, in 2005, his official coronation didn't take place until 2008. Great celebrations were planned, and in the process, he'd become the youngest monarch in the world. In every village we visited there was a palpable sense of change and excitement about the new elections. I imagined it was not unlike America's first election in 1789.

I hiked back up the hill and waited for Peter's cue and when it came — "Okay!" — started back down, hiking methodically and mindfully.

"Thanks," Peter said, clicking off his video camera as I reached the bottom.

"No, problem," I managed, still winded from the uphill.

Peter asked if I minded hiking up again.

"Again?"

As Peter nodded, I suddenly had a new appreciation for my dog McGee, who used to constantly run up and down the trail on family hikes to make sure everyone was all right. When I protested, Peter told me he really wanted to get a close-up of my hiking boots coming down the trail and justified it by reminding me God was in the details.

I agreed. Not only was I excited about helping Peter out, but

I'd also become enamored by a twisting tree beside the trail that appeared to have been sliced down the middle by lightning. In fact it was the most beautiful and ancient-looking tree I'd ever seen, with long great strands of green moss dripping beneath its branches. When I first came tromping down the trail, I didn't even see the tree. But after Peter stopped me, it suddenly appeared in all its ancient splendor. I could only imagine all the tree had witnessed over the centuries — invading armies, wandering sorcerers, monks, saints, madmen, and smugglers. Suddenly I realized traveling with Peter would be great, for his artistic eye would help me awaken my own.

"You ready?" I yelled down to him from the top of the hill after I caught my breath.

"Okay," he hollered, gazing into the small, square video screen.

I plodded down the hill again, gazing at my tree as my trekking poles tapped the rocky trail. When Peter yelled cut and looked up, I asked if he needed anything else.

"Can you go up there one more time?"

Before I could protest, Peter laughed and thanked me with a hard candy he'd bought at a shop in Gunitsawa yesterday. "I'm going to run ahead and catch Tom and Ryan. Want to join me?"

I thanked Peter but told him I was going to hang beside the tree for awhile because it looked like it had something to teach me. "Who knows?" I said. "Maybe I'll find myself!"

"Well, if you do," said Peter, smirking, "mind looking for me?"

ROB WAS ALSO FILMING THE TREK, BUT HE WAS ENTIRELY different in his filmmaking approach. Whereas Pete was methodical — you could see shots slowly growing on him and then he'd gently reach down for his camera as if a sudden movement might scare away the object of his attention — Rob would just yank out his digital camera and start firing like a Wild West gunslinger.

My first impression of Rob was of him roaring into Paro on his classic Royal Enfield motorbike. Having just ridden all across India and Nepal, he slapped a business card in my hand, which read:

Introducing . . .

ROBERT H.

Ambassador of the Arts	*Hero of the Oppressed*
Soldier of Fortune	*World Traveler*
Adventurer	*Philosopher*
Dragon Slayer	*Philanthropist*

Specializing in: rivers run, wars fought, tigers tamed, revolutions started, steers ridden, mountains climbed and trees planted.

How could I not like a guy with a business card like that and immediately hire him on as my new best friend? When I asked Rob about his past trips, he spoke in excited half sentences that described adventures that were, no doubt, very full. "Ah yeh, well Kev, let's see," he began, "in 1984 I traveled China as an early independent traveler and then Inner Mongolia staying in yurts. 1987 took me down the Chilkoot Trail, Yukon Territory, Alaska, following the route of Buck in *Call of the Wild* by Jack London. Found my Scottish collie pup there, named him 'Buck' and had him for fourteen years. Even taught him to pull my bicycle laden with groceries three kilometers from the shops!"

"Any other trips?"

Rob told me he toured Zimbabwe, Zambia, Botswana, Kenya, Uganda, Tanzania, and Zanzibar in 1994. "Then I did th' Okavango Delta safari in a Toyota troop carrier, where it sank in a crocodile and hippo swamp, and we had to perch on the roof. Met Kee-ra in Papua, New Guinea, in 1995, ran a few ree-vers. In 2004 I rode my Royal Enfield Bullet to Rajastahn Desert, Karnataka, Kerala,

Tamil Nadu, in southern, western India. Also been to Sikkim, West Bengal, northeast India, and went trekking in New Zealand. But that's jes' the short list!"

Rob and I continued up the trail, and when we arrived at a fork in the trail, marked by a large pile of rocks and decorated with prayer flags, Rob slapped his video camera into my hand.

"You want me to film you?" I asked.

"Ah ye," said Rob, retracing his steps. "Jes' press the red button and hava' go!" Rob pointed to the fork in the trail. "Just think, hike eight miles up to th' left and yar in Tee-bet!"

"Cool."

"Not just cool, mate," he said, "Amazin'!"

As I started filming, Rob immediately became animated, crouching and whispering like a secret agent. "It's day two of the Snowman Trek," he said, "and behind me is the turnoff to Tee-bet. This trail leads to the *Tremo La. La* means a "mountain pass" in Dzongkha, Bhutan's national language. This trail has been used for centuries by all kinds of crazy blokes like saints, shamans, and like journey men like m'self."

As the camera shook with my chuckles, Rob tightened the shoulder straps of his backpack. "But today, we're not going to Tee-bet—we're going on the Snowman Trek, which follows the river up the trail to tha' right." With that, Rob started off, but not before turning around and gazing at the camera ominously. "Wish me luck!"

"And cut" I said, lowering the camera, "So who's this movie for anyways?"

Rob told me he films all his trips for his parents. "My father jes loves watchin' my advenchas!"

When I asked how he paid for all his trips, Rob told me he works as a building project manager or a tourist information officer for a few years, saves up money, and then sets off. "I got professional goals like everyone else," he said, fixing the top button of his khaki safari shirt, "But I got to indulge my spirit for advencha too!"

"And it all just works out, huh?"

"Aw, Kev," Rob said, gazing back at me. "If ya' set your mind to it, you can d' anythin!"

FOLLOWING LUNCH, THE TRAIL CONTINUED ITS UNRELENTING route, slogging over moss-sweatered stones and around ankle-deep mud sections. Despite hiking through lush broadleaf and conifer forests, I had my eye on the river — it had picked up speed considerably since the first day and traded its slow Paro glow for raging whitewater that echoed across the forest and pulsed through the rocks with an impressive energy. Despite the difficulty, I found hiking beside the Paro River to be wonderful, its rushing sound was an audible reminder for me to breathe. As I slowed my heart rate with deep, Buddha-belly breaths, I decided there's something wonderfully inspiring about rivers — about the determination with which they set their sights on the sea and weave around the infinite obstacles in their path while never losing their sweet trilling song.

The Himalayas often get top billing, but equally impressive are Asia's mighty rivers. Indeed, the mountains and rivers are forever locked in the dance of creation and destruction — mountains rise, creating deep river valleys, which, in turn, sweep the mountains back into the sea. Bhutan is both geographically and economically defined by its rivers. Hydroelectricity is Bhutan's main revenue generator and the rivers have created fertile and wide valleys on which nearly 70 percent of the population depends for farming. Most Bhutanese rivers share similar features — they have their headwaters in the high peaks of the north, exit into India through one of the eighteen *duars*, or "gates," and eventually feed into the mighty Brahmaputra. And as is the custom in Bhutan, most rivers have multiple names or change names many times.

With such a vast network of rivers, it's easy to see why Bhutan invests so heavily in hydroelectric power — it's renewable, sustainable, and if based on a run-of-river concept, has minimal environmental

A timber bridge delivers a horseman and his animals over the Paro River. Photo by Peter McBride.

impact. Bhutan's hydropower provides more than 40 percent of the economy and not only lights up homes and businesses in Bhutan but also in India. Bhutan has the potential to generate more than 30,000 megawatts of energy and has a goal of producing 10,046 megawatts by 2020. While the Snowman Trek is famous for the six mountains over 23,000 feet, the trek is really a route of rivers. Since river valleys are the only semi-flat sections of Bhutan, it's natural that the hiking trails follow these paths of least resistance. Over the twenty-four-day trek, we were rarely ever without a crashing river or meandering stream nearby that, along with song, provided another very important element — drinking water.

As I hiked beside the Paro Chhu on day two, I remembered the river that ran through my backyard as a boy. Kristine, Sean, and I used to spend hours fishing in the river, dreaming of catching a trophy-sized trout. Most days, we'd just end up catching the same darn bluegill, a junk fish, about five times. In fact, we'd become so frustrated at catching the same bluegill, we'd decide to just keep the fish on the line to use as bait to catch something larger. The river I grew up near was wide and welcoming with a gentle murmur — nothing like the furious froth of the Paro Chhu.

Two hours after lunch, as I hiked on slippery rocks above dark, misting gorges, I started to get a little worried I would fall in. I could hear rocks clapping and crashing underwater and knew if I fell in I'd be halfway to Paro before anyone realized I was gone. Then, as I was crossing a steep landslide section, I did something you should never do when crossing a precipitous part of the trail, I stopped and looked down. Dizziness coursed through my veins like a narcotic and I had to throw myself against the steep, uphill slope to avoid falling. As I looked up, I noticed the whole hillside had just let loose, causing large granite boulders to crumble like blue cheese into the river.

"Help," I said weakly.

This worry wasn't like me at all, and indeed, it felt as if someone else had momentarily entered my body — someone who was scared and hesitant. It was probably due to my lack of sleep and jet lag but that still didn't solve my dilemma of how to get across.

Suddenly I heard a voice. "Hello, Mr. Kevin."

I turned and there was Sonam, trotting up the trail behind me with a thermos of tea in one hand and a candy cane–colored umbrella in the other.

"Very steep," he said, navigating by my side and glancing down at the sheer rockslide.

"I've noticed that," I said, standing up slightly. "Any thoughts on how to get across?"

"Take step, sir," Sonam said.

When I looked at his face, I saw he wasn't kidding.

"Take step," he said again, pointing up the trail. "Then other step."

"One step?" I asked. "And then another?"

"Yes, sir," he said, nodding me forward with his gaze.

When I looked across the landslide again, instead of seeing one vast muddy slide of rocks, roots, and gnarled tree branches — the problem — I focused on the individual rocks I needed to step on to make it across — the solution. I remembered the Chinese philosopher Lao-tzu who said, "A journey of a thousand miles begins with a single step."

After the landslide, Sonam and I hiked together, up sheer hillsides, through dense thickets, and over impossible rocks. The climb was relentless but manageable with Sonam's good company. Through broken English, Sonam spun tales of hardship of how his parents fled to Bhutan from Tibet during the Chinese occupation and ultimately settled in Thimphu. Sonam went to school for a few years in Thimphu before having to drop out to help his dad around the farm. At twenty-three he spent most of his time farming and picked up trekking jobs during the fall and spring tourist seasons. In Thimphu, Sonam told me he lived near Tango Monastery. "Very beautiful," he said. "One day, I will show you."

By late afternoon, we crossed a bridge to the west side of the river, and high up on the hillside, the trees thinned and gave way to broken rocks and what looked to be ancient meditation caves. We passed another bridge, this one leading back to the east side of a river and by a large chorten. We continued up the river for thirty minutes, passing little clearings with stone fire rings, footprints frozen in the dirt, and by the time I reached the campsite, I was exhausted. Having been up since 5:00 a.m., there was no doubt that Sonam was too, but before he went to the kitchen tent to help Achula, he insisted on hauling my duffel bag to an empty tent.

Sonam threw open the rain fly and, like a Bhutanese bellhop, said "Enjoy, sir!"

6

OUR SECOND CAMP ON THE SNOWMAN TREK WAS ANOTHER grassy meadow beside the Paro Chhu called Thangthanka. Dinner had started off normal enough — Sonam and Sangey had passed out bowls of rice, tuna, beef cubes, vegetables, and soup, and we all compared the bumps we'd received on the day's grueling hike. Then Paul told us about his past adventures in Tanzania, Rwenzori, Uganda, Mongolia, New Zealand, and cycling from coast to coast in Costa Rica. But at some point — and I'm not sure how it came up — Paul started telling us how he'd survived one of the worst maritime disasters of the twentieth century. On September 28, 1994, just after midnight, the Estonia ferry, en route on the Baltic Sea to Sweden, suddenly lurched forty degrees starboard and minutes later disappeared from radar screens forever. Of the 982 people on board that night, only 141 survived. Paul was one.

"When I knew the ferry was going down," recalled Paul somberly, "I climbed up the pipework of the promenade deck, and the next thing I knew, I was alone on top of this massive ship with forty-foot waves crashing over it. And there was just this dull, ghostly moonlight illuminating everything."

"What happened then?" asked Kira in a low whisper.

"It was either jump in the water or go down with the ship," continued Paul. "When I jumped in the water, it was just complete chaos. Pure carnage! Everyone was screaming and shouting and bodies were floating everywhere. The sea had turned into a human soup."

By then, everyone in our dining tent was silent and frozen with shock. Forkfuls of uneaten food had been set down on plates and cups of hot tea sat cooling on the table.

"How did you survive?" inquired Larry from the head of the table.

"What kept me alive was that I was always looking for another life-saving technique," replied Paul. "When the ship went down, I struggled to find a life raft. When a huge wave flipped that over, I grabbed a life jacket and climbed back on. If I lost both the life raft and the jacket, I would've swam."

"The water must've been freezing," I said. "How did you not get hypothermia?"

Paul told us he was so cold he couldn't think properly. "But I knew the adrenaline was no help at all, that it would just zap my energy resources. So I tried yoga breathing to lower my heart rate and prevent shock." Paul paused and took a sip of tea. "When I clambered back onto the life raft, there were eleven people. By dawn, I think there were five. I'll never forget the look on peoples' faces as they just disappeared into the depths. By the time I got into the rescue helicopter, I was so spent, I just told the medic, 'I'm done' and collapsed. It was the worst thing I could have done because I gave up in that moment, you see? Luckily though, the medics kept me alive."

Paul told us that because of where the ferry went down in the Baltic, they couldn't raise the Estonia, so they just sealed it off like a tomb and declared it a graveyard. Most of the people never made it out of their bunk rooms that night, and no one under the age of twelve survived.

Joe just shook his head, as the lantern cast long shadows.

"I'm sorry," said Tom. "I'm so sorry."

As we all nodded, Paul told us that for months following the tragedy, he occasionally suffered a crippling sense of survivor's guilt — a normal reaction to an overwhelmingly stressful situation. "But I got through it," Paul said, nodding.

Paul's confession prompted Kira to mention that she, too, had suffered immensely after her brother Marc drowned in the Kunene River near the Namibia-Angola border in Africa. Then, moments later, Ryan confessed sadly that his brother had also died in an outdoor accident.

As I heard these tragic stories of lost loved ones, it dawned on me that everyone on this trip had brought something with them that no horse could carry, some worry or wound that they alone must bear the burden. I'd heard that people began to lose their social conditioning after spending time in the wild, but I hadn't expected such honesty and disclosures on the second day. Already I could tell the Snowman Trek was working on us and inviting us all to open up and examine our lives.

When Ryan's head dropped in sad recollection, Tom patted him on the back and the unspoken but fully felt message was that we were all there for one another on this trip. While soldiers in the army say it's about the guys in the trench with you — the ones to your left and right — on the Snowman it would be about the trekkers on the trail with us, the ones in the front and back. Despite the sad nature of the conversation, a part of me smiled deep down for I knew a divine work had been done that night. In the space between the clink and the drink, we had bonded like friends, like family, and like soon-to-be-sent-out soldiers such that, if something did go wrong on the trail, I knew we'd all put our lives on the line for one another. It was quite a nice feeling to have when I was about to travel into one of the most remote and dangerous places on earth.

LATER, I FOUND SONAM WAITING FOR ME BESIDE MY TENT, holding a flashlight in his mouth like a cigar so he could use both hands to hold open the tent door for me. As I crawled in he said, "Sir, if a horse runs over your tent during the night, wake me. I put your tent back together."

I wanted to tell Sonam that if a horse runs over me during the night, forget the darn tent. Instead, I took this comment for what it was, a generous and well-intentioned offer. "Thank you, Sonam. I will."

As I crawled into my sleeping bag, I wondered about the nature of wounds. Could the broken heart of a bad experience ever truly be healed? Or did that submerged part of ourselves have to be, like the Estonia ferry, sealed shut and never salvaged?

7

PRIOR TO MY TRIP, NO ONE COULD GET OVER THE FACT THAT I was traveling alone. When I tried to tell them that I was traveling with eight other trekkers, a Bhutanese support staff, and thirty horses, they'd sip their wine politely and say, "Oh." However, the truth is the world is full of kind hearted people and you're only traveling alone until the airport, at which point you meet your first friend. I made fast friends with the people sitting next to me on my flight from LA to Bangkok, met Tenzin on the flight to Bhutan, and on the third morning of the Snowman Trek, was fortunate to leave camp hiking alongside Tom, a tall and lean literary man whose idea of light reading on the Snowman Trek was *The History of the Roman Empire*.

Tom lived in upstate New York with his wife and two daughters. Recently retired, he had taught high school history and social studies and coached soccer for years. Despite being fifty-seven years old, he was still more active than most people in their twenties. Tom now owned a climbing gym and took numerous adventure travel trips each year.

As we started up the trail, I asked if he'd done any big trips before.

"A few," he said nonchalantly.

"Like what?"

Tom said he'd done a few ice and rock climbs in the Adirondacks.

"Ever climbed out West?" I asked. "I hear Joshua Tree is amazing."

"Yosemite was fun."

When I tell Tom I'd heard about this sheer, insane vertical wall called El Capitan, he smiled broadly.

"Don't tell me you've done it?" I gasped.

"Just once in 2003," he said, modestly.

"Did you sleep in a tent fixed to the rocks hanging in midair?" I asked.

"Nope," Tom replied. "We slept on little ledges tied-in with our harnesses on."

Not only was I in disbelief about Tom's accomplishments but also his modesty. I'd met many "toppers," or people who felt the need to top everything I said in my life, but evidently Tom wasn't one of them.

When I asked what else he'd done, with near embarrassment, Tom told me he'd climbed Mount Kenya in Africa, the Matterhorn in Switzerland, and Pumori in Nepal.

"Pumori?" I exclaimed.

Tom asked if I'd heard of it.

"Have I heard of it?" I gasped. "Pumori is known as Everest's daughter! That's a 23,000-foot monster!"

Tom just smiled and then told me Pumori was the trip that pushed him physically harder than he thought possible, led to a spiritual awakening, and opened his eyes to the opportunities in life that he shouldn't let slip by. As I heard this, all I could do was shake my head with surprise and good fortune. There are two kinds of people on the planet — those who make your world larger and ring with possibility and those who make your world shrink. Clearly, my trekking companions belonged firmly in the first category.

As I stopped for a water break, Tom hiked on and Ryan, Paul, and Joe passed soon after. I drank the water I'd collected from the Paro Chhu last night and decided pure cold water from a mountain stream is like sunshine for the stomach. You can actually buy holy water to drink in Bhutan. Kuje Drubchu natural mineral water is bottled in the valley of Bumthang and sells for about thirty cents a bottle. According to legend, the pure spring water was extracted magically from a rock face by Guru Rinpoche and is endowed with eight qualities that can cure physical and mental disease. While I wasn't sure if the water from the Paro Chhu was holy, it sure tasted like it was.

Day three of the Snowman Trek would take us 10.5 miles with an elevation gain of 1,530 feet to Jhomolhari Base Camp, and as I continued on, I kept my eyes peeled for the elusive blue poppy, Bhutan's national flower. The blue poppy is the snow leopard of flowers — it is rarely seen, imbued with mystery, and inhabits high rocky crags where few people go. There are thirteen species of the blue poppy in Bhutan, and its flowers can range in color from blue to red, yellow, and purple. The plant grows above 11,000 feet, and like Anne Fowler's affection for me in seventh grade, blooms once, briefly, then withers and dies. As the trees began to thin, rhododendrons appeared in glorious greens on the hillside. Trudging on, I found myself strangely ambivalent about the prospect of going above treeline. Sure, I enjoyed hiking on the sun-warmed rocky slopes and loved the inspiring effect such openness had on my spirit, but that day, I had a strange sense of foreboding. As the trees thinned into twisting, storm-smashed appendages and the Paro Chhu raged harder, I had a sense of leaving behind the protective shelter of the forest and venturing out into a violent, high-altitude expanse.

Suddenly I saw two trekking poles stuck in the ground beside the trail.

"Hello?" I tossed out.

In the dense underbrush nearby, something moved — something big.

"Hello," I said a little louder, tightening my grip on my trekking poles. "Anyone there?"

When I saw the bushes move again, to my great surprise I discovered Paul, peering down at a flower.

"Hey, Kev," he said, still gazing down.

I eased my grip on my trekking poles. "Hello," I said, "I was, um, just coming over to see what you are looking at."

Paul snapped a photo and stood. "This orchid is amazing. Take a look."

Bhutan is often called the Land of Orchids, there are more than 369 varieties. I crouched down and took a look. The orchid was beautiful, with a lovely long green stem and pink petals, fragrant and fragile.

"That's great!" I said, pulling out my camera. "You know a lot about the plants around here?"

"You bet," he replied. "And if you'd like to come along, I'll teach you a thing or two."

After only three days, I realized that I could pick my experience on the trail based upon who I hiked with: hike with Kira and learn about Buddhism and the travel writer's life, hike with Tom and learn amazing historical anecdotes and cool mountaineering tips like the rest step, hike with Peter and see the trail with a photographer's eye, hike with Ryan to learn the intricacies of the oil business and the best indie bands on the planet, hike with Rob to hear swashbuckling tales of near escapes and mob fights, hike with Joe and learn about undiscovered travel destinations, and hike with Larry to learn about chemical engineering or simply to have good company. It was wonderful, I would be spending twenty-four days with some of the most interesting and accomplished people I'd ever met.

As I hiked with Paul, a whole new side of the forest opened up

A shining path leads up through an enchanted forest. Photo by Peter McBride.

to me. I'd never noticed how colorful and alive the forest floor could be, brimming with a surprising variety of plants among the orchids and rhododendrons. Thanks to Bhutan's plentiful rainfall, 72 percent forest cover, low population, and progressive environmental policies like its pledge to keep 60 percent of the country wooded forever, to hike in Bhutan is to hike in an enchanting, wooded wonderland.

Along with the orchids, there are more than 5,500 vascular plants, 300 medicinal herbs, and 46 varieties of rhododendrons. In addition, Bhutan is home to 770 species of birds, 24 of which are threatened, and more than 160 mammals including the red panda, musk deer, blue sheep, snow leopard, royal Bengal tigers, and golden langur, a primate found only in Bhutan. In 1998 the Convention on Biodiversity ranked Bhutan in the top 10 percent of countries with the highest species richness per unit acre in the world. In 2007 Bhutan recorded twenty-one new species of birds (such as the Brahmin starling and white-rumped vulture), and in the far northern streams near Lingshi, scientists recently discovered a new fish called a loach, bringing the total number of fish species in Bhutan up to fifty. It's as if the word on Bhutan is getting out around the animal kingdom, and animal species from all over are swimming, flying, and crawling to this remote Himalayan Kingdom for refuge. Bhutan was so lush and beautiful that I couldn't help but think it was a place where one could conjure answers to the larger questions of life.

"WHAT'S THAT?" I ASKED, POINTING TO A PLANT.

"That white shrub is called Daphne," said Paul, taking a picture. "People pound the bark of Daphne to make paper."

I pointed to another flower. "What's that?"

That's *Arisaema,*" answered Paul, "also known as the cobra lily."

"What's this?" I said, turning again. It was like I was three years old, pointing and asking what everything is.

"That little golden flower is *Delphinium*."

"What's that?" I said, pointing to a crooked tree.

Paul said it was juniper.

"And that?"

"That, my friend, is a common fern," said Paul with a chuckle.

I apologized. "I thought it looked rare."

Paul just laughed. "We started our hike in mixed broadleaf and conifer forests and now we're entering subalpine meadows and scrub."

As we trudged on, the first yaks appeared wandering high up on isolated ridges. Paul stopped about every ten minutes to check out a new flower, which not only allowed me to learn something new but also allowed me to rest. A glance down at my altimeter revealed that we were above 12,000 feet, and as I saw that, I also realized my breath was shallow and rapid and my head throbbed with pressure.

Not good. As the trail turned east, entering another valley, I saw Joe and Peter talking to a Bhutanese man in a big cowboy hat who was spinning a long knife in his hand like a drumstick.

WHAT IS IT ABOUT TRAVEL THAT MAKES YOU FEEL MORE alive, more open to experience, and more willing to take risks? Moments later, I was standing alongside Joe, Paul, and Peter, conversing with that man who had the long, sharp knife. This would never happen in the United States. I would never be walking in, say, Los Angeles, see a stranger with a long blade and rush over to make his acquaintance. However, things were different in Bhutan — I immediately felt safe, more trusting, and confident that if Guru Rinpoche vanquished flaming-haired demons then he probably also took care of the muggers and murderers too.

Peter introduced us. "Hey guys, meet Karma!"

I assumed I'd experience karma in the Himalayas, but I didn't think it'd be a man with a sharp knife.

"Pleased to meet you, sir," I said, shaking his hand.

We learned Karma worked as a forest ranger with the Jigme Dorji National Park, which was named after the Third King, Jigme Dorji Wangchuck. The park is the largest of five national parks in Bhutan. Along with these, Bhutan has four wildlife sanctuaries, one nature preserve, and multiple wildlife corridors that connect the protected areas and serve as a kind of highway for hooves. Together, these corridors and protected areas cover more than 34 percent of Bhutan — a remarkably large number for such a small country.

"What do you do up here?" Paul asked.

"We have one-month rotations," said Karma, twirling his knife. "During that time, we assist trekkers, look for Tibetan smugglers, and during the summer, monitor the *Cordycep* collection."

"*Cordyceps*?" I asked

Karma informed us that Bhutanese *Cordyceps*, or *yartsa goenbub*, grow in the northern highlands and are one of the most prized medicinal mushrooms in the world.

When I asked to see his knife, called a *dozum*, Karma handed it to me and informed me that most every Bhutanese man living in remote areas carries a dozum that hangs from his belt or is tucked in the chest fold of his gho. Karma's knife had an eight-inch steel blade and a leather handle. I gave it a twirl, and when I nearly lost a finger, handed it back.

"Knives and treadmills," I said to Peter. "My nemeses."

Karma continued to tell us about Bhutan's national parks. "In Bhutanese national parks, there are few established tent sites, no toilets, roads, or trail signs, and the local people are able to live on the land," he said, accenting the end of each statement with a knife twirl.

"So people could be standing in a national park and not even know it?" asked Paul.

"Yes, sir," said Karma.

I loved that there was no visible difference between national parks and private land. It was a far cry from the United States where some national parks are bordered by gateway towns full of arcades, fast food restaurants, and amusement parks.

"Jigme Dorji National Park is the largest protected area in Bhutan, and the route of the Snowman Trek lies almost entirely within its 2,683 square miles," Karma explained. "The elevation ranges from 4,000 feet to 24,734 feet, and in addition to the people who live there, is home to over 300 species of birds, the takin, mule deer, snow leopards, Himalayan black bears, and the royal Bengal tiger."

Bhutan is the first country in the world where the royal Bengal tiger has been reported leaving its subtropical habitat to venture above treeline. In previous studies done in India, Bangladesh, and Nepal, the tiger never ventured above 8,500 feet, yet in Bhutan, there has been evidence of tiger kill sites at elevations exceeding 11,000 feet. This means, for the first time, the habitat of tigers and snow leopards is overlapping. It is estimated there are between 115 and 150 tigers in Bhutan.

"Why do you think the tigers are here?" I asked.

"It could be global warming," Karma said, "or they could have been here all along and no one knew it."

Before we left, I had to ask Karma if it is true that Bhutan has a national park specifically designated for the Yeti, a large hairy beast that in other parts of the world goes by the name of Sasquatch, Big Foot, or the Abominable Snowman. The Bhutanese Yeti has a hairless human face, backward-facing feet to avoid detection, has the power to become invisible, and from what I read, has a terrible stench.

"The Sakten Wildlife Sanctuary in eastern Bhutan is for the Yeti," said Karma, dead serious.

"Let's hope the Snowman Trek steers clear of there," said Paul.

"Ahhh," replied Karma, his eyes lighting up, "You are bound for Lunana?"

"We are," I said.

"Thanza is very beautiful," said Karma, his face lighting up. "I wish you well and may you have a long life."

I thanked him, but as we left, I wasn't sure if that was a wish or a warning.

SOON AFTER WE LEFT KARMA, WE PASSED A SMALL WOODEN house, enclosed by a fence with some stacked wood and a flagpole flying both the Bhutanese and the Indian flag. As we trekked past, three dark-skinned Indian men came running out.

"Wait, sir!" one yelled out, waving.

They hustled out to us, all wearing brightly colored red, green, and gold sweatsuits and baseball caps. Paul, Joe, Peter, and I stopped.

"Hello!" said the man in a red sweatshirt. "I am Amit."

The two others introduced themselves with handshakes, Badal and Manish. They were soldiers with the Indian Army. India and Bhutan have been friendly neighbors for almost fifty years. India purchases hydroelectric power and nearly 80 percent of Bhutan's exports and, in return, provides laborers and military support. Bhutan also provides a nice buffer for India from the world's other most populated country, China.

Peter, Paul, and I introduced ourselves and then Joe extended a hand. "*Mera ghand phat gaya.*"

Amit, Badal, and Manish burst into hysterics.

"Excuse me, sir?" asked Amit incredulously.

Joe made a pained expression. "Mera ghand phat gaya."

With this, Amit, Badal, and Manish launched into another round of wild, hand-clapping laughter, and Peter discreetly pulled out his camera — a sure sign a "moment" was happening. I reached for my camera.

"Is that Hindi?" I asked, knowing Joe was fluent.

"It is," he replied.

Since Bhutan welcomes few trekkers each year, it's rare for Amit, Badal, and Manish to meet trekkers, let alone one who speaks Hindi. As they wiped away tears of laughter, Joe gave his real name, and I was reminded what a great exercise laughter is and its ability to cross cultural divides and connect people. Amit invited us in for tea. "You must come in now that we are good friends!"

"We'd love to," Joe replied. "But our group is waiting on us for lunch."

Suddenly we heard barking and a friendly looking dog hustled out to meet us. He stood about knee-height, had scruffy white and black fur, brown paws, and a spotted tongue.

"His name is Lucky," replied Badal.

I loved this — a dog named Lucky who lived three days from the nearest road, without another dog in sight, in a land of perpetual ice, tigers, and snow leopards!

We snapped a few pictures, waved good-bye to Amit, Badal, Manish, and Lucky and started up the trail.

"What did you say to them?" asked Peter, "I've never seen people laugh like that!"

Joe looked over at us. "You mean, 'Mera ghand phat gaya'?"

When we nodded, Joe told us about the need to make a connection with the locals when traveling and bridge the gap between cultural and linguistic differences, "Because even a simple encounter can last a lifetime."

"So what did you say?" I asked, as our lunch spot appeared beside a white chorten in an olive green field, "Something about world peace and the oneness of humanity?"

"Something like that," said Joe with a smile, "*Mera ghand phat gaya* means 'My ass is broken.'"

8

AFTER LUNCH THE MIGHTY HIMALAYAN RANGE BEGAN TO assert itself. The trees thinned, shrinking as if scared, and the soft rolling mountains transformed into immense ridges, rocky folds, and scree chutes. This change in the external environment was mirrored in me internally—my breath grew shallow, the pressure in my head increased, and the altitude popped my ears like kettle corn.

The Himalaya is not only the tallest mountain range on earth but also the most scenic. The range stretches more than 1,500 miles and rises from sea level to 29,092 feet. At 4,500 miles, South America's Andes Range is the longest, and at 250 million years, Russia's Ural Range is among the oldest, yet neither can match the glorious height and grandeur of the Himalayas. The Himalayan Range is so vast that it covers nearly a tenth of the earth's landmass, and so tall, it affects the weather patterns across the planet. Stretching through regions of Pakistan, Afghanistan, Nepal, China, Tibet, India, and Bhutan, the Himalayas were created some 50 million years ago when continental plates decided to play a game of bumper cars—the Indo-Australian plate drifted north and collided with the continent of Eurasia. As the Indo-Australian plate subducted into the earth, granite, gneiss, and sedimentary rocks crunched like car metal, glaciers splintered like glass shards, and the Himalayas were born. As I followed the river up the valley, the scope of the Himalayas was jaw-dropping. Unmapped, unmeasured, unnamed, and untamed mountains extended in all directions. I felt like I'd been set down in some towering, mountainous maze, and that day, it would have been hard to convince me that there existed a flat spot anywhere on earth.

Up ahead, I saw Sangey waiting for me. He sat on a dumpster-sized rock that had rolled down the adjacent hillside. I smiled and tried to increase my pace, feigning fitness, but it didn't work. I was forced to stop ten feet from him to catch my breath.

"Okay, sir?" said Sangey, jumping off his rock.

"Yes," I said, plodding on.

Like Sonam, Sangey spends most of the year farming, except during the busy trekking season. He lived in a small village called Sephu, which we would pass through on the last day of the trek.

We hiked on, past yak tracks zigzagging under high rocky outcrops and increasing mountains and waterfalls cascading down from unseen lakes up high. Half an hour up the trail, wood fences and modest stone farmhouses appeared. Rather than the two-story structure and elaborate decoration of the Bhutanese homes in Paro River valley, these single-level, stone homes squatted low to the earth as if there was no time to decorate at that altitude, only survive. It was obvious winter was close — braided grasses hung from the rooftops, yak patties — to be burnt instead of firewood — were stacked alongside stone walls, and the small gardens surrounding the homes had been freshly tilled.

"Why aren't you married?" asked Sangey suddenly, as if we'd been talking relationships for hours.

I shook my head and laughed — it was one thing being psychoanalyzed on a couch but it was quite another thing slogging uphill at high altitude.

"Why don't you marry Kira?" Sangey said, like the whole process is so simple.

To be honest, I didn't know why I wasn't married. Growing up, I'd always thought I would've been by now, but I was learning life had its own timeline.

"You've had girlfriends, sir?"

"Of course," I managed, "But it was never perfect."

Sangey didn't seem to understand.

"You know, perfect," I said. "Everything perfect all the time."

"Yes, I know perfect," Sangey replied in such a way that made me think maybe it was I who didn't.

"How did you become a guide?" I asked, changing the subject.

When you travel to Bhutan, it is required that you travel with a guide, and they take their jobs very seriously. On more than one occasion during my 2004 trip, I had to stop my guide at a bathroom door and say, "I can probably handle this one on my own." Making tourists travel with a guide is a great idea — it gives locals work, aids the economy, helps protect the resources, and creates great friendships. Sangey told me that because he was a member of the kitchen crew, his training was different than Norbu's. Trekking guides like Norbu are required to have graduated from twelfth grade and take a month of classes on first aid, environmental policy, sustainability, Bhutan's culture and history, as well as the logistics of tour management. After these classes, the students must give an oral presentation, write three papers, and pass a final test.

"What is the best part of guiding?" I asked.

I expected a long-drawn-out answer, perhaps one Sangey had been given to memorize about the importance of people from different cultures learning about one another, but he beamed and said, "Pretty girls, sir."

When I asked if there are a lot of young pretty girls who visit Bhutan, Sangey just said, "One Korean girl . . . very pretty, sir!" before blushing like a schoolboy in love. I couldn't help but smile too, and we spent the next few minutes plodding on in silence, each of us recollecting someone special.

As we neared Jhomolhari Base Camp, the trail leveled off and Paro Chhu softened and slowed and the whole valley widened and rang with a drizzly, dreamlike air. I expected the hike to be easy with the slowed pace and leveling trail, but my respiratory rate remained rapid and my heart boomed a techno beat in my chest. Last night's worries returned: *You have altitude sickness.* No, I don't. *You've had it before.* So what? *You'll have it again.* I'm better prepared this time. *No, you're not.*

As Sangey and I ascended a small hill, Jhomolhari Base Camp spread out before us — a circular tourist bungalow, scattered colorful settlements of tourist tents, and a crumbling dzong. To our right, an immaculate side valley led up to a white screen of clouds that covered Mount Jhomolhari, Bhutan's most sacred peak.

"Jhomolhari is shy," said Sangey.

I struggled to smile, but at that moment, my motivation for attempting the trek seemed likewise hidden. While I knew why I'd traveled to Bhutan, due to my altitude worries, for a moment it didn't seem worth it — not the physical effort or financial or emotional cost. In fact, part of me wanted to turn around and run for home, which would've been fitting because the name of that night's campsite — Jangothang — translates as "land of the deserters." According to legend, a tyrant king wanted his dzong on top of a mountain so he made all the local villagers build it for him. However once it was built, the king discovered a nearby mountain was restricting his sunlight. The king then ordered the villagers to cut off the top of the mountain blocking his view and build him a new dzong. However, the villagers were smart. They convened and decided that it's much easier to kill a king than to cut off the top of a mountain, lest it anger the resident deity. After the king was disposed of, the villagers were afraid of retribution so they deserted the area and the Tibetans destroyed the dzong during one of their many attempted sieges of Bhutan. Today, all that is left are a few crumbling walls just up the valley from the tourist bungalow.

Sangey and I found our camp nestled between yellow bushes beside a small stream, two hundred yards down the trail from the tourist bungalow. I wearily stumbled over to the tarp to find my bag, but it wasn't there. "This isn't good," I thought.

Just then, Sonam appeared wearing my duffel bag like a backpack, but staggering under its weight. "Which tent, sir?"

"Any tent."

We wandered through the tents and found one without two trekking poles out front. Sonam unzipped the tent and threw in my bag as a rainbow arched majestically over our campsite. But instead of comforting me, it seemed like a sinister frown.

THAT AFTERNOON AND EVENING WERE A BLUR. I DON'T recall who sat where at dinner, what was served, or what was talked about. I was present but absent. Looking but not seeing. Listening but not hearing. Perhaps the greatest tragedy of not feeling well is that it plunges you inward, and you are not present to your surroundings. Absolutely nothing in me desired to take a bite of the wonderful dinner of onion soup and ema datsi Achula made that night. It was very strange knowing I was sitting before a wonderful spread of food, that I'd just done one of the longest day hikes of my life, burning well over 5,000 calories, and that I was not the least bit hungry. I forced bites in, but by then, I had no doubts about the symptoms of altitude sickness — it feels like you're breathing through a straw as someone plays racquet ball in your brain, while nausea slithers like a snake through your intestines. *Turn around!* I wanted to argue with my inner critic but I had little strength left, and to be honest, it was probably right. I could predict the future because it would be exactly like my past. As was the case on my first trip to Bhutan and my recent failed attempt to summit California's 14,496-foot Mount Whitney, I wouldn't sleep that night. The pressure in my head would progress to a pounding headache. My lack of appetite would turn into worse nausea, perhaps vomiting, and

I'd have to lie awake, staring at my tent ceiling until morning. Then, I'd have to inform everyone at breakfast that instead of spending a rest day exploring with them, I'd have to turn around for home. "Some people are just not made for the mountains," I'd tell them. "I'm not a quitter but altitude sickness leaves you no choice." I'd try to act strong, finding a bright side and then I'd go back down to Paro, where I'd catch the first Druk Air flight out of Bhutan. Sure, I could stick around, but staying in Bhutan would only be a reminder of where I wasn't — on the Snowman Trek. The only problem was I wouldn't want to go home either because there I'd just have to tell everyone I built the trip up to — friends, family, and coworkers — that I didn't finish. That would be bad, but the worst part would be, I'd never find that elusive answer I was looking for about lasting grace or hike that trail blazing up the valley. I'd never make it to the Lunana District or get that special twinkle in my eyes when someone said "Thanza." I'd also lose the eight thousand dollars I'd invested in the trip, but compared to the other lost riches, that seemed like a paltry sum.

"Everyone cries on the Snowman Trek," Peter had said on the first night. As I crawled into my sleeping bag in Jangothang, I felt like crying. I wanted to cry and needed to cry. But no tears arrived.

9

MOMENTS AFTER I CRAWLED INTO MY SLEEPING BAG, SOMEONE tugged at my tent door. "Wake up, sir!" the voice said, "She is out!"

I rolled over, assuming I was dreaming. But the voice continued. "Come quick, she is out!"

"Who is out?" I said sleepily.

"Jhomolhari!" the voice said. It was Sonam and his insistent tugging on my tent door continued.

"It's the middle of the night," I stammered.

"Mountain is out!" he said quickly. "Come quick."

I slowly blinked my eyes open, expecting my tent to be dark. But instead it had a gray dawny glow. Not expecting that, I checked my watch and its green florescent numbers announced 6:30 a.m. "It's morning," I said to myself. "I slept!" Forget hiking more than thirty-three miles in three days and climbing from 8,460 feet to 13,260 feet — getting eight hours of sound sleep felt like the greatest physical achievement of my life. Sleeping meant my body was adjusting to altitude, and I could continue trekking. I could follow that trail leading up the valley to the treasure chest of Thanza village! I did a quick body scan: I shook my head — no headache. I checked my stomach — no nausea, and my breath was smooth and deep. "I slept!"

Suddenly, something rumbled. "The Thunder Dragon," I thought.

The thunder sounded again, only that time I realized it was not coming from the sky — it was coming from my sleeping bag. I may not have had high altitude pulmonary edema or high altitude cerebral edema, but from the sounds of it, I had an ailment my trekking mates referred to as HAFE — high altitude flatulent edema. I needed to go to the bathroom. And fast. Since I hadn't used the toilet tent on the first three days of the trek, this was welcomed news, but as I went to unzip my sleeping bag, I found myself stuck.

On my first trip to Bhutan, I froze every night. There is nothing worse than waking up from the cold in the middle of the night because there's nothing you can do about it, save eat a candy bar and hope your digestive fires provide some warmth. So prior to the Snowman I bought a fancy sleeping bag. At the time of purchase, I thought I was buying a four-season synthetic down sleeping bag with welded seams and good loft, but that morning, I realized I'd purchased a two-hundred-dollar "Dutch oven." When the roar came again, I realized a horrible truth about sleeping bags — that which holds the heat in might also not let you out. Unable to move, trapped in the toxic air, I now saw why the manufacturer called it a "mummy bag." All I could do was worm around the tent, wriggling and writhing, sliding and gliding while struggling with the zipper. If I had an accident then, it really would've been tragic. When the roar sounded a third time, I realized it was literally "Go time!" I maneuvered my right hand up across my waist and grabbed a hold of the zipper beside my left ear. With my mouth, I bit the fabric in the zipper, then, using every ounce of energy, yanked down. The zipper released with such abandon that for a moment I thought I'd severed an appendage. I threw on my shoes and sprinted toward the toilet tent, which was hiding between the bushes.

"I'm in here!" yelled a voice from inside as I grabbed the zipper.

"Are you kidding me?" I shrieked.

"One minute!"

What were the odds? The toilet tent was empty for about twenty-three hours and fifty minutes each day, and I had to pick the ten minutes when it was occupied. Suddenly the toilet tent zipper lifted and someone — I have no idea who — exited, and I rushed in.

How would I describe the toilet tent? In a word . . . painful. The toilet tent was not the kind of place where you'd sit and read the paper because, for one, there's no place to sit — you must squat over a shoebox-sized hole in the ice-crusted earth and use a roll of pink toilet paper hanging from a stick dug into the ground. The toilet tent was like a lethal combination of Sartre's *No Exit* and Milton's *Paradise Lost*. Squatting there, I was crippled with claustrophobia and felt terribly trapped. Since the stench was terrible, I tried to beat the system by holding my breath. But, alas, I'd forgotten at high altitude, my lungs received less oxygen with each inhale so the result of my holding my breath was that my body went into panic mode and forced me to take big hyperventilating breaths, completely opposite of my intentions. Could the toilet tent be the reason only 50 percent of people finish the Snowman? The toilet tent was enough to make me question continuing on the Snowman Trek that morning, but the moment I hurried out, *paradise lost* became *paradise found*, and I exalted in a panorama of pristine peaks gleaming in every direction and thought, "Ain't life great!"

MOMENTS LATER, I FOUND JOE, LARRY, PAUL, AND ROB near the tourist bungalow, snapping pictures of Jhomolhari in the frosty morning air. Unbeknownst to us, Achula had given Sonam the task of mountain watching. Sonam's job last evening and at five o'clock this morning was to keep his eyes glued on Jhomolhari for a break in the clouds and to rouse us the moment she appeared.

Mt. Jhomolhari (23,995 ft.), Bhutan's most sacred peak, hides behind a veil of clouds. Photo by Peter McBride.

I looked up the valley, and despite being partially covered with a thin sheet of clouds, Jhomolhari was breathtaking. The mountain soared nearly 24,000 feet into the sky and looked like Mount Rainier on steroids. The symmetrical shape of Jhomolhari was particularly rare in the Himalayas which, thanks to a daily cataclysm of ice, sun, and snow, is famed for its spiky peaks and twisting ridges.

"She certainly is stunning," said Paul.

"Come on, clouds," said Joe. "Clear for us."

We watched Jhomolhari and waited. The clouds coyly shifted and swirled about the mountain but yielded only brief glimpses of immense snowfields and splintered mouthwash-blue glaciers.

After fifteen minutes, Joe suggested going back to breakfast, even though much of the surrounding valley was clear. "Mountains create their own atmosphere," said Joe. "It could be days before we get a clear view of the mountain."

While I wished it were otherwise, my surfing experience has

taught me that when it comes to nature, there are no guarantees. As I looked back up at Jhomolhari, I realized that in surfing terms this morning was a day of no waves. "Breakfast, it is," I said putting away my camera.

THERE IS A WONDERFUL BHUTANESE FABLE CALLED "THE Four Friends." It is a story about a peacock, a rabbit, a monkey, and an elephant who are all hungry and decide to work together to get some food. The peacock finds a seed and plants it, the monkey fertilizes the seed, the rabbit waters it, and the elephant guards it. Their efforts prove immediately successful, but their tree grows so tall that none of the animals can reach the fruit. Faced with another challenge, they decide to work together again. The monkey stands on the back of the elephant, the rabbit stands on the back of the monkey, and the peacock stands on the top of the rabbit. Using this ladder of cooperation, the peacock grabs the fruit and the four friends enjoy the shade of the tree, the nourishment of the fruit, and spend the rest of their lives in mutual harmony.

TWENTY MINUTES INTO BREAKFAST, I SAT IN THE DINING tent, and instead of the four friends, there were Joe, Larry, and Paul — a guide, an engineer, and an architect — working together on the very important matter of pressing a cup of Paul's gourmet coffee. The only problem was, they didn't have a very important item — a coffee strainer.

"We could use a bandana," suggested Larry.

"Or a sock," added Joe.

"We are not using one of your filthy socks to filter my gourmet coffee," smirked Paul.

As a coffee drinker who could just as easily go to 7Eleven as Starbucks, all the effort seemed a little ridiculous to me. But I was to learn there were few delicacies on the Snowman Trek, so what few there were — cookies and coffee — tended to take on a life-

or-death urgency. Just then, Sonam entered with a small circular strainer the size of a magnifying glass.

"What is that for?" asked Larry.

"Who cares," said Joe, "it'll work."

Sonam handed Paul the strainer. "Thanks, you're a star," said Paul with a grin.

And thus, the three friends made their magic—Paul filled the strainer with coffee grounds and held it over the coffee mug. Larry poured the hot water into the strainer, and Joe held the coffee cup stable. Moments later, a rich aroma perfumed the tent and three cups of coffee sent strings of steam up toward the tent ceiling.

The tent door opened and Norbu hurried in. "Morning, gents," he said, taking a seat. "Where is the rest of the group?"

Joe told Norbu that Peter, Tom, and Ryan rose early to climb up the ridge behind camp and catch the sunrise. And Rob was helping Kira, who had an eye infection.

Despite being our lead Bhutanese guide, I knew Norbu the least. Since Norbu was always at the front of the group, and I was always at the back, the only time we saw each other was in camp. As Norbu joined us at the breakfast table that morning, I discovered he was married, lived just outside of Paro, had a one-year-old son, and had done the Snowman Trek five times.

"Hey, Norbu," I said, "know where Chuni Dorji lives?"

Norbu looked impressed. "How do you know about Chuni?"

"I've been reading *Kuensel* online for the past few months," I said.

Kuensel was Bhutan's only newspaper until the *Bhutan Times* and *Bhutan Observer* went to print in 2006. *Kuensel* was started in 1986, and today *Kuensel* (which translates as "clarity") is published twice a week in both English and Dzongkha and has a readership of more than 130,000.

"You want to find Chuni?" asked Norbu.

"If I can," I said. "He seems like an amazing guy."

"Let me go find out," said Norbu, stepping outside the tent to consult with some village women who had set up a blanket and sat to the side on their folded legs, selling souvenirs — silver necklaces, brass bracelets, colorful textiles, and little Buddha statues.

When Larry asked, I told him Chuni was the closest thing Bhutan had to a rock star. "He's this eighty-five-year-old musician who lives in Jangothang and wrote Bhutan's most famous song — the yak herder's song," I said. "Yak Legpai Lhadar Gawo" is about a yak herder saying good-bye to his yak who has been summoned to the slaughter by an evil king. The song is sung from the viewpoint of the yak and is said to be so sad that whoever listens to it immediately bursts into tears."

"Maybe that's why everyone cries on the Snowman Trek," said Paul.

In addition to the song, I told them that Chuni Dorji was gifted at *Lozey*, a verbal game of wits in which the contestants use metaphors and rhymes to outdo one another. In a game of verbal joust that would rival a Shakespearean play, Chuni would squash his opponents with his great oratorical skill, to the delight of onlookers and swooning women. "Local men were so scared of him that they used to bribe him with doma so he wouldn't compete or cast them as villains in one of his songs," I explained. "But what made Chuni's skill at Lozey more impressive was that he didn't have an education. He didn't go to school and he wasn't trained as a monk — the wisdom just seemed to bubble up in him."

"Chuni sounds like a fun guy to meet," remarked Joe.

I envisioned my going to meet Chuni like that scene in *Star Wars* where Luke Skywalker leaves Uncle Owen and Aunt Beru to find Obi-Wan Kenobi — I'd walk through the rocky ledges like Luke, but instead of sandmen, I'd dodge sharp-horned yaks. Then Chuni Dorji would come hobbling out in a hooded robe like Obi-Wan, whereupon, I'd bow reverently, introduce myself, and then we'd go have butter tea in his hidden mountain hermitage.

The tent door opened and Norbu shuffled in. "Chuni isn't here."

"Where is he?" I asked, standing.

"He expired."

"Expired?" I asked.

Norbu made a motion of slicing his neck with his index finger. "Expired."

I was taken aback by the word, *expired*. Comparing a deceased man to the three-month-old cream cheese in my fridge back home just didn't seem respectful. However, my sense was that to Buddhists death is like an expiration date. One day, the physical body just falls off, and while it is certainly a time of great sorrow, it is no more questioned than a wave cresting and crashing on the beach. Following death, the soul either achieves enlightenment or is reincarnated.

Since Chuni was unfortunately no longer around, I decided to spend the day by myself. Over the last few days, I'd been inspired by the time and care that Kira devoted to her inner life, writing in her journal, meditating, and chanting prayers with her prayer beads. Despite it only being the fourth day, I could tell Kira was going to get something big spiritually out of this trip, kind of like the way you see an athlete shoot a basket in warm-ups and know he or she is going to have a good game. Since day four of the Snowman was a rest day, I decided to follow her good example and honor time with myself. I made an immediate plan to hike to a nearby ridge and spend the afternoon reading, journaling, and perhaps napping on a sun-kissed ridge. That is until Joe and Paul invited me to join them on a day hike to see Jhomolhari's glaciers up close and personal.

"Count me in," I said, immediately.

When my critical voice lambasted me for not being able to keep a commitment with myself, I laughed at this self-criticism. While I could've spent the day searching for inner truths, I also couldn't deny an absolute truth — I'd never get the chance to see Jhomolhari's glaciers with Joe and Paul ever again. The truth was I can write in my journal or read a book anytime, but most of all, the truth was those guys were too fun not to hang with.

FOR THOUSANDS OF YEARS, THERE HAS BEEN A BELIEF among many different cultures around the world that there are special power places, or points, where heaven and earth intersect. It is said that at these sacred spots the four points of the compass meet and the spirits of the higher realm pass down blessings to the lower realms, and spirits of the lower realms ascend to the higher realms. From Japan's Mount Fuji to China's Mount Kun Lun, from Mount Sinai in Israel to California's Mount Shasta, from Tibet's Mount Kailas to Australia's Uluru and Bhutan's Jhomolhari, many mountains have historically been regarded as sacred power places. However, no mountain range is more revered for its spiritual benefits than the Himalayas, which translates literally to the "abode of the gods." The Himalayas are sacred in every respect—sacred to be seen, sacred to be spoken of, sacred to be trekked through, and sacred to be touched. In fact, I read in *So Close to Heaven* that there is a legend in Tibet of a divine rope hanging down from heaven. It was a "stairway to the immortals" in the Himalayas. But an evil king cut the rope, and the connection between heaven and the earth was lost.

Not only do monks and lay people pilgrimage to sacred peaks in the Himalayas, but they often do Tibetan prostrations to get there. Tibetan prostrations are hard—I did a sequence of them in a yoga class once and my abdominal muscles were sore for two weeks. As I learned it, you clasp your hands together in a prayer fashion at the top of your head (to bless your thoughts), bring them down to your mouth (to bless your speech), and then to your heart (to bless yourself). Next you bow to the earth on your hands and knees, bringing your forehead to the earth, sweeping your hands forward and sliding on your stomach. Then you stand back up, take three steps forward, and start the process over. It's not uncommon to see Tibetans prostrating around their sacred mountains, often wearing thick aprons, fortified shoes, and gloves with a wooden pad on the palm to protect their skin. While I didn't see any monks doing Tibetan prostrations along the Snowman Trek — probably because the rocky trails would make it impossible — soon after we finished our adventure, I read in Kuensel about a thirty-eight-year-old Bhutanese man who prostrated 120 miles from Pheuntsholing to Paro, dragging a wooden trolley with his sleeping bag and food, to generate positive spiritual merit.

Mountains have always played an important role in my life. Growing up, I could see Mount Washington, the highest mountain in the Northeast, beckoning in the far distance of my backyard and thought family hiking trips were the best way to spend a summer Sunday. In college, I explored the high Cascades around Seattle and took trips to the Olympics, Rockies, and Tetons. Part of my love of hiking in the mountains was receiving trail truths that ranged from small ideas to major life changes. I'd come to relish the simplicity and beauty of these ah-ha moments as much as the rock, snow, and scree that surrounded me. Mountains were magical places — solid and secure yet constantly changing and shifting, firmly fixed to the earth, but also pointing to something higher and beyond. Mountains had brought me sweet contentment and self-realizations in the past, so it was only natural that I packed my largest life questions with me on this trip to the Himalayas. When you come to a crossroad in life . . . go up.

Jhomolhari (or, Chomolhari, as it's also spelled) translates to "Goddess of the Holy Mountain," and along with being the most sacred mountain of Bhutan, the Tibetans revere it more than Everest. Frequently, both in Bhutan and Tibet, there are ceremonies of dedication, thanks, praise, and worship to the Goddess. In fact, Jhomolhari and every other mountain in Bhutan is considered so sacred that mountain climbing is forbidden. However, before the ban, Jhomolhari was climbed in 1937 by Frank Spencer Chapman, Charles Crawford, and three Sherpas. After a destructive flash flood, which the locals attributed to the angry gods, and two members of an Indian team died in 1970, the government closed it off indefinitely. That is on the Bhutanese side, but China still allows people to climb Jhomolhari from the Tibetan side. In 1996, Jhomolhari was climbed on the Tibetan side by a Chinese-Japanese team, in 2004, by two British climbers, and in 2006 by six Slovenians.

Paul, Joe, and I weren't so spiritually motivated to attempt Tibetan prostrations, but we did have a strong desire to get as close as we could to the sacred Mount Jhomolhari and bask in its icy majesty. From the dining tent, we leapt over a little stream, passed the smoke-stained bungalow, and followed the stream up through the swaying bushes under a windy, partly cloudy morning. Day four was technically a rest day on the Snowman Trek, but Joe told me hiking would help with acclimatization. "Hike high and sleep low," he said.

"My guess is we'll be hiking on all our rest days?" Paul asked.

Joe nodded. "Probably, there is too much to see and do in Bhutan to rest, eh?"

As I followed Joe and Paul through the thickets and small brush, I felt like a kid again, tagging along with my brother and his friends to the playground. By signing up for the Snowman Trek, you really receive a "Be a Kid for a Month" pass. Think about it, the trek is a complete regression to childhood — all your meals are made for you, your gear is carried for you, and a simple order like pack up your tent (i.e., clean your room) is a momentary intrusion upon a day full of play. However, I thought the regression to the childlike wonder of basking in the small details, living in the moment, and being open emotionally wasn't necessarily a bad thing.

"What's going on here geologically?" I asked looking up the valley.

I thought Paul would've been sick of all my questions, but he seemed excited that I was excited. "This is a U-shaped glacier valley," he explained. "A glacier is a river of frozen ice that moves downward in relation to gravity."

"As a glacier moves," Joe added, "it picks up some rocks, carves others, and grinds others to dust."

"What's with all the rocks?" I asked pointing to a large mound.

"Those are moraines," explained Paul. "As glaciers melt, they dispose of unsorted rocks called till, which form moraines. A terminal moraine forms at the end of a glacier, and a lateral moraine forms at the side."

A small milk-white stream poured from the moraine before braiding into a wide sandy plain. "Why is the water that strange white color?"

"Glaciers act like sandpaper against the rocks," said Paul, "creating what is known as rock flour, which changes the color of the water."

What a gift Paul had — to be on a first-name basis with every plant and flower and to be able to read the geologic story behind the scenery! I thanked them for their information and we hiked on in silence, soaking in the warm sunshine and the magic of this vast geologic system at work. As we hiked through mud and sand (an outwash plain), past rocks with lined surfaces (glacial striations), and shiny rocks (glacial polished), I could really feel a strange kind of power that was at once ancient and still active. After hiking two hours up the valley, a curtain of cloud closed over Jhomolhari, and we lost sight of her altogether. However, what Jhomolhari lacked in sight, she made up for in sound. I could hear water rushing, a rock crashing every now and then, and loud shifts of the snow.

When we decided to break, Paul pulled out some beef jerky and chocolate, and Joe wandered off, poking around the rocks. Paul and I ate in silence, sitting in the shadow of Jhomolhari's immense lower glaciers. The lower ice flanks were dirty with mud and rocks yet poured forth braided streams of runoff the color of Swiss coffee.

As I soaked in the splendor surrounding me, a feeling of

immortality arrived and I was certain Buddhism had it wrong: it wasn't life that was the illusory dream — it was death.

"Hey guys," Joe yelled, breaking my reverie. "Check this out, eh?"

Joe stood on a granite rock, holding up a sun-bleached skull with two curving horns.

"A blue sheep!" said Paul.

As Joe held the skull in front of his face, he morphed into a Satyr, the half man–half goat from Greek mythology.

"I suspect it was killed by a snow leopard," said Paul, scientifically. "In fact, that snow leopard may be watching us right now."

I scanned the ridges above for the elusive beige-and-black-spotted cat. The snow leopard, one of the most elusive and endangered creatures on earth, is found in twelve countries along the Himalayan spine — Afghanistan, northern Pakistan, Nepal, Bhutan, China and Tibet, India, Kazakhstan, the Kyrgyz Republic, Mongolia, Russia, Tajikistan, and Uzbekistan. Despite being placed on the endangered species list in 1972, according to the Snow Leopard Trust, there are only 4,000 to 7,500 snow leopards thought to be in existence and about a hundred cats are reported to live in Bhutan.

Joe set the blue sheep skull on top of a rock and wandered back to us. "Shall we head back?"

We hiked back to camp on a boot-wide yak trail, high up on the side of the valley. As we did my thoughts lingered with the blue sheep skull. Not only was it strangely haunting how the sun lit up the empty eye sockets, but it was also a jarring intrusion into such a peaceful valley.

I was reminded of the Divine Madman who said, "Look at the hundreds of large birds and thousands of small birds and realize no matter how high they fly, they are all bound for the city of death."

The historical Buddha, Siddhartha Gautama, had a similar experience of death in the story of the "Four Sights." In that story, Siddhartha escapes the sheltered life of his father's sprawling palace and sees an

A horseman displays skulls belonging to some *bharal*, or blue sheep. Photo by Peter McBride.

old man, a diseased man, a decaying corpse, and a monk. The first three sights taught Siddhartha that suffering and death are part of life, but the sight of the monk made him realize that release from suffering is possible. After Siddhartha saw the monk, he pursued the spiritual path until he received full enlightenment under the Bodhi tree.

I couldn't help but think my desire to do the Snowman Trek was an echo, however small, of Siddhartha's desire to leave the gilded cage of his palace life. Like Siddhartha, I wanted to reduce and simplify my life to the essentials with the hope of learning an elemental truth or two. That day, as we navigated a muddy little yak trail, I got the sense there was wisdom to be found by foregoing convenience and embracing difficulty. After all, wasn't that the message Bhutan was broadcasting by building monasteries on the sides of cliffs, stretching prayer flags across impossible abysses, and doing Tibetan prostrations from Pheuntsholing to Paro? Despite only being on the trail for four days, already I could feel a void opening up in that space I once filled with newspapers, television, and the Internet. I sensed the beginnings of a hearth-like opening in my heart and was certain the coals of my questions would soon light into the flames of insight. While Tantric Buddhists believe enlightenment can occur at any moment, I had the feeling mine would occur in Thanza, just thirteen days away.

THE TOPIC OF WOMEN WAS BOUND TO COME UP IN conversation because you talk and dream about things you can't enjoy on a trek — gourmet dinners, drinks, and desserts — and the whole point of it is to take your mind off the fact that you have eleven high passes yet to cross and 186 more miles of tough hiking ahead of you. Such conversations keep your mind away from thoughts of toil and tiredness, from the rain, sleet, and snow — such thoughts keep your feet moving.

Naturally, talking about women in front of Kira frightened me. Kira had traveled alone to the remote corners of the world most of her adult life. And how was she making her re-entrance into traveling with people again? By signing up for a twenty-four-day trek with eleven guys and a team of horsemen! I wanted to say, "Hey Norbu, how do you say 'disaster waiting to happen' in Dzongkha?" Since Kira was writing a feature story for a national magazine and I knew how a group of guys could get when they ventured into the woods, I had nightmares of seeing a mug shot–style picture of myself on the magazine cover with the headline: "He's a Cold-Hearted Snake." To my surprise, it was Kira who brought up the subject of girls at dinner on the fourth night — specifically one girl.

"What does Ingrid look like?" Kira asked, in between spoonfuls of our fruit cocktail dessert.

According to Norbu, Ingrid was a twenty-six-year old German girl doing the Snowman Trek with her mom. Ingrid and her mom were traveling with Hauser Exkursionen, an adventure company based in Germany that had a group of ten doing the Snowman Trek. They had arrived at Jangothang earlier that afternoon.

"Ingrid is cute," said Norbu, smiling slyly. "Very cute."

The prospect of a cute girl nearly my age traveling one day behind us on the trail was proof miracles could occur. Talk about a great story about how you met!

"Want a beer?" Ryan asked me.

"For sure," I hollered. "Let's get this party started!"

Ryan handed me a can of Pabst Blue Ribbon. I opened the flip-top, and just before I took a slug, it dawned on me. I am holding a can of Pabst Blue Ribbon in the middle of the Himalayas!

Before I could even ask, Norbu said, "Smugglers bring Pabst into Bhutan from Tibet."

"That answers all of my questions," I replied, "Except one small one—WHAT THE HECK IS PBR DOING IN TIBET?"

I was amazed, I couldn't even find PBR at my corner convenience store in Huntington Beach! I was to discover that Pabst Blue Ribbon licenses the name and recipe to breweries in China, and the name Pabst is held in such high regard for its quality and taste that Pabst also sells bottled water in China featuring the PBR label.

"Hey guys," said Joe, "I wouldn't recommend drinking at altitude. We're still acclimatizing."

Ryan pointed out that there were only two cans of beer for the nine of us, which amounted to about two sips each. "Drink up!"

As I brought the can to my mouth, I was not expecting much. I sniffed slightly, and when the beer smelled nice and aromatic, I took my first sip. It tasted wonderful, smooth, a hint of hops, light carbonation, and a crisp finish. However, I was certain that the great taste had nothing to do with the beer. Everything tastes better on a hiking trail. The peanut-butter-and-jelly sandwiches my mom made for family hikes tasted finer than filet mignon, and if it could happen with PBJ, then it could also happen with PBR.

"So when will we see the Hausers again?" asked Peter.

Norbu informed us we had about a week. "Since the Hausers are a day behind us, we will see them again on our rest day in Laya Village on day eleven."

"Aw, don't wait till then, Kev," said Rob, excitedly. "Do like we do in th' bush, jes' march over to tha' Hausers' camp, throw Ingrid over ya shoulder, and take her back to ya' tent!"

"Thanks, Rob," I said, "Maybe I'll be slightly more traditional and begin by, say, introducing myself first."

LATER, LYING WARM IN MY SLEEPING BAG, I CONTEMPLATED the trek thus far. I was acclimatizing and sleeping well, my stamina felt good, and one day behind our group, was a beautiful German fraulein whom I would soon meet. By all accounts, things were going perfectly. That was, until I remembered we would cross our first mountain pass in the morning, the 16,040-foot Nyile La. I realized the trek was just beginning to flex its muscles and the boxing match was about to begin.

10

I AWOKE AT SIX O'CLOCK THE FOLLOWING MORNING, EXCITED and ready for day five. Not only would I finally follow that profound path blazing out of the valley, but with every step from there, I'd be one step closer to the luminous district of Lunana. On day five, we would hike thirteen miles, cross the mighty Nyile La, and camp on the outskirts of the village of Lingshi.

Just then, I heard a "knock" on my tent door and Sonam and Sangey arrived with bed tea.

Some people say traveling to Bhutan is too expensive, but personally, I thought bed tea alone was worth two hundred dollars a day. You simply can't put a price tag on the feeling you get when you open your tent door and a panorama of pristine peaks explodes into view and a hot cup of tea is handed to you. And the feelings that arrive with that cup of tea — that today will be a good day, an active day, a day spent in the company of already-dear friends, today I will challenge myself, hear my heartbeat, laugh and love — today I will live.

Following breakfast and an unsuccessful reconnaissance mission to the Hauser camp to meet Ingrid, Ryan and I left Jhomolhari base camp and followed the stream up the valley and through the bushes. As we hiked, we discussed Bhutan's daily tariff. We both thought Bhutan's tourism policy was a good idea but had different views about the price — Ryan thought people labeled it expensive because they didn't have the money, and I thought people labeled it expensive because they didn't think nature was worth the money. People will gladly spend two hundred dollars for the manufactured experience of a rock concert, a day at Disney, or a night in Vegas. But when it comes to the outdoors, they put their checkbooks away.

As the trail approached three stone homes at the head of the Jangothang valley, we agreed a traveler couldn't get lodging, three meals a day, a personal guide, driver, and museum entrance passes for less than two hundred dollars a day at most major tourist destinations around the world. "When you compare Bhutan to places like Tahiti, New York City, or Paris, I guess it's not that expensive," Ryan concluded.

In addition, I told Ryan that around 35 percent of our daily tariff goes back into the country to improve infrastructure and to support social and environmental programs, such as keeping 60 percent of the country forested forever. "If you think about it, every tour is an eco-tour!" Still, as we passed the first of two bridges leading up to an alpine lake, we recognized that some people simply couldn't afford to travel to Bhutan, specifically younger travelers, and agreed that Bhutan should set up a scholarship program where young adults could apply to get discounted tariff fees.

"That would be smart," said Ryan. "About half of Bhutan's population of 700,000 is under the age of twenty-five, yet most of the tourists I've seen are over the age of fifty. There needs to be a dialogue between the young people of Bhutan and the young people of the rest of the world."

"I agree," I said. "The world needs to know about Bhutan and get hooked on environmental conservation and Gross National Happiness — like us!"

As Ryan hurried on, I stopped at the second bridge to fill up my water bottle and drop in two purification tablets. While Achula boiled water each night, I preferred drinking it fresh and cold from the streams we passed each day. To my left, a quaint, stone home exhaled thin wisps of smoke from the chimney, and I deeply inhaled that wonderful wood smell. Behind the home, a towering mound of mud and rocks rose up — the terminal moraine of Jichu Drake, a 22,925-foot mountain hidden in shadows and fog at the head of the valley.

I crossed the second bridge, decorated with prayer flags, and started up the steep hillside. The trail zigzagged up and up, and I was immediately out of breath and shedding layers. Looking down the valley, there was an amazing view — endless green mountains, glacial streams, and a smattering of colorful tourist tents. After one hour of arduous hiking, I arrived at a ridge and the trail veered off into a splendid, side valley. There I found Larry, resting against a rock and breathing heavily. Sangey sat beside him, ominously carrying a first-aid kit.

"How are you Larry?" I said, stepping up.

"So far, so good," he replied, in between labored breaths.

"How is the hike going?"

"Slowly but surely."

Larry spoke with a brevity born of the military.

"Want me to wait with you?" I asked.

Larry thanked me but said he'd meet me up the trail.

"You sure?"

"You bet," he said. "I've got Sangey with me."

"Then I'll see ya at the pass."

From the ridge, the trail entered a broad valley of brown hillsides dotted with marmot holes so big that they could easily house a hobbit. Overhead, large black ravens rode the thermals, their caws like warning cries. As the thin grassy hillsides surrendered to vast scree and rocky slopes, my thoughts fell on Larry. Along with breathing heavily, his nose was badly sunburned from his day hike yesterday, and I felt my first twinge of worry for him. The truth was, he wasn't outfitted correctly for the Snowman Trek. Sure, Larry had that sincere, salt-of-the-earth New Jersey quality, and I loved the fact that he didn't appear to care about brand names — that he brought a bright orange hunting coat instead of a fancy down jacket, he wore green army pants instead of wickable hiking pants, and he carried two coffee mugs instead of a fancy thirty-two-ounce, BPA-free water bottle. But I wondered: would his gear hold up over the course of the trek? On a twenty-four-day trek, your gear isn't an accessory, it's a necessity.

The problem for Larry was if his cotton pants got wet, they wouldn't dry. His orange hunting jacket didn't appear to be waterproof. The poncho he wore for rain protection seemed to lack any ventilation, which meant he'd soak his clothes with sweat from the inside. Plus, there was no way he was drinking enough with those two coffee mugs. Above 6,000 feet people exhale and perspire twice as much as they do at sea level. Increased breathing means you lose more moisture on each exhale. Making matters worse, moisture evaporates almost immediately from the skin, so often you're not even aware you're sweating, and you can be down a quart on liquids before you even feel thirsty. When I looked at Larry, I saw a courageous man with good intentions, but I also saw a man susceptible to dehydration, hypothermia, exhaustion, and based upon his labored breathing, cardiac arrest. Maybe Larry knew something I didn't about faith and determination. Maybe Larry had luck and superstition on his side, which wouldn't surprise me because Bhutan is a superstitious place.

The best — and only — guidebook exclusively on trekking in Bhutan was written by a man named Bart Jordans, who has led treks in the country since 1994 and spent four years living in the Dragon Kingdom with his wife and two children. *Bhutan: A Trekker's Guide* is a wonderful book, full of detailed trail descriptions, Bhutanese history, mountain folklore, and helpful advice, such as providing warnings against swimming in Bhutanese lakes because demons live there and letting you know that entering the central tower of some dzongs may have ill consequences, such as your untimely death. The book also lists more of the superstitions that abound in Bhutan: seeing seven black crows is good luck; a group of snow partridges means snow is likely; empty eggshells hanging from trees ward off evil spirits; it's bad luck to walk around a chorten counterclockwise; cloud formations can predict your future; cutting trees in the forest angers the forest god; white yaks are a sign of good luck; mountains can fly and switch places; throwing bones on a fire will bring on bad weather, and when crossing a river, you should always tip your cap and recite prayers to appease the river deity. Some of the superstitions made sense to me, but I was confused about others. For example, eating ravens is supposed to have medicinal powers, yet the raven is also Yeshe Goenpo, the guardian deity of Bhutan. And if you yell at the top of a mountain pass, it's supposed to bring a hailstorm, but yesterday Norbu instructed us to shout "*Lha Gyalo*," which means "Praise!" or "Victory to the Gods," at the top of each mountain pass.

The superstition I was fascinated with was blossom rain, or *metok-chharp*. According to Tibetan and Bhutanese folklore, the moment of rainbow light when it is raining and sunny at the same time is considered to be very auspicious. If something strange hadn't happened, blossom rain probably wouldn't have intrigued me anymore than, say, the good luck in finding a penny on the sidewalk in the United States. When I first read about blossom rain in Bart Jordans's book, I was sitting in my condo in Huntington Beach and the moment my eyes scanned over the words "metok-chharp," thunder shook the sky. When I stopped reading and lifted my head, the thunder sounded again. Was it really thunder? Probably not. In Southern California, it was probably just a jet flying overhead. However, that didn't matter — what mattered was the *timing* of the sound, that it set my heart pounding and seemed like an invitation, an audible omen. I understood that the moment of blossom rain is auspicious, but I wanted to know why and, more important, what it meant. I had a hunch it would help me on my own journey.

When I saw Sonam on the trail up ahead, leaning against a rock, I decided to ask him.

"Sonam," I said, marching up. "Do you know about blossom rain?"

Sonam gave me a look that said he didn't understand.

"Metok-chharp."

With this, Sonam's head immediately fell to one side, as if remembering an old, fond friend. "Metok-chharp," he said. "Very auspicious."

I took a seat beside him. "Yes, but why is blossom rain auspicious?"

"Rain and sun," he said, "at same time."

I thanked him. "But what does it mean?"

"Mean, sir?"

I asked Sonam why it was good luck. "Is there a teaching behind it?"

With that, Sonam gave me a crazy look and patted me on the back, like I'd just told a terrific joke, and started up the trail.

"Hey wait!" I yelled after him. "That's no answer!"

"You funny, sir!" Sonam called back.

As Sonam left, it started to drizzle. I looked up at the bruise-colored clouds, hoping the sun would appear and answer all my questions, but there were only low-flying, lint-gray clouds blowing up the valley. I quickly grew cold and started hiking again. From there, the trail veered left into another side valley, wound around steep ridges and smooth rocky slopes, and started its relentless climb to the pass. As my breath became labored, I realized it was going to be a tough haul.

BREATHING AT ALTITUDE WAS HARD. WHILE THE PERCENTAGE of oxygen in the atmosphere is the same at 16,000 feet as it is at sea level, the decrease in atmospheric pressure reduces the gas exchange between carbon dioxide and oxygen in the lungs. In fact, at 13,000 feet, you get 40 percent fewer oxygen molecules per breath. This was strange and my body didn't grasp the concept. When I'd inhale deeply, my head thought it was getting enough oxygen but my heart was screaming, "Hey buddy, I'm dying down here!" Thus, when I hiked at high altitude, my head and heart were constantly at odds with each other — one thought it was getting enough oxygen and the other was certain it was not. My head would tell me I didn't need to stop for a break. My heart demanded it.

When I found myself particularly exhausted, I stopped and waited for Joe, who came plodding up the trail with Paul. As they approached, it dawned on me yet again that my group really was the dream team of trekkers. Kira was one of the gutsiest travelers alive; Ryan could make beer appear out of thin air; Rob slayed dragons and started revolutions; Paul was an expert on plants and geology; Tom knew all about history and hiking at high altitude; and being a chemical engineer, Larry could probably make an explosive device out of sticks and stones. Lastly, Peter matched a poet's eye with an athlete's prowess, and Joe, along with being a very competent trip leader, seemed to know how to say "My ass is broken" in every language. As I fell into line behind Joe and Paul, I was seized with a burst of energy. "Hey guys!" When I found myself uncharacteristically quick-footed and nimble, I realized when you play with people better than you, your game improves. As I followed Joe and Paul up brown, storm-beaten slopes, I found myself leaping from tundra tuft to tundra tuft and darting from rock to rock with a talent I never knew I had — and may never have again.

But as we made the final, steep ascent to the pass, the wind kicked up and, by turns, hammered us from all sides. Nobody warned me about the wind before a trek, as if it didn't matter on account of its invisibility. Trust me, the wind counted. It made the pitch of the trail seem a lot steeper, the air feel a lot colder, and my stride a lot more off balance. Thus, I found myself walking with my knees bent and my arms up, expecting an imminent impact from any direction at any time, not unlike the mosh pit I once stood in at a Pearl Jam concert.

Summoning all my strength, I made the final slog to the saddle-like pass where I was greeted with a few scattered collections of rocks, called cairns, and torn prayer flags tied to weathered branches. The experience of hiking to a mountain pass in the Himalayas is like riding a roller coaster: going up all you can see is the hill directly ahead of you and as you slowly crest over the top, a whole new vista opens up, causing you to either scream with excitement . . . or lose your lunch. As Rob, Kira, Tom, Ryan, Peter, Paul, and Joe celebrated between windy shivers, I dropped my pack and stood tall to have a look around. When I peered over the other side of the pass, another valley of tundra and talus slopes beckoned in the swirling otherworldly fog.

Despite our good fortune, I decide to sway on the side of caution and not yell "Lha Gyalo," lest it summon a hailstorm as the superstition predicted.

Suddenly Rob yelled, "Lha-a-a-a Gyalo-o-o-o-o!" threw up his arms, and started down the other side of the pass with Kira.

One way or the other, I was going to find out if the superstition was true.

As Ryan, Tom, Paul, Sonam, and Peter followed Rob and Kira down the other side of the pass, Joe waited for Larry, and I knelt down to grab my prayer flags out of my bag.

The prayer flag tradition began in Tibet with the Bon religion. Sacred prayers were inscribed on multi-colored flags and then hung to promote good luck, prosperity, happiness, a long life, or to help guide a departed soul after death. Traditionally, monks used soot dye and wood blocks to press prayers and symbols onto the flags. The five colors represent the elements — blue for sky, white for air, red for fire, green for water, and yellow for earth. Hanging one flag is as good as hanging a hundred, but generally the more the better, and once hung, the flags and the prayers are activated by wind. The flags bless the person who put them up, the person they were put up for, and the person now seeing them. Some prayer flags hang vertically on a pole of blue pine, but most hang horizontally, in five colors, along a string tied between two points.

I took out my flags and made increasing efforts to tie them, but that was when all the trouble started — the gusting wind, numb fingers, and uncooperative knots. When Norbu removed his gloves and came to my assistance, it was immediately clear from his sense of purpose that the Bhutanese take their flags very seriously. Norbu stood for a moment watching the string of flags whipping in the wind, and when the wind suddenly died, he sprung into action.

"Gotcha," Norbu cried, holding up the untied end of the prayer flags like a trophy.

"You got the gift!" I mused.

As Norbu secured the second end of the string to the curving horn of a yak skull perched atop the rocks, he asked if I wanted to tie the final knot.

"Nah, just do it yourself," I said, standing and shouldering my pack. "I'll try again later up the trail."

As the knot was tied and the string stretched taut, the flags kicked into a colorful, wind-snapping song.

"Thank you," I said, handing him his pack. "Where to?"

Norbu pointed to the gravelly trail leading down from the pass. "To the beautiful village of Lingshi."

11

MY FIRST INTRODUCTION TO THE DISTRICT OF LINGSHI was the knee-jarring trail down from Nyile La. It was a gravelly trail that, while not terribly steep, seemed to travel down the valley in a straight line. Without rocks or switchbacks to buffer the descent, my knees did all the work and ached immediately. If going uphill was hard on the heart, going downhill was hard on the knees, and thanks to the small, slippery pebbles, my feet threatened to slide out from under me with every step. Consequently, my knees seized up, stalled, and ached with protective effort. Far down the misty trail below, my trekking companions looked like brightly colored confetti flakes with feet.

Five minutes below the pass, the wind suddenly stopped, as if someone hit a switch, and all fell silent. As it did, my internal critic began criticizing my performance with the prayer flags. Instead of listening, I tried to focus on the surrounding beauty for I was then hiking above a wonderfully scenic gorge with a river zigzagging along its floor. All around, Celtic-green rhododendrons clung to the hillsides in scattered glistening clumps, and I imagined that their beauty in spring bloom would hardly be bearable. There are more than forty-six varieties of rhododendrons in Bhutan, and over the course of the Snowman Trek, we would pass three varieties — *arboreum, cinnabarinum,* and *griffithianum.*

Despite the beauty surrounding me, I had to agree with some of what my internal critic was saying and laugh about the incident with the prayer flags at the pass. There I was, trying to tie prayer flags for happiness and peace, and I ended up fumbling the attempt and feeling frustrated. It was the trekking equivalent of tripping in line at church on my way up to receive Holy Communion. I wasn't really concerned about the botched attempt but rather the feelings of disappointment that accompanied it. When I watched Norbu, he seemed to have a special faith in the flags and a way of working with wind that I hadn't yet grasped.

Not paying attention, I suddenly discovered I was hiking lost in whiteout fog, the result of fast-changing Himalayan weather. I spun around, searching for an opening, a door of sunlight in this four-cornered cloud room, but everything was socked in and swirling gray. As I peered into the white void, I spotted a shadowy black beast creeping toward me. Was it a black bear? A Yeti? A demon? It wouldn't be the first time — tales abound in the Himalayas of dark forces, evil ogresses, and ghost armies. When I saw the shag coat and curving horns, I decided it was a yak. But not an ordinary yak — it was a ghost yak with sharp horns and black eyes. Uh oh, I thought. This isn't good! When the yak lowered its horns and grunted, I raised my trekking poles like swords and fixed my stance. Then suddenly the yak lifted its head, as if noticing something behind me, and bolted up the hill.

When I turned, two young Bhutanese boys stood there, shoulder to shoulder, their arms hanging straight down at their sides like Pinnochio. The older boy wore green pants, a striped sweater, and a dark coat with a wool cap. The younger boy wore blue boots, gray sweatpants, a red jacket, and a baseball cap. They were yak herders. Brothers. For a few moments, we stared at each other in mutual wonderment. They'd never seen anyone like me, and I certainly had never seen anyone like them. And thus, in that white fog silence, two different cultures looked each other in the eye and met somewhere in between and beyond the years. Just then, the younger boy burped, and as the older one gave him a gentle elbow to the ribs, I broke out laughing. The younger one started laughing and then the older one joined in.

"Kuzuzangbo la," I said.

"Kuzuzangbo la," they responded together.

"Do you speak English?" I said.

When they gave me an uncomprehending look, I pointed down the trail and said, "Thanza."

"Ahhhh," said the older one with twinkling eyes, a gesture I'd decided to name "the Lunana look."

"Lingshi?" I asked.

They nodded. They lived here.

The older one glanced up the hillside where their yaks, black smudges in the gloom, had begun to wander off. He nudged his younger brother — time to go.

"*Tashi Delek,*" I said, Dzongkha for good luck.

"Tashi Delek," they replied, hurrying up the hill.

As the fog bank slowly moved out, I took a few steps down the trail and had to ask myself — did that just happen? Were those boys real? Along with demons, the Himalayas are also said to be home to protective deities who look out for the devout on precarious pilgrimages. I stopped and turned, hoping for a farewell wave, but the boys had disappeared, swept up in the swirling fog.

FOLLOWING MY ENCOUNTER WITH THE YAK HERDERS, I traversed the trail past the glacial drainages of 21,405-foot Mount Takaphu and into a dizzying maze of rumpled mountains extending infinitely in the fog horizon. I hadn't expected Bhutan to be so lush. Like Ireland, it seemed to have a thousand shades of green. From a lookout ridge, I shuffled down to the valley floor on a trail flanked by bushes ablaze in brilliant yellows and oranges.

As I walked, I kept my eyes peeled for Ugyen Tenzin, a postal worker who for thirty-seven years has made the five-day walk from Thimphu to deliver mail to Lingshi. Ugyen Tenzin was the subject of filmmaker Ugyen Wangdi's documentary *Price of Letter*, which showed how the humble postman routinely risked his life, braving winter storms, and crossing swollen rivers, simply to deliver the mail. But of course, it was more than the mail he was delivering—he was handing off the hopes and feelings of the human heart.

Bhutan didn't start mail service until 1960, but when it did, it did so with the typical Bhutanese love of the fantastical. Thus, Bhutan has created some of the most original and sought-after postal stamps in the world—paper stamps, silk stamps, sticker stamps, steel stamps, scented stamps, talking stamps, 3D stamps, mini-phonograph stamps, and in the months following our departure, Bhutan would come out with a commemorative CD-ROM stamp with video footage.

While I didn't meet Ugyen Tenzin, as I started across the valley floor of knee-high grasses, I saw a monk hustling up the trail behind me, his saffron-red robes rustling in the afternoon wind. I waited for him because, hey, it's not every day I get to hike with a Buddhist monk.

There was something wonderful about hiking through Bhutan, a country where most of the people sought shelter under the luminous umbrella of Buddhism. The only thing I can compare it to is that buzz big cities in the United States get when their team makes it to the World Series. Suddenly everyone is wearing the team T-shirt, putting up posters, and displaying the flag and bumper stickers. People of different races and socioeconomic statuses—people who never knew the other existed, let alone interacted with one another—begin sharing taxis, buying each other drinks, and trading high fives. Rooting for the same team, for a few weeks, a city of millions becomes a city of one. I got a similar feeling in Bhutan, only here the World Series lasts 365 days a year, and instead of major league All-Stars like Alex Rodriguez, Ichiro Suzuki, and Derek Jeter, you have the Buddha, Guru Rinpoche, the Shabdrung, and the King of Bhutan. Walk into any Bhutanese home, temple, or store and you'll see this All-Star team of Bhutan — framed in pictures, on colorful, scroll-like *thangka* paintings, and displayed on pins and posters.

To me, Buddhism is at once the most simple and complex of religions. Since much of Buddhism deals with personal growth and your thoughts, some scholars don't even think it should be labeled a religion. More than 450 million people practice Buddhism, making it the fourth-largest religion in the world. Buddhism is complex; from the trunk of Buddhism shoots many branches of belief, which in turn blossom into flowers of localized color. You need only to look at the shape-shifting image of the Buddha himself to see the diversity of the faith. He is alternately portrayed as benign, wrathful, smiling, serious, standing, seated, skinny, and sometimes portly. Indeed, both he and Guru Rinpoche — Bhutan's favorite saint — seem to have more manifestations than Madonna. On the flipside, Buddhism is also incredibly simple. When asked by his students what Buddhism meant, the Buddha simply held up a flower and threw the question back to the students. And the student who got the question right — Mahakasyapa — was the one who smiled back at the Buddha.

Despite these regional variations, there are some basic core beliefs that all Buddhists share. All Buddhists believe the historical Buddha lived in fifth century BC India and achieved enlightenment under the Bodhi tree; all are concerned with identifying the cause of suffering and eliminating the source; and all believe in the doctrines of Karma, Nirvana, the Four Noble Truths, Eightfold Path, and Three Jewels. These beliefs combine as ingredients for enlightenment, providing a recipe for realization. There are three main traditions in Buddhism: Theravada, Mahayana, and Vajrayana. Each branch, or "vehicle," of Buddhism essentially offers a different roadmap to get to the same place.

Vajrayana technically falls under the Mahayana school, but because of its popularity and esoteric practices, it is often awarded its own school. Vajrayana (also called Tibetan, Tantric, Himalayan Buddhism, or simply, the Diamond Way) stresses the guru-student relationship and uses yoga, mantra, and meditation to purify the mind, body, and soul. Instead of viewing the body as a hindrance to enlightenment, Tibetan Buddhists embrace its potential to be a vehicle toward enlightenment. Because this school of Buddhism engages all the energies of the human mind and body in service of the spirit, it enables one to attain enlightenment in a single lifetime. Vajrayana Buddhism arrived in the Himalayas in the eighth century with Guru Rinpoche and is now practiced in Mongolia, Nepal's Mustang region, India's Ladakh region, Tibet, Sikkim, Bhutan, and elsewhere in small devoted groups around the world.

As the monk approached, I saw that he, like many Bhutanese, seemed to have mastered the art of swift walking and maintained a familiar posture of the Bhutanese on the trail — his hands clasped behind the back like a college professor, his head bent humbly, and his face wearing a wide smile.

"Kuzuzangbo la," I said as he approached.

"Kuzuzangbo la," he replied, eyes twinkling.

From there, our conversation consisted of pointing — to him, to the trail, to me, to the trail, to my camera, to him, to me, to him. He seemed eager to have me take his picture, and when I pulled out the camera, he stepped back and fixed his hair like a high school student before his senior picture. This wasn't a vain gesture but rather a generous one — he wanted Buddhism to look good. I snapped a few pictures and he scurried over to have a look at the digital image.

"Ahhh," he said, smiling.

"You look cool," I said with a smile.

He didn't understand.

"Cool," I said again, giving him a thumbs-up.

Lingshi Dzong floats mysteriously in the clouds. Photo by Peter McBride.

"Cool," he repeated in a heavily accented voice.

We hiked on together, crossing the Lingshi Chhu on a rickety wood-plank bridge and started up a steep trail, traversing a pyramid-shaped mountain. After fifteen minutes, we arrived at a towering ten-foot chorten and a fork in the trail. One trail led across the hillside and around the bend toward Lingshi village — my trail. The other trail headed up the peak, where it disappeared into the clouds — his trail. At first I couldn't see anything perched atop the pyramid-shaped peak, but as I kept looking, the clouds swirled magically and a structure slowly began to reveal itself, the faint outlines of a building, an imposing castle-like structure with white stone walls and a red roof.

"Lingshi Dzong?" I asked.

As the monk nodded enthusiastically and I rejoiced in my discovery, I couldn't help but think that this was the role of priests and monks all across the planet — to open up the eyes of their congregation to a fabulous kingdom that exists just beyond their perception. Lingshi Dzong looked exactly like the castle in a fairy tale — isolated, mysterious, floating in the clouds, forbidding, yet strangely inviting.

The monk gestured for me to join him.

"Tomorrow," I said pointing to the trail I was to follow to our campsite.

"Tashi Delek," he said, shaking my hand with both hands.

As I watched him float up the trail, all the foolish, lingering disappointment of my incident with the prayer flags disappeared. There was something in that compassionate monk's gaze and smile that made me feel tremendously hopeful. Living in a monastery without heat, running water, or electricity, it was doubtless the monk lived a hard life. Yet what radiated from him was a joy totally unaffected by external events. I thought of the definition I'd once heard of an enlightened individual as someone who has "laid down the burden." Like Siddhartha's Fourth Sight, I got the sense from that monk that everything in my life would be all good. At the Nyile La, I'd questioned the universe for not helping me out with the prayer flags, but as I plodded on, there arose the idea that perhaps Norbu helping me *was* the universe helping me out. Suddenly I knew, not only that everything would be all good, but that it always had been and forever would be. The feeling didn't last long, but for a few steps it sure felt nice.

12

IN NOVEMBER 1995 RON AND DEBBIE PLOTKIN OF SAN DIEGO were trekking around the upper lakes of Nepal's Goyko region when tragedy struck. After finishing dinner one night and chatting with their friendly Sherpas, they headed off to their tents to sleep. A few snowflakes were falling but nothing serious — they were the kind of snowflakes you might see floating in a Macy's store window around the holidays. Without a second thought, they crawled into their sleeping bags and went to sleep. At 2:00 a.m. their guides woke them and hurried them out of their tents. Those small flakes had turned into a raging snowstorm. No sooner had Ron and Debbie crawled out of their tent, than an avalanche thundered down the mountain, sweeping away four of their Nepalese staff, their tents, and all their gear. While the four Sherpas who were buried managed to struggle free and survive, one of their guides died of hypothermia. It would take Ron and Debbie three days of crossing icy rivers and trudging around huge snowbluffs without any gear — at times only managing twenty feet an hour — before they made it back to the safety of a village. All across Nepal, similar dramas played out, although many people weren't as fortunate as the Plotkins. Twenty-six people died in Panga village when an avalanche buried their cabins as they lay sleeping. Eleven other people died in a landslide in the Manang region. Hundreds others were stranded and would have faced a certain death if the Nepalese government hadn't launched a swift and successful rescue mission. The cause of this "perfect storm" of snow? A cyclone in the Bay of Bengal traveled north and dumped more than six feet of snow in hours. It was to become the worst trekking and mountaineering disaster in Nepal's history. In that storm a total of 46 people lost their lives and 517 more were rescued.

ON THE MORNING OF DAY SIX, I FOUND JOE OUTSIDE THE dining tent and asked him how he checked the weather on the Snowman Trek.

Joe gestured to the sky and smirked. "You look up."

As I looked up, I noticed it was a cool and overcast morning, but it didn't look like a cyclonic storm was blowing in. Despite the clouds, I couldn't deny how good it felt to be in weather again. At home in California, the weather rarely changed, and inside my house I controlled all the elements. With a flick of a switch, I could light a fire in my fireplace, control the air temperature, and summon water in the shower and bubbles in the Jacuzzi tub. Making me feel more disconnected to nature, fake plastic plants decorated my house, my dinner salads came in pre-prepared packages, and landscapers took care of all the lawn maintenance. While one part of me cursed the drizzle that fell for the first six days of the Snowman Trek, another part of me celebrated surrendering control and being out in the ever-changing elements.

Lingshi was a small village of 118 homes with three to four hundred people, many of which live a few hours' walk from the dzong. The homes in Lingshi — constructed of stone with corrugated-metal and wood-shingled roofs — were perched on a gently sloping hillside above the Lingshi Chhu. Along with the homes, there was a school, a livestock extension center, and a Basic Health Unit (BHU), a satellite clinic the government of Bhutan sets up in remote areas.

After a steep, sweaty hike, our group assembled under the stone archway announcing the entrance to Lingshi Dzong. As the group arrived, Norbu told us that Lingshi Dzong is one of the oldest dzongs in Bhutan, and historically, a checkpoint for people traveling from Tibet. The dzong's original foundation was destroyed in the 1897 earthquake, an earthquake so strong it bounced large boulders into the air and set them down a few feet away. The evidence of that earthquake was still apparent, the structure of Lingshi Dzong looked horribly unstable, its stones resembling crumbling sugar cubes.

"A reconstruction effort was launched in the 1950s," Norbu explained "and, most recently, Germany has donated funds to assist with rebuilding the central tower."

"Hear that, Kev?" said Rob with a nudge. "A *German* fund."

Even though none of us have yet to meet Ingrid, I could tell I was going to have eighteen days ahead of me of similar jokes and nudges. Norbu said there are about eighteen young monks at the dzong and one head monk. "I think I met him on the trail yesterday," I volunteered.

We followed Norbu past the front of the dzong to the back entrance where, suddenly, two dogs rushed us, snarling and barking. I braced myself for the attack, but before fangs punctured flesh, the dogs' metal chain went taut and wheeled them up on their hind legs, their sharp claws slicing the air.

"Tibetan mastiffs," said Joe. "Do not pet."

"People in the north use mastiffs as guard animals," said Norbu. "They fend off snow leopards, tigers, and robbers, so they have to be tough."

When a young monk with a shaved head ran out, the dogs turned into tender black and gold teddy bears. As the boy gave them a hug, the dogs decorated his face with big ice-cream-cone licks.

Norbu led us into the main dzong courtyard where six monks were carrying large wood beams into the central tower. "This is probably part of the German-based restoration project."

Behind them, a pile of about twelve more beams waited to be hauled in.

"Let's give them a hand," cried Peter, grabbing a beam.

"Great idea," added Rob, joining him.

"I'm in," I said. "I can use all the merit I can get!"

However, when I picked up a beam and turned, it swept through the air like a helicopter blade and the monks had to duck. That couldn't be good for my merit. With our combined help, the beams were quickly carried into the dzong. The monks didn't allow us into the central tower, which is just as well — superstition says if we enter this tower, we might die. Following this we sauntered back into the center courtyard and past some underground cells that used to hold prisoners.

Upstairs, I ran into the monk from yesterday, and Norbu introduced him as the head monk. When he saw me, his face lit up as if we'd been friends for years (which I was beginning to believe we were). The monk led us into another room to see some paintings, statues of local gods, as well as pictures of the King, Guru Rinpoche, and the Dalai Lama. Then he opened up a cabinet that was full of swords, helmets, and shields from a bygone era. Kira grabbed a sword and gave it a little twirl.

"Wow," I thought to myself, "She really is a real-life Lara Croft!"

It was clear from the weapons that in the seventeenth century, war was a close contact sport and that Buddhism in the Himalayas shared some of the violent past of other religions. We spent another fifteen minutes looking around, then we all gathered in the central courtyard to leave, but not before the head monk took my right hand in both of his and wished me well with a nod.

Outside the dzong, eight young monks were now washing laundry in large silver washing bowls, overflowing with suds and soapy water. The monks had shaved heads, wore burgundy robes, paraded around in blue plastic sandals, and had ruddy cheeks, the result of windburn, sun, and living at a high altitude. I expected the monks

Laughter and laundry for the young monks of Lingshi. Photo by Peter McBride.

to be scrubbing with a Zen-like rigor, but instead, they were scurrying around, whipping each other with their robes. It was refreshing to see such youthful mischief along with the austerity. It was also quite visually stunning — flashing red robes amidst the background of green mountains, under a highway gray sky.

When one boy whipped his robe, the wind caught it and held it afloat, and for a moment, he was transformed from a monk into a matador. Seeing this, I was reminded of the Buddhist story of the ten bulls or ox-herding pictures, a series of twelfth-century poems and woodcuts that illustrate the difficult path of attaining enlightenment. Taming the bull is, of course, a metaphor for the mind, which, as I knew, had an occasional habit of running away and rearing its horns.

When the wind died, the monk twirled his robe with a grand gesture, looked at me, and bowed gracefully.

OUR NEXT STOP WAS AT THE LINGSHI COMMUNITY SCHOOL, A single-story stone structure with a corrugated-metal roof, surrounded by deep cement gutters. There was a swarm of schoolchildren out front, and when they saw me coming down the hill, they immediately raced over and gave me a rock star moment, crowding around, pleading for a picture, and jostling for my attention.

"Sir, over here," cried one boy in a white and gray checkered *gho* with a big freckle decorating the side of his nose.

"No, over here!" yipped a little girl in a blue sweatshirt and maroon *kira*, the traditional ankle-length dress that women wear in Bhutan.

"People please," I said, hamming it up. "Let me pass by."

The children of Lingshi were adorable—they all had their hair short and wore ghos and kiras. The girls sported flip-flops and the boys tromped around in little blue boots. Like the monks, all had ruddy cheeks and smiling faces. When the children clung to my legs and refused to let go, there was nothing I could do but break out my air guitar, and their laughter was a sweet soundtrack.

It was a wonderful scene at the school, as many villagers wandered down to meet us. To my right, Ryan was taking pictures of a bunch of kids who squealed when they saw their digital image. To my left, Kira was kicking a soccer ball with two schoolgirls; Rob was using his two index fingers as horns and stampeding around like a yak. Peter was demonstrating a handstand, and Tom was helping some kids practice their English.

What's that?" the children said, pointing to a thin, titanium stick.

"Trekking pole," Tom replied.

"TREKKING POLE," they squealed, before pointing to his nose.

Tom told the kids those were sunglasses.

"SUNGLASSES!" they sang.

On my left, Joe was handing out pictures he took in Lingshi on his 2005 Snowman Trek, and Larry was presenting the Lingshi school teacher with our gift of pencils, pens, and markers. "On behalf of

Canadian Himalayan Expeditions," he said formally, "we'd like to present these gifts to the schoolkids of Lingshi."

Norbu told me Bhutan is very adamant about tourists not giving local children gifts. "We don't want them to start begging. That is why Larry is giving your gift to the teacher, who will then give it to the children."

"Why are the children here on Sunday?" I asked.

Norbu told me that most of the kids in these remote schools are boarding students. "It's safer than walking hours to school each day. They get to spend time with their friends, and their family is assured they're eating well."

While typical school sessions in Bhutan go from February to December with two months off for winter, the remote schools in Lingshi, Laya, and Lunana have adjusted schedules and curriculum. "Depending on the snow," Norbu explained, "these kids start school in late April or May and go until late October or early November. They also have classes in the evenings and sometimes on the weekends. The real problem isn't the short school year," he continued, "but that many kids drop out to help their parents with little siblings and the yaks."

When a soccer ball rolled over, I give it a great kick and Norbu told me that he thinks keeping kids in school longer will be a goal of the next five-year plan.

Since 1961 Bhutan has planned its national development in a series of five-year plans. The plans generally focus on improving universal education and healthcare, building roads, providing safe drinking water, improving sanitation, improving agriculture, lowering the number of people living below the poverty level, and providing rural electrification since only 40 percent of Bhutanse homes are currently lit.

When I asked who decides what goes into each plan, Norbu told me that prior to instituting a new five-year plan, the king travels the country, often on foot or horseback, and holds question-and-

Dressed in their traditional *ghos*, school boys in Lingshi smile for a picture. Photo by Peter McBride.

answer sessions with local villagers to find out their needs and concerns. "Based upon these meetings, as well as some existing goals from the previous five-year plan, the king draws up the new five-year plan.

"Wow," I said, "the king really does work for the people."

When the soccer ball rolled over once again, I thanked Norbu for answering my questions and joined the fun. At that altitude, I was winded in less than two minutes. So I took some pictures, let some children practice their English, and played a stunning rendition of Guns N' Roses' "Sweet Child O' Mine" on air guitar to an applauding audience.

As we left, the children ran after us yelling "Bye," and I hadn't walked two hundred yards before I was missing them. I walked a few more paces and then turned to wave one last time, but when I did, the children were already hard at play, kicking the soccer ball in front of the school. "God bless children," I thought, "forever living in the moment."

THE TEN-MILE WALK FROM LINGSHI TO THE VILLAGE OF Chebisa on day six followed a flat, sun-caked trail, high above the river. As I hiked the flower-carpeted slopes, I thought of the prayer flags at the first pass and the unpredictability of grace, and had to shake my head that at thirty-three I was still searching for answers. It just didn't seem fair. All through my adolescence, I'd gone to catechism and attended church on Sundays. When my early adulthood brought a burgeoning interest in Buddhism, I read books on the Buddha, listened to dharma discussions on CDs, and watched movies about the Dalai Lama. After college, when I realized an open heart was more important than an active mind, I began practicing yoga six days a week at local studios and in the dancing-candlelight dawn of my bedroom. Over the years, I'd read the Bible, the Upanishads, Yoga Sutras, Tibetan Book of the Dead, Bhagavad Gita, parts of the Koran, the collected works of Joseph Campbell on mythology, Huston Smith's classic *The World's Religions,* and many more books explaining the meaning behind those epic texts. You'd think all the effort would have yielded lasting results, yet I was still searching. And it wasn't that I didn't believe — I believed in loving your neighbor and the Golden Rule of "Do unto others as you would have them do unto you." I believed heaven wasn't so much a patch of real estate but a state of mind and a way of looking at the world. I believed joy was our birthright and was to be found within oneself. I believed all of this right to the depths of my being, yet these firm beliefs didn't translate into lasting feelings of contentment. And thus, I was still searching. Would being in Bhutan yield that elusive key to me? I hoped so because, at thirty-three, I was tired of searching. I wanted answers.

FROM THE RIDGE, I FOLLOWED THE TRAIL DOWN INTO THE lovely town of Goyok, a little hamlet of twenty-five homes and 100 inhabitants with a small white monastery built right into the side of the cliff. As I wandered the dirt walkways between stone homes, the villagers were busy readying for winter by threshing barley, stacking straw, and harvesting potatoes. At 13,120 feet these are some of the highest farm fields in the world. The potato is not native to Bhutan but was introduced by an Englishman named George Bogle, who was sent by the British East India Company to tour the country in 1774. Evidently, Mr. Bogle believed in getting drunk, and if you can believe it, planting potatoes. Prior to Bogle, the first westerners in Bhutan were two Portuguese Jesuits who visited in 1627, and after Bogle came a long line of British explorers, often sent by the East India Company.

We had lunch a hundred yards outside of town. Some local kids followed us out and, as we ate, pretended to hide behind a large rock near our table, staring and giggling. Since tourists were still rare in Bhutan, villagers would often just watch us do simple things with the utmost amazement — handling silverware, tying our shoes, and reading a book. That afternoon, one little girl in a red sweater with magnificent eyes like brown marbles, approached our table. When Peter set her in his lunch chair, she beamed like a princess and our cameras were a chorus of clicks.

The remaining hike that day took about an hour and was pleasant and beautiful with open vistas of the surrounding valley and colorful alpine pastures. A grassy knoll decorated with tall prayer flags announced our arrival in Chebisa, a quaint little village tucked in a V-shaped valley. At the far end of the valley, a majestic waterfall poured from a hanging lake, crashed among craggy rocks and juniper trees, and then murmured past fifteen houses that huddled together on the hillside.

As I strolled into camp and found my trekking mates milling around, Norbu informed us that beyond the waterfall was a trail to Tibet and many of Chebisa's villagers were Tibetans who fled to Bhutan in the '50s when China launched its "peaceful liberation" of Tibet, which involved burning monasteries and persecuting people.

"The pass is closed now," explained Norbu. "But that doesn't stop smugglers from trying their luck."

As we settled into Chebisa camp, it dawned on me that, given the low numbers, trekkers must still be a strange sight in these small Bhutanese hamlets. Groups like ours — sixteen people with thirty horses and twelve tents — would waltz in without reservations and literally set up a traveling village in someone's front yard. Imagine if the Bhutanese decided to do the same thing in the United States? Imagine if one day the Bhutanese got all their horses together and decided to hike through and camp in, say, Beverly Hills? I suspect the police might receive a frantic phone call or two. But not only did we set up our village in their front yard, but we also started taking pictures of their children, sweeping them up in our arms and running around pretending to be yaks. If we weren't parading around as farm animals, we'd be strolling the narrow paths between homes. And of course, we must've looked positively hilarious rolling into town with our reflecting glacier glasses, bandanas, glowing headlamps, and adjustable trekking poles. Now I understood why the children rushed out to meet us with such joy — the carnival had, indeed, come to town.

THE SIXTH NIGHT WOULD FOREVER BE REMEMBERED AS THE "Night of the Normans." The night got off to an interesting start when Achula whipped up a meat dish that, with our best guesses, could only be described as "hairy bacon." Then Sonam and Sangey brought out some cookies that immediately had us all laughing about the food names in Asia that had been lost in translation. On the trek we had eaten peanut butter from India made with "unsaturated rat" and cookies made with "plam oil," "natural identical flavor," and "orange crystals." Making matters more humorous, the cookies all had strange names like "Naughty Boy," "Little Panda Shape Cookie," and best of all, "Yo Dutch Orange Yoghurt Creame

Puffs." When the laughter finally died down, Paul gestured to the cookies and said, "Could you please pass the Normans down to this neck of the woods?"

"The what?" asked Ryan, incredulously.

"The Normans," Paul exclaimed, gesturing to the plate.

We all stared at him quizzically.

"Ah hell," he said, frustrated, "the bloody cookies!"

Of course, we were all in stitches because calling cookies "Normans" made absolutely no sense, which for us, slap-happy at high altitude, meant it made perfect sense. Following an impassioned and hilarious discussion about "Normanology of cookies," Kira led us in a psychology game in which ambiguous words were given to a person on the assumption that their responses would reveal hidden beliefs and aspects of their personalities. The game was based on Freud's idea that we can project aspects of our personality onto objects and events.

"You're walking in the woods and you come upon a cup," Kira tossed out, glancing around the table.

"What does the cup mean?" I asked.

Kira said she couldn't tell me. Instead, we just had to respond with the first answer that came to our minds and that was the fun part of the game. "So, what kind of cup is it, guys?" she continued, "And do you pick it up?"

"A beer stein," declared Ryan. "And I definitely pick it up."

"A golden chalice," I barked. "But I don't touch it, I admire it from afar."

Sonam and Sangey huddled in the tent corner with bemused grins.

"Mine is a Dixie cup," added Tom. "I pick it up. And then I rip it apart and toss it over my shoulder."

At the end of the game all the answers were exactly the opposite of what we expected. For instance, Kira told us the cup symbolized our views on love and Tom, the only married one among us, had declared it a Dixie cup and ripped it up. Whereas I, the single guy, had chosen a golden chalice.

"But you admired it from afar," noted Larry. "You didn't embrace the cup."

"Yeah, Kev," said Joe, smirking. "You should really get that checked out, eh?"

After this, we played Find Your Porn Name, which was decided by taking the name of your first childhood pet and name of the street you grew up on.

"Ladies and gentlemen," I announced, "I will now be known as Frisco Pleasant."

By then, I was certain the villagers of Chebisa thought we were crazy because our laughter was bouncing off the canyon walls — especially when someone would trip over the tent ropes. The good part of having a big lantern as the centerpiece of our dining table was that it threw off a lot of light and heat. The bad part was when you ventured out of the dining tent, your eyes took about five minutes to adjust to the darkness, often causing you to trip over the ropes that radiated from the tent like spider legs. Over the past five nights, everyone had tripped at least once — Peter, Ryan, Sonam, Achula, and even the horses. But when I stood that night to use the toilet tent, I vowed to myself that I would practice Buddhist mindfulness and not trip on the tent ropes. I didn't either. I navigated safely to the toilet tent and emerged moments later to the "paradise found" of Chebisa village at night.

As I clicked off my headlamp, I was surrounded by the darkest night I have known, and yet the stone homes of Chebisa, lit by butter lamps, glowed with a festive, First Night radiance. There were no stars overhead, just blowing black mist, but there were eight "stars" in the dining tent in laughing orbit around the one sun of the lantern. As I saw the larger-than-life shadows of my trekking companions splashed across the canvas of the dining tent and heard joyous laughter echoing through that timeless valley, I thought to myself, “Home isn’t a place, it’s a feeling.” Our tent was a collection of canvas flaps and metal stakes clinging to the rocky face of a planet floating in infinite space. And yet, solidarity and human friendship had made this modest shelter feel as strong and secure to me as one of Bhutan’s mighty dzongs.

A feeling of immense gratitude arrived for this journey that I was on. In a world of perpetual distraction, of constant arrivals and departures, how rare to be part of a team that shared the dream of a common destination. I took a moment to say thanks — for Bhutan, the Snowman Trek, and my trekking companions.

And then, yes folks, I tripped on the tent ropes.

13

I NEEDED TO MAKE EATING ADJUSTMENTS, AND IT WASN'T just due to hairy bacon. Not only did I give up control over what I ate, but I also surrendered control of when I ate. If I hiked over a ridge and saw Sonam and Sangey standing beside a table full of food, it was lunchtime — whether I was ready or not. I couldn't stroll up to them and say, "I'm sorry, my reservation wasn't until noon." And while I had entrée selections within each meal, my choices were limited to what was served. Coming from a country where I had unlimited food options and could control my meals down to the fat content and calorie count, it wasn't an easy adjustment during the first day or two. But after six days on the trail, I'd learned to be flexible with food again, to let go of control, and to find a five-star meal in a single slice of buttered bread. I'd been reminded to appreciate what is set before me.

The meals on the Snowman Trek followed a typical pattern: breakfast preceded a big climb that usually involved a pass, and lunch came immediately after. Tea and "chocolate Normans" greeted us as we arrived in camp, and the dinner bell rang around seven. On the Snowman Trek, I ate three meals a day with the same people every day — for twenty-four days. Most married couples don't even do this! The funny thing was, after a few days on the trail, we started to resemble a married couple—I'd see Kira graciously accepting a bowl of soup from Sangey and immediately know to pass her the spice rack. Tom would pour some tea, and Paul would hand him the sugar, and we'd all automatically leave the seats at the ends of the tables for Joe and Larry.

Day seven would take us from Chebisa to a camp called Shakyapasang. It was a nine-mile hike that featured the second pass of our trip—the 14,560-foot Gombu La.

"Piece of cake," I said, as the trail snaked up through Chebisa village. "That pass is nothing compared to the Nyile La."

Tom reminded me that this "piece of cake" was about the size of Switzerland's Matterhorn—one of the highest peaks in the Alps.

"Good point," I said. "I won't get cocky!"

It was always beautiful hiking out of Bhutan's valleys and gazing down at our camp each morning. Seeing our tiny tent village and the staff loading up the horses, I always had the same deeply spiritual thought: "Thank God, I don't have to carry my bag!"

As the trail opened up into alpine pastures, awash with red and autumn gold grasses, I fell into step with Larry.

"How's it going, Larry?"

"Slowly but surely, Frisco."

No sooner had Larry said this, than he ducked behind a bush. "Get down!"

When an ex-army guy tells you to get down, you hit the deck.

"What is it?" I whispered, crouching behind a bush.

Larry peeked through the branches. "Blue sheep," he whispered. "Just up the hill."

A herd of fifteen blue sheep were grazing on the hillside a hundred yards from us. Standing around three feet tall and with a grayish coat and curving horns, blue sheep looked a lot like the goats I had in my backyard growing up. In Bhutan, blue sheep graze the high-altitude, grassy slopes during summer and then migrate to the warmer lower valleys in winter.

"Let's see how close we can get," suggested Larry.

Together we scampered over to a little sand bunker and hunkered down. While we may have thought we were invisible, the truth was we couldn't be more obvious — Larry wore a bright orange jacket (which was then probably registering on Google Earth), and the bright sun reflecting off my glacier goggles was sending out a thousand points of light. It's not that the blue sheep didn't see us, they didn't care. This mattered not the least — what mattered was that, with our imagination, we were invisible and having fun — like those precious children "hiding" behind the rock in the village of Goyok.

My brother and I used to track animals in the woods growing up in New Hampshire, and there was nothing like the magic of stumbling upon a footprint in the mud or snow, speculating on the species and knowing, perhaps only moments before, a wild animal had walked that way.

"That's a deer for sure," I said one time when I saw fresh tracks in the snow. "Probably a six-point buck."

"A deer?" Sean guffawed. "Whatever made that print was no bigger than a rabbit."

It really didn't matter. In my fourth-grade mind the hoof print was made by a beautiful buck with a shiny regal coat and antlers that extended majestically, the king of the forest.

"But this is a deer trail," Sean said, pointing to another set of tracks. "Let's see if we can find it!"

"Cool," I said.

Off we raced down the trail, leaping over muddy patches, ducking under trees and tiptoeing when we thought the deer was close. Like Larry and me, we were probably the loudest and most obvious thing in the forest, but we felt invisible. Most times, Sean and I never saw anything, but that January morning all of our unsuccessful backyard tracking games finally paid off. Suddenly, something swept over both of us at exactly the same time. We quickly hid behind a bush. A kind of ESP had taken hold of us and told us an animal was near. Old instincts, passed down from our ancestors, had risen up within us, instincts that were understood on a cellular level and needed no interpretation. We both crouched behind a bush, motionless, waiting. Sticks snapped, leaves cracked, and we knew an animal was approaching. As we held our breath and waited, the animal suddenly stopped. A soft wind was blowing from behind us, and we immediately knew it had delivered our scent to this animal, whatever it was. Sean and I looked at each other, agreed without saying anything, and slowly peeked over the bush. Two deer, a buck and a proud doe, stood frozen against a backdrop of snow and bone-white birch trees. Our eyes met the deer's briefly, profoundly, and then the deer disappeared into the silence of the snowy forest.

That morning, when Larry and I crept too close to the sheep, they bounded up the hill a hundred yards and continued grazing with grinding teeth.

FOLLOWING OUR BLUE SHEEP STAKEOUT, LARRY AND I continued traversing up the ridge for thirty minutes, and then from behind, we heard the sound of our horse team charging up the trail.

"Shall we wait and watch them?" asked Larry.

I was always up for a break. "Sure thing."

I took a seat on a tuft of grass and closed my eyes so as to open my ears. The whistling shouts of the horsemen, the silver-studded harness bells, and the vibration of hooves on hard ground—that glorious soundscape rivaled any landscape I'd seen and will forever remind me of Bhutan. As the horse team approached, I blinked my eyes open to watch the grand choreography of a scene that hadn't changed in hundreds of years. The horsemen orchestrated the direction of the horses with all the artistry of conductors. While a conductor might use a baton, these mountain maestros tossed rocks to keep the horses in line. They never hit the horses with the rocks, but if they wanted a horse to turn left, they'd throw a rock on the right side of the horse and vice versa. Watching Achula, Sonam, Sangey, and the horsemen running alongside their animals, steering the squad with great yells and rock tosses, I realized another thing — their aim was impeccable. As they thundered up, Sonam waved me on. "Come, sir!"

"Me?" I asked, standing.

Larry smiled. "I don't think they're talking to me!"

Sangey tossed me a rock. "Come, sir!"

I caught the rock, shouldered my pack and started running alongside them.

"What do I do?" I hollered to Sonam.

"Like this," Sonam yelled, tossing a rock. It was a perfect shot. It landed on the left side of the horse, veering him right back in line.

"Nice shot!" I yelled.

"Sir," cried Sangey, pointing to a horse wandering off to my right.

I stopped running, reared back and threw with all might. My rock soared far over the horse and nearly hit Achula.

"Sorry!" I yelled.

"Yes!" Achula called back with a merry wave, dashing on.

Sonam sprinted around me, threw his stone, and the horse fell back in line.

When the horses slowed down, Sangey and Sonam gave them encouraging slaps on the side and yelled, "HAW!"

"Haw," I said, city-shy.

"HAW!" Sonam thundered in a wild cry, born of the backcountry.

"HAW!" I bellowed.

Sonam's eyes lit up. "YES, SIR!"

"HAW" I yelled, supremely happy.

The horse team thunders over another towering pass. Photo by Peter McBride.

What a feeling! Running horses through the Himalayas like a true cowboy! While I wanted to run forever, my heart had other plans.

"Sir," Sonam said, pointing to a horse out of line to my right.

"I . . . can't," I managed, between heaving breaths and tossed my rock to him, "keep going."

"Long trek," replied Sonam, smiling. "We try again."

With that, Sonam patted me on the back, yelled "HAW," and ran to catch up with the horse train, which chugged over a flowering ridge and out of sight.

THE HIKE TO OUR SECOND PASS, GOPHU LA, WAS TIRING BUT beautiful with clouds splashing cottony shadows on surrounding peaks and tiny blue flowers smiling at my feet. An hour and forty five minutes after leaving Chebisa, the path leveled and I found myself walking on a thin trail on a sheer mountainside that disappeared three hundred feet down and out of sight. Up above a bird floated frozen in the blue sky with an impressive wingspan that seemed to extend five feet in each direction. Was this the Garuda, the mythical Buddhist eagle that hatched fully formed from the egg and could travel from one end of the universe to the other with a single flap of its wings? Perhaps. But more likely it was a lammergeier, or bearded vulture, a bird of prey that had come for a sky burial taking place on Inela Peak, the towering spire to my left.

Not only does Jordan's *Bhutan: A Trekker's Guide* list campsites, mileage, and trail maps, but it also points out burial sites along the route. When a guidebook recommends where you can safely stash a teammate who unfortunately "expires," it's never a good thing. However, if the lammergeier was flying overhead for a sky burial on Inela Peak, it would be a very auspicious sign.

There are four practices following death in Bhutan — burial, cremation, sky burial, and water burial. With a water burial, the body is placed in a river for predation and decomposition by natural elements. A sky burial is similar, only the body is placed on an isolated ridgetop, and the appearance of a bird of prey, such as a lammergeier means the soul of the departed has either reached nirvana or attained an auspicious rebirth. Since some Buddhists believe burial inhibits a soul's migration to the other realms, cremation is the most common form of burial in Bhutan, and age-old practices such as sky and water burials are slowly dying out.

To westerners the idea of a sky burial can seem morbid, yet it is built upon a fundamental truth — all life lives on other life. Buddhists accept this truth, and are comforted knowing that when they die, their body will support the life cycle that supported them. That dead bodies are also left out in the open, albeit on high ridges, also speaks volumes about the way Buddhists approach death, namely death should be out in the open. This idea is not morbid, for when you know life is short and can end at any minute — you have an increased impulse to live.

When I arrived at the pass, I sprawled out on my back, resting my head in the pillow of my interlaced hands, and watched the lammergeier soaring and swooping on the thermals. With its massive, motionless wings, the bird appeared to steer with its eyes or an imperceptible tilt of its head, which seemed to be a lesson about intention being just as important as action. When the lammergeier did finally flap its wings, it disappeared behind the clouds, no doubt into another dimension.

FOLLOWING A SHORT NAP IN THE SUN AT THE PASS, NORBU and I traversed down a valley radiating with rhododendrons, where a single dew drop glistened in the upturned hand of each leaf. As we hiked down a steep and straight trail leading to the valley floor, where the rest of our team was waiting for lunch, I asked Norbu what he thought was the biggest danger on the Snowman Trek. The altitude, snow, remoteness, drinking Pabst Blue Ribbon at high altitude?

"Getting lost," Norbu said without a second's delay. "There are no signs on the Snowman Trek, and there are hundreds of yak trails leading everywhere — all of which are as wide and well traveled as the Snowman route," he explained. "You could easily be walking toward Tibet and not know it."

When I asked Norbu if there was any way to avoid being lost, he noted our large number of pack horses and instructed me to follow the manure. Switching subjects, Norbu then asked if I did a lot of pre-trip research on the Internet.

"You bet," I said. "I did a Google search about every aspect of the Snowman Trek."

"What happened when you Googled Lunana?" Norbu asked.

I told him when I Googled Lunana, I discovered Lunana was a forty-six-year-old woman from eastern Europe with a MySpace webpage that said she liked David Bowie, Khalil Gibran, David Hasselhoff from *Baywatch*, and her son. "And sadly, it was in that order!"

Next, I told Norbu I visited Google Earth, which allowed me to take a satellite tour of the country. "What immediately struck me was the topography." Bhutan was a country exploding with mountains, and on the screen they appeared in terrifying shades of dark green, brown, and spine-shivering white. The only flat parts of the country seemed to be the icy tongues of glaciers, alpine lakes, and floss-thin rivers. I told Norbu that when I zoomed in on the northern regions of Bhutan, I didn't see the magical Himalayan Kingdom, I saw a wild land of snake-like glaciers, knife-sharp peaks, and inhospitable terrain. "In fact, I clicked off my computer and for the next twelve hours, reversed my decision to do the Snowman Trek."

"What happened on the thirteenth hour?"

"I spoke to a woman named Marie Brown."

"And then what?"

"I fell in love with a place called Thanza."

AT THE BOTTOM OF THE VALLEY, WE SKIRTED A MUDDY section and crossed a little creek to find everyone having lunch on a small plateau with a good view of the pass from which we'd just hiked down. High up on the mountains behind us, a few blue-tarp tents of yak herders dotted the landscape.

I'd come to Bhutan excited to see a traditional *ba*, or yak-hair tent, because from what I read, they were quite amazing. To make a traditional yak-hair tent, a large, square hole is dug in the ground, and around it, rocks are stacked chest high and filled in with mud and dirt to keep out the wind. After this, the yak herders assemble two tall wooden posts to provide support inside the tent. Long strips of yak hair are sewn together and draped over the posts for the roof. The roof is connected to strings of yak hair and sinew, which are stretched tight to a half dozen wooden posts outside the tent, giving the whole construction the resemblance of a yurt. Yak-hair tents also seemed to have magical abilities: they allow light in and smoke to waft out but when it rains, nothing gets wet. Despite repeated inquiries in Bhutan, I never found out the science behind this.

"Does anyone still use the yak-hair tents?" I said to Norbu.

"Yes," he said, "But it's changing — tarps are easier to set up and lighter."

Following lunch, after thirty minutes of hiking in a yak-infested forest — where I'd be hiking carefree and suddenly a grunt would alert me to a half-ton beast hulking inches away — the trail opened up and delivered me to a lookout ridge with an awe-inspiring view of the surrounding mountains. Those moments where vistas suddenly opened up, like scenic satoris, made all the hard uphill slogging worthwhile. Sure, I knew a few lucky others had hiked there before, but I still had a Lewis and Clark moment, where I felt as if I was discovering the area for the first time. And I was . . . for myself.

After that brief glimpse of the high pastures of tomorrow's route, the trail wound back into the woods, passing little black cliffs and tiny caves hidden among the trees. An hour and twenty minutes after lunch, the trail descended through a forest filled with dazzling spruce, cypress, and birch trees on a muddy trail that made loud, digestive gurglings as I slogged through it. As I slowly descended, I grew concerned about the river crossing that the guidebook said waited at the bottom of the valley, and my mind warned of Class V rapids. *You will fall in!* No, I won't. *Your backpack will hold you under.* I'll unfasten the straps before I cross. *The current will be too strong.* I can swim. *You'll bash your head on the rocks.* I won't fall in. *You'll drown.* No I won't. *You will!* Won't. *Will.* Won't.

Up ahead, the trail brightened, signaling an end of the forest, and the sound of the rushing river increased. I slowed my pace and approached the river like a criminal might go to the gallows. But when I rounded the corner and saw the river, I had to laugh. There was no need to remove my backpack shoulder straps or put a spotter downstream to catch me when I fell in. While the river was wide and certainly could be dangerous during spring runoff, that afternoon, it was but a shallow, trilling stream.

Moments later, as I stepped across holding my boots in my hands, my feet rejoiced in the cold, clear river rush and round-stone massage. As I crossed the river and thought about how my mind tried to build up the drama and dangers, I remembered a quote by Guru Rinpoche who said, "By realizing all discursive thoughts to be the mind, the threat of horrifying gods and demons does not intimidate me."

With this in mind, I arrived on the other side of the river where our tents waited in a campsite called Shakyapasang, a small clearing with dense bushes in a beautiful U-shaped glacial valley. Pewter-gray clouds had socked in the valley, but there was a hint of surrounding snow peaks. As I entered camp I noticed it was a virtual minefield of yak and horse patties. Nothing was constant on the Snowman Trek — not the trail, not the weather, not the food, not the villages, and of course, not the sleeping surfaces. That night, my tent would not only have a doormat of yak dung but would also be horribly sloped.

"Looks like I'll be sledding in my sleeping bag tonight," I said to Tom.

Tom didn't seem to care, but then again, he was a guy whose idea of fun was sleeping on a ledge, hanging a thousand feet above the floor of the Yosemite Valley. "Just put your big duffel bag at the end of your feet," Tom instructed me. "Then you won't slide."

The real message, of course, was that I couldn't change the campsite, but I could change me in the campsites. I thanked Tom. "Got any other suggestions?"

"Yeah," he replied. "You might want to remove that piece of toilet paper clinging to your boot."

AT DINNER, STILL BASKING IN THE GLOW OF LAST NIGHT'S special evening in Chebisa, I also felt the good fortune of not having a television around. If there was a TV in the dining tent, we wouldn't have had half the conversations we did, and I would've never learned important things like my porn name, or that Rob and his fellow Australians refer to Speedo swimsuits as "budgie smugglers," or thanks to Paul, that it's polite in England to call sex "rumpy pumpy" around your grandmother. If there was a TV in the tent, instead of talking, all of our energy would be focused on the blinking screen. Some might argue this point and say that no way would people sit in front of television in an exotic foreign country, but I can attest to the fact that they do.

One of the great surprises of the Snowman Trek was that it made me fall in love with reading again. I used to love to read as a boy. Sean and I would slip into our one-piece pajamas — the kind where you had to be very careful zipping up around the midsection — and crawl into our bunk bed, armed with a book and flashlight. Sean was into Choose Your Own Adventure books at the time, and I was reading all the great stories about boys and their dogs: *Old Yeller*, *Sounder*, and *Where the Red Fern Grows*. Mom and Dad would tuck us in, turn off the lights, and moments later our flashlights would click on. As a kid, there is something wonderful and rebellious about reading a book under your bedcovers with a flashlight — your bed suddenly becomes a magical cave, and the book you're reading morphs into a secret scroll. At the time, I thought my parents had no idea of our late-night reading binges, but looking back, I realize that they did — come morning our bed covers were always snug around our shoulders, our flashlights turned off, and our books neatly stacked on the bed stand.

Despite the varied campsites, my nightly ritual on the Snowman Trek was the same. I'd crawl into my sleeping bag after dinner, zip it up, and immediately hunker down to wait for the bag to work its warm magic. Even a four-season sleeping bag is freezing when you first crawl in, but within a few minutes it'd grow toasty. Once warm, I'd crawl out slightly, as if emerging from a cocoon, click on my headlamp, and reach for my book. As in elementary school, reading on the Snowman Trek felt rebellious, the "cave" of my tent replacing my bedcovers and my headlamp substituting for a flashlight.

I brought Rainier Maria Rilke's *Letters to a Young Poet* on the Snowman Trek. While the book is about poetry, it's really about bringing forth and crafting the work of art that is yourself. *Letters to a Young Poet* is a great book—the kind of book you can read over and over because it says different things to you at different times of your life. The section that spoke to me that night, reading under Shakyapasang's swirling night clouds, concerned a lot of things in my life at that moment: blossom rain, the outcome of the Snowman Trek, my love life, and all the other unanswered questions of my life that caused countless sleepless nights. "Be patient toward all that is unsolved in your heart and try to love the *questions themselves* like locked rooms and like books that are written in a very foreign tongue. Do not now seek the answers, which cannot be given you because you would not be able to live them. And the point is, to live everything. *Live* the questions now. Perhaps you will then gradually, without noticing it, live along some distant day into the answer."

14

YOU HAVE TO LOVE ROB AND PEOPLE WHO ARE LIKE him — people who get excited about anything and everything and crank up on the motorbike throttle of life, zooming into one adventure after another, making friends and memories across the planet, and ending each day with cheeks sore from smiling. After seven days on the trail with Rob, I'd learned his excitement didn't depend on the subject — he could be just as excited to see a snail as he would a snow leopard. Hence, when I heard Rob running through camp on the morning of the eighth day, yelling in his Aussie accent that "It looks like Switzerland out he-re!" I didn't pay attention. I rolled over and tried to go back to sleep. But when I heard Ryan, Peter, Paul, and Kira's tent zippers, followed by their excited exclamations, I sat up in my sleeping bag.

"Wow!" said Ryan. "That's amazing!"

"Magical," added Paul.

"It's the best morning so far!" declared Kira.

"Truly magnificent," announced Larry.

"Amazing," said Peter.

That was it, I was out of my sleeping bag and throwing on my shoes. When a professional photographer thinks something is

Dawn hints at a day of sunshine and snowy peaks. Photo by Peter McBride.

amazing — you take a look. I stumbled out into the frosty grass and found everyone standing outside their tents. When I looked up the valley, I saw the source of all their amazement. Last night's clouds had disappeared, and in their place an alpine wonderland of snowy spires and lofty meadows glittered with morning dew. A waterfall crashed down the rocks in the distance, its roar echoing through the valley.

That day was the first completely clear morning of the trek, and I'd forgotten how good white peaks looked against a blue sky and how such a view made my spirit soar. I snapped pictures of the mountains, of me, of my trekking companions, the horses, and even the toilet tent, I was so happy. A view like this makes you fall in love, which, of course, makes you lazy. Why go anywhere? Why do anything when you can just relax and stare into the eyes of your beloved?

"I'll tell you why," said Norbu, "because we've got a 10-mile hike and a 15,695-foot pass ahead of us."

"Good point," I replied. "I'll get dressed."

As always the trail ascended steeply through bushes behind camp, and as I climbed out of the trees, I was captivated by the frozen-in-time feel of that valley: the sunlight streaming through the trees and the gentle river. It was the kind of day where you feel glad to be alive and want to suddenly start sprinting just to see how fast you can run. After thirty minutes, the trail turned east and started up another side valley that was prime yak-grazing country. Miles of sun-lit meadowy slopes extended in every direction, punctuated by distant gray smoke curling up from the blue-tarp tents of yak herders.

Up ahead I saw Paul taking a rest and removing his coat. "What d'ya say, Paul?"

"Just breathtaking, Kev!"

I asked Paul if he ever thought he could feel so good.

"Not without a pint of ale."

It made sense we were happy because Bhutan is serious about Gross National Happiness. Bhutan is so serious about happiness that they have a whole branch of government, the Center for Bhutan Studies, devoted to it. The Center for Bhutan Studies is like the Federal Reserve Bank of the United States, only instead of prioritizing their country's economic future, it studies the economy of bliss and makes every effort to ensure there is never a recession in Bhutan's bank vault of joy.

The idea of promoting Gross National Happiness over Gross National Product began with the Fourth King, Jigme Singye Wangchuk. He believed that rather than a more conventional economic model, a country should focus on the happiness of its people, with the idea that a happy citizenry will lead to a productive and profitable country. While you can't really legislate happiness — anymore than you can force enlightenment — you can set up a situation in which it might arise. Wangchuk grounded his Gross National Happiness plan on four principles — equitable and sustainable socioeconomic development, preserving and promoting cultural values, conserving the natural environment, and good governance. While skeptics may scoff at such a New Age idea, Gross National Happiness seems to work: Bhutan's economy has risen at roughly 7 percent each year since the 1980s and a recent study found that over 69 percent of the population labeled themselves as "very happy." Bhutan also seems to realize that achieving happiness is a practice that, like tending a garden, must be cultivated daily and they're not afraid to ask for outside input.

One such meeting took place a few months before we arrived when the Center for Bhutan Studies invited Professor Richard Layard, an economist at the London School of Economics and a member of the House of Lords, into the country to discuss happiness. Based upon a study of income in proportion to the population size, Professor Layard found people living in Third-World countries were not as happy as people living in rich countries, and he also discovered that the transition from a subsistence life to a higher level of income made people feel better and content. And how could it not? Knowing there will be enough food on your child's plate and a roof over your head will, of course, make you happier. In addition, not being dependent on a harsh environment for food and the physical toil it takes to harvest that food tends to raise one's spirits. But here's the interesting point, as a country transitions out of a subsistence way of life, their happiness increases for a period of around fifty years and then abruptly stops. Countries like the United States and Japan, which have had huge economic increases in the last fifty years, have not had any increase in happiness. In fact, happiness has plummeted in the United States. In 2007, with over 118 million prescriptions written, the U.S. Centers for Disease Control listed antidepressants as the most prescribed drug in America — far more popular than drugs for high blood pressure, cholesterol, asthma, and headaches.

Professor Layard theorizes that the difference between richer and poorer countries is that in poorer countries, people want to be rich in the absolute sense — they want to get their basic needs met. In richer countries, people want to be rich in the relative sense — in relation to someone else. In addition to this competition with our neighbors, we're constantly bombarded by the media reminding us of everything we lack — the perfect car, the perfect body, and the perfect house. Given aspirations we can never achieve, it's only natural that anxiety and depression result. Another interesting thing Professor Layard discovered was that people in rich countries take far too little leisure time. Historically, it used to be that as your income increased, so did your leisure time, but not anymore. These days, your workload increases along with your income until you're left with a lot of money and no time or good health to enjoy it. Were the Bhutanese truly happy? Or was my perception merely a case of Western wishful thinking? It was too early to tell about the Bhutanese, but I knew I felt great that morning.

Despite my happiness, I couldn't say the same for Larry. Twenty-five minutes up the trail, I found Larry sitting on a rock, and he didn't look good. He was pale, his breath was labored, and thanks to the sunburn on day four, his nose had gone from being deep red to being white and flaky. My worry from a few days ago returned. Still, when I asked Larry how he was doing, he smiled cheerfully and said, "So far, so good."

"Need any water?" I asked.

"I've got my two water bottles," he said, gesturing to his coffee mugs. "Beautiful scenery, huh?"

"It's amazing," I replied. "Looks like a tough climb to the pass, huh?"

"Slowly but surely," he said grabbing his trekking poles.

While Larry wasn't worried, everyone else on our trek was. We were worried about Larry's labored breathing, how he convulsed when he coughed, and how, when he fell asleep each night at dinner, his face froze and looked like a death mask. Over the last few days, the subject of Larry and whether he should continue on the trek had become a constant source of conversation on the trail. In two days, we would arrive in the village of Laya, the halfway point of the trek and the last opportunity to exit before the high passes of Lunana. If Larry, or any of us for that matter, was to leave, Laya would be the place to do it.

"Shall we head out?" I asked after a few moments of rest.

Larry told me he was going to sit and enjoy the view. "I may crawl to the pass," Larry said, "but I'll make it."

I hoped so.

"HOW WAS THE HIKE?" NORBU ASKED AS I ARRIVED AT THE 15,695-foot Jare La later that day.

Breathing heavily, I dropped my pack and collapsed to a seat. "The hike was horrible," I said. "I hate false passes!"

One hour previously, I was standing atop a ridge that I thought was the Jare La. It wasn't and upon reaching it I realized I still had an hour of tough hiking up steep scree slopes ahead of me. False passes are terrible. There is nothing more heart wrenching than to set your sights on a goal, hope and struggle for it, and then arrive to find you still have a long way ahead of you. Disgruntled, I trudged on, under massing clouds, across ankle-deep scree chutes, past rocky corridors and the abandoned stone camps of yak herders. Then, with semicircular sweat stains under my neck and each arm, I arrived at the finish line of prayer flags.

As I took my seat at the pass, a beautiful vista opened to rocky ridges, granite cirques, and clouds clinging to icy summits. When my breath returned, I pointed my face to the sky and smiled.

"How do you feel now," asked Norbu.

"Like I've arrived," I said, proudly. "And I'm going to enjoy this moment of having nothing to do and nowhere to go for as long as I can."

Norbu gestured to a string of snowy peaks looming before me and pointed to one specifically. "Know what that mountain is?"

"What?"

"Tomorrow's pass."

As Norbu chuckled, I told him he was mean — very mean.

FROM THE PASS WE FOLLOWED THE TRAIL DOWN THROUGH the lichen-freckled rocks and barren brown slopes to have lunch beside the white ribbon of a stream, overlooking the giant massifs we would meet tomorrow. When lunch was finished, after everyone else started off down the trail, I wandered over to Sangey. He was busy rinsing dishes in the stream, listening to the iPod Peter let him borrow.

"Hey Sangey," I said, tapping him on the shoulder.

Sangey stopped scrubbing and removed an ear bud. "Rock 'n' roll — good stuff."

I asked Sangey if he'd please tell me what blossom rain means.

"Sun and rain at same time," he replied casually.

"But what's it mean," I asked. "You know — like the appearance of snow partridges means it will snow."

Sangey told me blossom rain is good luck.

"Yes," I said. "But why?"

"Why not?" Sangey said, smiling.

I asked him why he wouldn't tell me.

"When you see, you know," he replied, putting the ear bud back in and scrubbing once again.

"And what if I don't know?"

"Then you won't know."

AN HOUR AFTER THE PASS, I ARRIVED AT TWO TREKKING poles stuck in the ground and waited for Paul who was taking a picture of a flower in the woods. There I noticed what looked to be some kind of pine tree with beautiful, brown dripping branches.

"What kind of tree is this?" I said to Paul as he emerged from the forest.

Paul told me it was a weeping cypress, the national tree of Bhutan.

"Even the trees cry on the Snowman Trek," I said, gazing at the branches that radiated with a kind of heartbreaking beauty.

As for the probability of my crying on the Snowman Trek, it wasn't good. It had been years since I'd cried, and to be honest, I wasn't quite sure why. It just felt like everything had just dried up.

Paul and I continued down to the valley floor where we crossed a sunny bridge that led to a fork in the trail.

"Which way?" I asked.

"I'm not quite sure," said Paul.

One trail went upstream to the left and the other trail followed the river downstream to the right. When I told Paul how Norbu said the other day to follow the manure, he rightly noted that yak and horse patties lead in every direction.

"When in doubt on the Snowman Trek," I said, "Go up."

Paul agreed, but no sooner did we take a step, than a loud whistle sounded from the forest.

"Go right," yelled an unseen Wizard of Oz–like voice.

It was Norbu, but he was nowhere to be seen. Over the last few days I'd become convinced that Norbu had mastered the art of levitation and spontaneous presence because he seemed to be everywhere on the trail at once and always suddenly appeared like a genie.

"Where are you, Norbu?" I called out.

"Right here," Norbu said as he and his red baseball hat materialized on a boulder, half-hidden behind yellow bushes. "Left will take you to Tibet."

As Norbu waited for the others, we continued downriver and came upon a sign nailed to the tree:

A mad saint created the takin when he ate a goat and a cow and belched them back into the universe. Photo by author.

We were hiking toward the Tsharijathang Valley, which serves as an autumn grazing ground for the *takin,* the national animal of Bhutan. The takin stands about four feet tall, looks somewhat similar to a moose, but has a rounded and broad nose. According to legend, the takin was created when Drukpa Kunley — the Divine Madman of Bhutan — ate a cow and a goat to impress a crowd of disbelievers and then promptly burped up his meal and set the goat's head on the body of the cow. Such a fanciful story is easy to write off, but science actually seems to support this explanation: taxonomists can't relate the takin to any other animal species — it's not a goat, antelope, cow, or a moose — although it seems to share some characteristics of each. Making the takin even stranger, it takes on characteristics of a herd animal out in the open but in the woods becomes solitary like a deer. The more I read about the takin, the more I thought it made sense that it was "burped" into the universe.

We followed the river down through a forest of perfect pine trees, past ravens cawing from gnarled, broken branches, and hiked out into the bright sunshine of Tsharijathang Valley. According to the guidebook, multiple valleys meet here, and apparently, multiple yaks do too. The sight of yaks meant we wouldn't be seeing any takin that day, for yak herders are forbidden to graze their animals when the takins are present. If we wanted to see a takin, we'd have to go to the national zoo in Thimphu at the end of the trek.

As we started toward them, the yaks grunted warnings and lowered their horns. I decided there really should be a safety book on what to do when you encounter a yak on the trail. After all, they are hulking beasts that have knife-sharp horns. If there are books about animals you rarely see in the wild titled *Bear Aware* and *Lion Alert* — and my favorite, *Don't Get Eaten* — then it stands to reason there should be a book about an animal you encounter all the time. Yaks aren't normally dangerous and certainly don't have a taste for trekkers, but they did seem to get very skittish around us. When I noticed a few beasts trotting behind me, I broke into a sprint, bolting around muddy bogs and across a small log bridge with such speed that I almost missed a shepherdess kneeling by the river's edge, silently washing her laundry in the reeds.

The remaining hike to our campsite at Robluthang was absolute hell — as was any short uphill at the end of a long day of trekking in Bhutan. With a towering mountain pass, you can prepare yourself mentally and physically for it, and if you're Tom, cue up AC/DC's "Highway to Hell" on your iPod. When someone described the hike as "a little uphill" — as Norbu did at lunch — you toss it off, forgetting that a short uphill on the Snowman Trek is a major day hike anywhere else on the planet.

From the river, Paul and I hiked up the sparsely vegetated hill toward our campsite, past wind-ravaged trees, scattered rocks, and stubby pines.

"What's with this uphill," asked Paul, "couldn't we have camped on the valley floor?"

"Norbu said this uphill will make tomorrow's hike shorter."

Paul said he'd heard that before. "If you're always hiking to make tomorrow's day shorter, tomorrow never is actually shorter."

"Good point," I said. "Norbu's been tricking us."

After twenty minutes of tough hiking, we arrived hot and sweaty at Robluthang, a meadowy campsite on a plateau with broad views over the surrounding valleys. We found everyone seated in the dining tent. When I took my first sweet sip of hot chocolate and my first bite of a "Yo Dutch Norman," all lingering thoughts about the end to the day dissolved. One bite and one sip and I was right back to feeling great. That is, until an hour later and I saw an unclaimed yellow duffel bag sitting alone on the tarp. This wasn't good and meant one thing — a trekker was missing.

Along with the model of trekking poles and jacket color, I'd also begun to identify people by their duffel bags — a green army bag meant Larry, a large maroon backpack was Peter's, and a yellow

North Face Camp duffel bag belonged to Ryan. That afternoon it meant Ryan was missing.

I raced to the dining tent. "Has anyone seen Ryan?"

Everyone looked and asked around and it was the classic case of "I thought he was with you."

When Joe asked for help, we all quickly volunteered. Of course, there was no need for all of us to search for Ryan, two people could do the job, but in a way it was not Ryan lost out there — it was all of us. Within seconds, we were all standing outside the dining tent, dressed in warm clothes with backpacks full of extra food, headlamps, matches, space blankets, and water, ready to launch a search-and-rescue operation.

"We'll go to the point of last sighting," declared Joe. "Who saw Ryan last and where?"

We quickly went around the group and discovered the last time anyone saw Ryan was before the bridge at the bottom of the valley. This wasn't good — Ryan may have gone left at the fork and could be hiking toward Tibet right then. It was a terrible thought, and I could just see Ryan, the optimist, thinking surely camp would be around the next corner all the while getting closer to Tibet, closer to night, closer to hypothermia, closer to . . . I cut myself off right there.

"We'll go back to the bridge," said Joe, leading us off down the trail. "And stay together — we don't want to lose anyone looking for a lost person."

With this, we raced out of camp, hurrying along the high ridge that would take us down the heartbreak hill we only recently slogged up. As I hurried behind Peter, my mind was wild with worry about Ryan. Was he injured? Had he fallen in the river? Was he alive? Overhead, the sun dropped behind the western peaks, filling the valley with cold shadows.

As we were just about to start down the steep downhill, Peter noticed another trail traversing the lofty ridge in the other direction. "Maybe Ryan went that way?"

Joe pondered this a moment. "Half the group will wait here with a radio, and the other half will continue down the hill and back to the bridge with the other radio."

Suddenly, we heard a voice. "Guys!"

We turned and there was Ryan, stumbling toward us down the trail Peter had just pointed to.

As Ryan hustled over to us, his face was a mixture of fear and relief. "I was taking some pictures of the yak herder girl by the river," he explained. "And I guess I took a wrong turn at the top of the hill!"

"Doesn't matter," said Paul, taking his backpack. "You're here now."

"Let's get back to camp before it gets dark," added Joe.

THE MOOD AT DINNER THAT NIGHT WAS SUBDUED AND somber. The brief incident was a reminder that things can go wrong on the Snowman Trek — and fast. We didn't talk much, and when we did, we spoke in hushed cadences, as if loud voices and broad gestures might upset the house of cards our trek had become. There were no jokes, no games, and the moment everyone finished their fruit cocktail dessert, we excused ourselves for bed. But before we left, Rob told us he had a surefire solution to all our problems. "It's called Cooee," he said. "And I'll tell y'all about it at brekkie."

15

ON THE MORNING OF THE EIGHTH DAY, WE WOKE TO another blue sky with amazing views of alpine ridges and distant icy summits, and at breakfast, an introductory lesson on *cooee*. Based upon Rob's excitement that morning, cooee seemed to be the Australian equivalent of *Om*, the mystical and sacred syllable revered throughout Asia to be the sound of the universe.

"Cooee will save ya' life," Rob declared, as we sat around the breakfast table, slurping up Achula's wonderful oatmeal, toast, and eggs. "Ya' can use cooee hikin', yellin' to ya mates while surfin', anywhere!"

"What do we use it for?" I asked.

Rob told us cooee was originally used by the Aborigines in the bush as a way of attracting attention, locating a missing person, and indicating your position. "But it was also used by World War I soldiers who went marchin' through Seed-ney shoutin' "cooee" with hopes of making blokes enlist."

"How do you do it?" asked Tom very scholarly.

"Jes like this," said Rob, bringing his hands to his mouth and taking a big inhale, "C-O-O-O-O-O-E-E!"

"Wow," said Larry, "that's loud."

"And when someone hears them," continued Rob, nearly knocking over the table as he stood up with excitement, "They yell C-O-O-E-E-E-E-E!"

I wanted to say, "Coowee please stop yelling — my eardrums are about to burst." But, before I could, Joe politely thanked Rob for his demonstration.

"Nah problem, Mate," said Rob, sitting down. "Any questions?"

We didn't have any questions, which I decided was because we could no longer hear ourselves think.

DAY NINE OF THE SNOWMAN TREK WOULD TAKE US 8.5 MILES from Robluthang to a camp at Limithang and over our third pass in three days — the highest pass we'd crossed so far — the mighty 16,400-foot Sinche La. There was no doubt the day would be tough. I followed Ryan and Tom out of camp as the trail climbed gently for twenty five minutes through sparse autumn orange and yellow bushes and passed a little yak herder hut before zigzagging up a side slope and starting up another valley. After twenty minutes of thigh-crying uphill, we reached a scenic plateau with some prayer flags and a 360-degree panorama of peaks, one of which had let loose half its side in a tremendous granite rockslide.

"Now that is a lesson in impermanence," said Tom.

I decided to hike by myself for a bit, and I let Tom and the others hurry on. As I hiked up the trail of low tundra beside a grassy moraine with peeking marmots, my thoughts drifted to Lunana District. While Tibet's King Songtsen Gampo believed there was a supine ogress reclined across the mountains of Tibet and Bhutan in the year AD 659 — so much so that he built 108 temples to pin her extremities to the earth — I imagined Lunana to be a princess, presiding over a court of precious streams, bride-white peaks, and invincible glaciers. Based upon my conversations with Marie Brown and the response of the Bhutanese people when I said the words

"Lunana" and "Thanza," I'd begun to think that if I was fortunate enough to make it to Thanza, it wouldn't be so much because I conquered the trail, but rather that Lunana had let me in. My experiences with yoga and surfing seemed to be hinting that some things in life — perhaps the best things — couldn't be forced, they had to be surrendered to, eternally wished and waited for. While it certainly didn't make rational sense, I had the strange feeling Lunana could grant wishes and make dreams come true. With this in mind, I stopped on the trail on the ninth day and decided to compose a little letter to her. "Dear Lunana," I whispered, bowing my head and closing my eyes, "Please let me in."

Well, my little love letter must've worked because moments later, as I hiked over a ridge, Lunana thanked me with the sound of bells, bells, bells, ringing victoriously in all directions, and the whole flowering valley shook with the sweet sound. Then I saw the source of the bells — ten yaks were charging straight toward me. But unlike the day before, I didn't feel the least bit afraid. It was as if the yaks were floating, I didn't hear any hooves, only the sound of glorious bells. I immediately assumed *Tadasana*, the eyes-closed, equal-standing mountain pose that begins most yoga classes, and received this sweet sound of bells like sunlight. The yaks thundered by on both sides of me, but again I had not the least fear of getting trampled. When the yaks were gone, I followed the sound of the bells as they wound down the valley with the same kind of wondrous, run-to-the-window rapture a child might listen to Santa's sleigh disappearing into a silent night, a holy night. When I blinked my eyes open, all I could do was shake my head with wonder and say thank you. In fact, I never would have believed the incident happened if I didn't find Peter standing with a similar rapt stare a hundred yards up the trail.

"What was that?" I gasped.

"Spiritual," Peter replied, shaking his head.

THE HIKE TO SINCHE LA WAS UNRELENTING BUT BEARABLE because I was buoyed by the sound of those yak bells. We had a good laugh at the pass when Peter discovered Paul had hidden five cans of fruit cocktail in his backpack, which was already heavy with multiple cameras and batteries. But it was only fair — days earlier, Peter had woken Paul up by saying, "The horses are eating your hiking boots!" which prompted Paul to leap from his tent in his pajamas to look for the culprits.

After watching Peter chase Paul around the rocks and prayer flags decorating the Sinche La, I took a seat to savor the scene. Norbu came over and pointed to the mountains in the far distance. "Hey Kev, know what those mountains are?"

"Let me guess," I said, cutting him off. "Tomorrow's pass?"

Norbu shook his head. "Not tomorrow. But soon. Those are the mountains of Lunana."

"Really?" I said, sitting up. I couldn't wait to see all that I'd heard about.

The mountains of Lunana look nothing like a princess. Black clouds clung to snowy, storm-beaten peaks. Rather than a gateway to paradise, those mountains looked like an entrance to some forbidden, evil kingdom.

"We're going there?" I gulped.

Norbu smiled. "That's what you signed up for."

I HAD TO GIVE LARRY CREDIT, HE WAS ATTEMPTING THE Snowman Trek at age sixty-six. Sixty-six! There are two sports I want to be doing when I reach age sixty-six: twelve-ounce curls and the couch luge. Yet Larry was hiking with us, snapping photos, slugging tea . . . and wheezing and coughing and sounding as if he was about to die. We were worried. Over the last twenty-four hours, the conversation had switched from debating whether or not he should continue to resolutely declaring that he shouldn't. It was a tough question — should we demand he quit the Snowman Trek at Laya on day eleven, even though nothing had really happened? Or do we let him continue on to Lunana and risk something serious happening? It was the perfect "damned if you do, damned if you don't" scenario. While we'd been swaying on the side of optimism, Norbu and Achula were certain Larry should not continue. When Achula, a man who had spent the first nine days saying "yes" suddenly says "no," we took note.

From the pass, we trudged forty-five minutes through boulders and grassy ridges down to our lunch spot, and after lunch we hiked past snaking moraines, tumbling waterfalls, and jagged coal-black spires. When I found Tom taking a water break beside the side of the trail, I hurried over.

"Have you seen Larry? He looks like he's going to die," I said, amped up with concern. "He should totally leave at Laya."

I regretted the words the moment they came out of my mouth.

Tom didn't respond. He grabbed his pack, said, "I'll see you at camp," and started off.

I was concerned — sometimes words just slipped out of me that I knew weren't really me. As I looked back up the trail, I saw Larry in the far distance leaving the pass. There was no way he heard, yet in a strange way, I felt like he did. Feeling embarrassed and ashamed, I hurried on.

The notion of abandoning Larry would be almost unheard of in Bhutan and other Asian countries where the elderly have traditionally been the most exalted in society. They are revered for having lived a long life and respected for their knowledge of generations and rites and are believed to have a special life force and wisdom. In fact, it is such a blessing to be in the company of an old person that young people will touch the elderly and sit in the room with them simply in hopes of receiving some of that life force wisdom — a far cry from the youth-obsessed West. Personally, I knew some of my fondest memories growing up were those spent with my grandparents — reading on my grandfather's lap, helping my grandmother handle the lobsters for that night's dinner, and staying at my other grandmother's beach house in Florida. They were special moments at the time but in the years since have become great gifts and as much a part of me as my DNA.

As I continued down the trail, I couldn't help but feel that I'd not only let Larry down but also my grandparents in a strange way. I had to wonder — what if we'd spent the last few days encouraging Larry instead of debating whether he should continue? Wouldn't that have been a better use of breath? If Larry did leave at Laya, maybe it was not he who had failed but we who had failed him.

FOLLOWING THE LARRY INCIDENT, I NAVIGATED OVER A section of shiny black rocks, under which ran an unseen stream. The trail opened up into a colorful meadow where a tiny wood cabin sat before the tremendous moraine of Gangcheta, or Tiger Mountain, a 22,435-foot skyscraper of snow and ice hidden in the clouds. As I hiked closer, I saw Rob, Peter, and Paul were standing on the top of a towering moraine.

"Come on up, Kev," cried Rob.

I hesitated.

"Why not?" Peter yelled down to me.

The "why not" was easy. I was exhausted, hungry, and when I first saw the huge moraine I had not the slightest inclination to climb. In fact, I had plans of taking an afternoon nap in the cool, canvas shade of my tent.

When they asked again, I gave into peer pressure and consented.

I regretted my decision from the first step. The rocks were horribly unstable, and as I clambered up with my arms and legs, I got dizzy. I increased my pace, hoping the top of the moraine might grant me some respite, but when I arrived there, the other side dropped abruptly to the glacial lake fifty feet below. I quickly took a seat, wedging my feet between the rocks and grabbing hold of the boulders to my left and right for support. The moraine wound around the valley, where it had poured forth majestically from the glaciated flanks of Tiger Mountain. But I didn't care, I immediately

Paul navigates the rocky moraine pouring forth from Tiger Mountain (22,435 ft.). Photo by Peter McBride.

wanted to leave — the unstable rocks, the sheer drop on both sides, my exhaustion — it was just too much. As my breath returned, I realized my dilemma was just beginning, for I still had to get down.

"I'll see you down below." I called out to the others.

As I stood and took a step, the boulder I chose rolled, causing me to take another step quickly. That boulder shifted too, which forced me to take another step and suddenly, to avoid turning an ankle or falling, I was literally running across the top of that horribly unstable moraine. When I spotted a big boulder, wedged between two others, I literally fell into it, giving it a great hug to avoid falling. As my lungs heaved for breath, I reprimanded myself for not listening to my instincts.

Thankfully, Rob came to my rescue minutes later. "Y'alright?"

"How do you get down?"

"Jes folla me," said Rob, slowly clambering down the hill.

Following his lead, taking it step by step, rock by rock, I managed my way back down to the dirt trail.

"Piece of cake, huh, mate," said Rob, slapping me on the shoulder.

"Sure," I said, wiping sweat from my brow.

From there, the trail crossed a bridge and descended into a dry cedar forest, leading down the valley. I arrived safely at Limithang, a grassy campsite surrounded by tall conifers, but the trouble was just beginning.

I'M NOT SURE IF IT WAS THE WHOLE LARRY INCIDENT, THE moraine mishap, or simply being exhausted, but I arrived in Limithang in a bad mood. Everyone has bad days, and on the Snowman Trek, they were compounded by exhaustion, the rough trail, and lack of sleep. With this mood arrived an internal avalanche of self-doubt. Doubt isn't healthy. Guru Rinpoche said, "Doubt is the enemy of dharma," and evidently it was also the enemy of the Snowman Trek. My mind used this opportunity to create uncertainty: *Can you finish the Snowman Trek? Will you win the screenwriting fellowship? Will you find out what blossom rain means?* And the worst part of it was, over the past few days, I'd really felt as if I was on the cusp of some great realization. But that afternoon, I was hobbling around again with the sprained ankle of doubt.

As I searched for my bag amid a sea of sacks, bamboo baskets, and propane tanks, I felt totally wiped out. While Guru Rinpoche's body may have been a "divine mandala" and he may not have been "subject of flaws of discomfort and misery," I felt wasted, bruised, and broken. As I zipped my tent open, I noticed Sonam and Sangey setting up Tom's, Paul's, and Ryan's tents by the river and Kira's and Rob's tents near the shade of the forest. The rest of our tents were huddled around the kitchen tent. Certainly, it was understandable that they wanted to sleep next to the river, but that afternoon, through the sweat-shrouded eyes of exhaustion, I interpreted it as a bad sign. No longer were we one united group camping together, we seemed to be splitting off in little cliques and the trek wasn't even half over. If this was happening on the ninth day, what would happen on the fifteenth?

When Larry staggered into camp, he looked dazed and defeated and the only remaining tent was next to mine.

"How was your hike?" I asked and he dropped his bag beside his tent.

"Hard," he said.

It was the first time Larry hadn't said, "Slowly but surely" or "So far, so good," and it came as such a shock that I was speechless.

"Yeah . . . well . . . ," I said, my voice trailing off. "Just hang in there—you'll make it."

Larry thanked me, but I felt as if he knew what I and the rest of the group had been saying about him. Later, as I crawled into my sleeping bag, I felt a little lonely for the first time on the trek. I opened my ears, hoping for laughter coming from somewhere in camp, but all I heard was the rainfly of my tent being slapped by the wind.

16

I AWOKE EARLY AND ANXIOUS ON THE MORNING OF THE tenth day. I didn't feel rested and what little sleep I had didn't repair my mood. Only Achula was awake, starting to boil water and prepare breakfast, as I sat up in my tent and crossed my legs. It was freezing, my breath was visible, so I hiked up my sleeping bag over my folded legs and bundled up in my winter jacket, hat, and gloves. With breakfast not yet made and the water not yet ready for tea, there was nothing to do but sit there. Despite the early hour, my critical mind was already awake *you are a failure* so instead of listening, I shut my eyes *quit the Snowman Trek* and tried to focus on my breath *Disney will reject you* but instead I heard the rushing river *you will never find love* and the water seemed to enter my body as I inhaled *you will never find grace* and rushed down my arms and legs *you won't stand beneath blossom rain* to pool in my fingers and toes *you will always be searching* and began washing away all my thoughts and then even my body began to disappear, bones, muscles, ligaments, tendons, and organs blotted out, gone, rinsed away, and then suddenly even the river ceased to exist, and all that was left was just the rushing, a glorious, ecstatic, radiant rushing.

"Bed tea, sir," called out a voice suddenly.

A glorious rushing. Photo by Peter McBride.

I blinked my eyes open. Sonam and Sangey stood at my tent with bed tea. As my legs sprung out of their cross-legged position, I realized I'd just meditated — something I swore I'd never do in the Himalayas. Prior to my trip, I couldn't understand why anyone would travel halfway around the world to the most beautiful mountains on earth to then sit and shut their eyes! Take me to a strip mall in the United States and I'd gladly sit and close my eyes, but not in Bhutan. Not only that, but I never truly believed sitting could lead to enlightenment. I'd spent much of my life sitting — in the car, at work, on the couch — if sitting led to enlightenment, I assumed I'd be a Buddha by now. But that morning's seat felt different, and after, gazing out of my tent door, I felt as if I'd been granted a new set of eyes. Suddenly everything was beautiful — my mood, our camp, the rising shafts of sun on Tiger Mountain, and the river giggling like a tickled child. There was no doubt, meditation was awesome.

WE ATE A QUICK BREAKFAST AND STARTED OUT ON THE trail. That day, we would hike 5.5 miles and descend 1,180 feet to the village of Laya, the halfway point of the Snowman Trek. Laya promised a rest day, a traditional Bhutanese hot-stone bath, and meeting a certain German fraulein named Ingrid.

The morning was bright with sun streaming through the trees. Leaving Limithang, the trail followed the river through lush cedar and fir forests, past smoke-stained rocks and yak herders wandering up the trail with their waddling beasts. It was a scenic 5.5-mile hike, but it was not easy. While the trail technically led down the valley, there were a lot of little elevation gains and descents that if added up, I would be willing to bet, would amount to one small mountain. After two hours of hiking, I found Norbu creeping through the shadowy forest.

"What is it?" I whispered.

Norbu ducked behind a tree and pointed at a shady patch in the woods. "A blood pheasant."

It took me a few seconds to locate the bird, which was camouflaged, but then I saw him, pecking in the lichen shadows. His plumage was bright red and streaked with yellow and black. Blood pheasants live in Nepal, Tibet, Sikkim, Bhutan, and Burma. Like many animals in the Himalaya, blood pheasants travel with the season, spending summers near the snow line of subalpine meadows and, in the winter, moving down to coniferous mixed forests. I pulled out my camera, but the pheasant took flight in the space between the photo click and flash and left only floating red feathers in its wake.

As we stopped for a water break, I picked Norbu's brain about blossom rain. "Twenty dollars if you tell me what it means."

Norbu recited something along the lines of the Buddha who said: "Rely not on the expedient but on the definitive meaning; rely not on the conditional but on the unconditioned. Rely not on the words but on the meaning."

"That's what I'm trying to find out," I told him, "the meaning."

Norbu smiled. "I can guide you to some things. But not others."

I waved him off. "Look, Yoda," I said, "can you just please tell me?"

Norbu said he couldn't. "The truth is, I've never even heard of blossom rain or *metok-cahrrup*."

"Chharp!" I said, correcting him. "Are you serious?"

"I swear."

"Fine," I said, "let's talk about beyuls."

The idea of *beyuls*, or "earthly paradises," has existed for more than two thousand years. According to lore, Guru Rinpoche empowered 108 beyuls, hidden valleys throughout the Himalayas, as sacred refuges in times of war, avarice, and strife. Beyuls have gone by different names such as Pemako, Shambhala, Lotus Land, Utopia, or Shangri-La. In the fourth century, the Chinese poet Tao Qian wrote about a never-ending "peach blossom spring" in a lavish spiritual oasis where people never grew old. The mention of such valleys also appeared in Buddhist texts and, more recently, in James Hilton's 1933 novel *Lost Horizon*. There is some debate about where Shangri-La is located — Sikkim, the isolated valleys of Huza in northern Pakistan, the city of Kham in China's Yunnan Province, the Khumbu Valley around Everest, Tibet's Yarlung Tsangpo Gorge, but if Guru Rinpoche did empower 108 valleys, it could be all of these places . . . and more. When I asked Norbu why the number 108 is auspicious, he told me that along with the beyuls, the mala has 108 beads for prayer, and there are 108 earthly temptations one must overcome to reach nirvana. When I asked why there were 108 mala beads and 108 earthly temptations, he told me the number 108 is auspicious. And as we went around in circles, I realized Tibetan Buddhism answers some spiritual questions with the same kind of kill-the-rational-mind koans as Zen Buddhism.

"Do you think Thanza is a beyul?" I asked.

Norbu said all of Bhutan is a beyul. "But they are only accessible to people with pure hearts."

My heart sunk. "There's no way I'll get into Lunana now," I lamented.

When Norbu asked me why, I told him Sean and I used to tee off on frogs while golfing as teenagers. "We'd sneak up to the water hole, take a swing, and you'd just see a pair of frog legs flying through the air."

Norbu laughed at me brooding in the midafternoon sun and told me if I was really, really good from there on out, he thought Lunana would let me in.

We continued down the trail for an hour and presently arrived at a chorten, marking the beginning of the village.

"Welcome to Laya," said Norbu.

"Thanks," I replied, relishing that moment of arrival. "Please don't point to any tall mountains we have to hike next."

Norbu smiled.

SITTING ON A FORESTED RIDGE HIGH ABOVE THE RIVER, the village of Laya — with a Basic Health Unit, school, telecom center, temple, and 140 households — is home to just under a thousand people. Laya was a quaint hamlet with terraced farm fields of barley, mustard, and turnips, with wandering horses and children dashing down dirt paths. Overlooking the village was Tsenda Gang, a 22,960-foot mountain piercing the clouds in the distance.

From the chorten, we trod down winding trails through a village whose people were busy threshing wheat, stacking wood, and plowing fields with teams of yaks. Since Bhutan is a country of isolated valleys and high peaks, it's not uncommon for villages to have their own dress and language. Nowhere was this more evident than in Laya, where the women wore a unique conical-shaped bamboo hat with a wooden spike at the top and adorned in the back with white, orange, and blue beads. Instead of a traditional kira, the women wore black, yak-wool skirts, decorated with thin vertical stripes of maroon and orange. Unlike many women in rural villages, the Laya women wore their hair long. As we saw them threshing wheat with rotating sticks, their black hair sparkled in the sun.

We began our visit by having lunch on the second floor of a

traditional home of a family that had kindly volunteered to host us for two days. The home was great, as pleasing to navigate as to look at. I squeezed up the narrow staircase, which was little more than steps notched into an ancient tree trunk, to discover two rooms upstairs; one contained a woodstove and rolled mats for sleeping and the other was used for praying. Water-filled silver offering bowls, candles, and incense sticks lined the altar in the prayer room, and pictures of the King of Bhutan, Guru Rinpoche, and the Shabdrung decorated the mantle. Up above, the walls were adorned with colorful flags and *thangkas*, or painted scrolls.

Sonam and Sangey had set up our lunch table in the large upstairs room, and as I sat down, I delighted in the amount of space. Two soft solar-powered lights cast a dull glow throughout the room and a dozen large silver bowls and pans hung on the back wall.

"Why the bowls?" I asked Norbu.

Norbu explained that bowls and extra bags of rice were a sign of prosperity.

"So the people who live here are rich?" asked Paul.

"Not rich," Norbu explained, "but they're content."

As we ate, Norbu informed us about Laya. "Like Lingshi, Laya is mainly composed of yak herders who also farm buckwheat, cabbage, radishes, carrots, barley, mustard, asparagus, and potatoes during the short, dry cropping season," he explained. "With the goods they farm and the yaks, they travel to the villages of Wangdue and Punakha to barter for rice and other products."

"What is the five-year-plan for Laya?" I asked.

Norbu told me the government was focusing on improving the lighting for the school, rural electrification, running a trial nursery, improving vaccination and breeding programs for animals, and improving the mountainous trails to and from Laya.

"Would they run power lines up here?" inquired Tom.

"Perhaps from the village of Gasa," Norbu said. "But they might also build a mini-hydroelectric plant."

Norbu continued to tell us that along with education, Bhutan offers free health care to its residents through a collection of hospitals and, in remote areas, Basic Health Units (BHUs). Historically, medicine in Bhutan has involved powders, lotions, blood-letting, acupuncture, medicinal herbs, and hot-stone baths in which fire-heated stones are placed in a tub of water to create the Bhutanese version of a spa. However, nowadays these traditional medicines are often used in conjunction with Western medicine. Since everyone in Bhutan now has access to health care, the emphasis of the upcoming years is to improve the standard of health care, beginning with increasing the number of doctors and specialists and updating equipment.

Joe entered and informed us that there would be a cultural dance that night, complete with a campfire, and then told us options for the afternoon. "You can wander up to the temple, see the school, visit the village shop, or take a nap."

From the end of the table, we heard a snore. It was Larry, of course.

Decisions were quickly made: Tom would catch up on reading *The History of the Roman Empire*, Kira would visit the temple, Peter and Rob would wander the village with their video cameras, Larry and Paul would nap, Joe would arrange our hot-stone bath for tomorrow, and I would visit the telecom center with Ryan.

From camp, Ryan and I followed a path of painted white stones across the well-trod dirt of the village and found the telecom center across from the stone school. The telecom center was a little stone building with a metal roof and a satellite dish pointing to the heavens from its side yard. Needless to say, the satellite dish looked positively out of place in Laya.

We were just about to enter the telecom center when a little girl came hurrying along in the other direction. Instead of the traditional Laya dress, she wore black sweat pants, a pink sweater, and looked to be about twelve. Her cheeks were dirty from play, her shoulder length hair tasseled, and there was a big wad of bubble gum in her cheek.

"Kuzuzangbo la," I said.

The girl stopped and stared at us. She had wide, chestnut eyes, dark hair, and cute, tuggable cheeks.

"Kuzuzangbo la," she said.

I asked her name in Dzongkha. "Cho meng gaci mo?"

"Nge meng Tshokyi," she said.

"Nge meng Kevin."

When I extended my hand, she took a step back and I realized she'd probably never shaken a hand before. I turned and shook Ryan's hand to demonstrate and then turned back to her. With a smile, she went to take my hand, but before she could, her friend appeared, squealed something, and Tshokyi skittered off, blushing.

"Awww, you're her first crush," Ryan joked. "How cute!"

As we entered the telecom center, we found a young monk and a sixteen-year-old boy in jeans and a sweater seated at the computer. When they saw us they immediately stood up and gestured for us to sit.

"Can I help you?" said the boy in impressive English.

"I'd like to use the computer," replied Ryan. "But only if you're done."

The boy pointed to the computer. "Please."

As Ryan sat down and double clicked the Internet Explorer, the boys immediately crowded around him, leaning in so close that Ryan was literally nearly knocking them in the eyes with his elbow.

"Ever get the feeling you're being watched?" said Ryan, laughing.

As I watched the boys, I saw they weren't watching the screen but rather Ryan's fingers on the keyboard. Clearly they'd never seen anyone type so fast, and to them, Ryan was the typing equivalent of Lance Armstrong.

Ryan finished typing, hit "Enter" and the Internet Explorer

hourglass icon appeared. Ryan looked down at his watch. "This might take awhile."

Both the Internet and television arrived in Bhutan in 1999, and it is estimated that approximately 10 percent of households now have televisions and 3 percent have computers. The arrival of television and the Internet have prompted mixed results — young kids love watching Bollywood movies and sport matches, yet many older people think the advertisements will create precisely what Buddhism seeks to extinguish: craving and consumerism.

Ten minutes later the hourglass figure was still on the screen and Ryan's e-mail account was still pending. He looked up at me. "I'm not having any luck. You want to try?"

I told Ryan of my plan to go twenty-four days without a computer, television, or cell phone.

A final glance back to the computer screen revealed Ryan's e-mail still had yet to come up. We thanked the monk and the telecom boy for their assistance and stood to leave. As we did, the monk sat back down at the computer, logged on, and his e-mail account appeared perfectly and effortlessly, like enlightenment.

WE LEFT THE TELECOM CENTER TO FIND THE VILLAGE ABLAZE with excitement over our arrival and the cultural show. A stone fire ring with stacked logs had been assembled directly in front of the house where we'd had lunch, and Sonam and Sangey had set up our folding seats like bleachers. Village kids and stray dogs loitered about, and an hour later when I saw Tshokyi for the second time, I barely recognized her.

I was on my way to dinner when she appeared. Her face glowed with a fresh washing, her hair was pulled back, and she now wore the traditional skirt, sweater, and conical hat of the Laya women. She beamed like a little flower girl at a wedding, but when she swept past me, she immediately ducked her head shyly and I pretended not to notice her. Like a young actress in costume, I knew I was not supposed to see her before the show. Still, after she passed, I had to turn and steal a glance because she could've been the cutest sight I had ever seen. Gone was the little girl covered in playground dirt and in her place had awoken a sweet little Cinderella, and her blue sandals sparkled like princess slippers. As Tshokyi hurried up the hill, I had the feeling that tonight would be her first dance with the adult ladies of Laya — tonight would be her welcome to womanhood.

The night got off to a great start after dinner when Ryan bound up the wood ladder, carrying a big box full of Hit beer.

"Aw, how d'ya do it, Ryan?" cried Rob.

"Magic!"

As Ryan handed out the beers, I realized that like a great host, he was more interested in others having a good time than himself. Ryan didn't necessarily like to party in the big drinking sense, he just liked to have a good time and was always serving himself last. Once we all had drinks, Peter raised his glass. "To our rest day tomorrow!"

"Cheers!"

After we toasted, Paul threw out the idea of making dinner for the kitchen staff tomorrow. "Let's give the boys the night off and whip up something special ourselves. What do you say, lads?"

"Are there any microwaves in Laya?" I mused.

Needless to say, everyone quickly volunteered. After that, it was just like old times — eating, drinking, laughing, and telling stories. Night slowly descended in dark hues, and from outside, we heard the crackling laugh of campfire logs and relished the oaky incense of camp smoke.

Twenty minutes later, Sangey scuttled up the steps and peeked his head in the door. "The women are ready."

We filed down the steps one at a time, mindful not to spill our beer, and came upon a sacred scene no doubt repeated throughout the ages: ten Bhutanese women, all wearing full traditional Laya dress, stood in a circle around the fire. Tshokyi waited in line with the women, still chewing her blessed bubble gum. Then, like theater ushers of Radio City, Sonam and Sangey escorted us to our appointed seats. When we were all seated, they made the rounds like wine stewards, refilling our cups with generous pours of Hit beer. The night was cold, but the fire and the gusting wind combined to throw off great waves of heat.

When the cultural show started, the women started singing, clapping, marching, and spinning in circles methodically and joyously. Watching them, I had the sense they'd be dancing exactly the same way for one spectator as they would for one hundred. While they were dancing before us, they weren't dancing for us — they were dancing for something else, something higher. As my eyes fell on little Tshokyi, I realized something timeless and true was happening before my eyes. I could tell by her beaming face and hesitant dance steps that this was, indeed, her first dance with the adult women.

The dance looked simple but it was actually quite complex — requiring all kinds of twists and turns and claps. Naturally, Tshokyi got a few steps wrong. Yet when she turned the wrong way, the woman in front of her with graying hair gently encouraged her in the other direction. And moments later, when she forgot to step forward, the woman with long black hair directly behind her, encouraged her ahead. As I looked at the three women in procession, it dawned on me the woman in front of her was her grandmother and the woman behind her was her mother and I was watching three generations, dancing and singing under the stars. Yes indeed, that night, Tshokyi would be initiated into womanhood the way her mother was and her mother before her. Watching Tshokyi's beaming smile, it was all right there — I saw the young lady that she was, the woman she would become, and thanks to the big wad of chewing gum, the little girl she was leaving behind.

When Tshokyi danced past, I clapped enthusiastically and nodded.

Wearing their traditional conical hats, the women of Laya perform a cultural dance. Photo by Peter McBride.

She didn't respond, for already the importance of this sacred rite had filled her gentle little soul. She had no time to smile for there was more important work to be done. She had to sing. She had to dance and clap. She had to pray.

The night rolled on, my cup was refilled, the fire grew higher and by the time Norbu suggested we join the dancing, we all immediately rushed forth — Kira, Rob, Ryan, Tom, Larry, Paul, Joe, and me, all following Peter's lead. Moments later, Achula, Sonam, Sangey, and the horsemen joined in, and in no time the rest of the village was also dancing, even the stray dogs paraded around the circle, yipping and barking with excitement.

There was something intangibly magical about that night, something infinitely hopeful that bypassed my head and spread its scented petals of promise into my heart. All I can say is circling around that fire with joyous representatives from five different countries — Bhutan, England, Canada, Australia, and the United States — made me feel lucky to be alive and filled with such infinite hope that no matter what any cynic said about wars and humanity going to hell, I knew our world would be all right.

My critical mind told me it was just the beer talking, but I didn't believe it.

People were still singing and dancing at midnight when I crawled into my sleeping bag. That night was amazing, but already I couldn't wait until the next day, a rest day, and the chance to do laundry, soak in a traditional Bhutanese hot-stone bath, and of course, meet Ingrid.

After eleven days on the trail, I no longer found falling asleep difficult. No longer did I fear the sound of horse hooves stepping precariously close to my head, the harness bells and night wind lulled me to slumber, and my sleeping pad now felt like a king-sized mattress. In fact, I could hardly remember my bed back home and the person who once slept there seemed like a stranger.

17

I AWOKE THE NEXT MORNING TO THE SUN STREAMING IN my tent window. I laid there, listening to the sounds of Laya village waking up — the river, a dog barking in the distance, a crow overhead, and despite the early hour, already a spade working the soil. Lying in my sleeping bag, my head resting in the palms of my interlaced hands, I felt supremely happy. Buddhists — who believe that joy is internal, infinite, and always available — would say that the happiness I had that morning had nothing to do with Laya. I was happy because, with nothing to do and nowhere to go, I had relinquished my attachment to fear or desire, such that I could now reside in my natural state — boundless joy.

However, my non-attachment to external desires didn't last long because, seconds later, I had a hankering for coffee, and at breakfast, the conversation was slightly singular in nature: Operation Ingrid. As we feasted on pancakes, everyone seemed to have a different opinion on how I should woo Ingrid. I wasn't sure why I had been elected, but on the other hand, I wasn't exactly arguing. Paul thought I should get in good with her mom, Peter thought a few bottles of Hit might help, Larry believed being friends was the best way to begin, and Rob suggested a tried-and-true Australian formula: girl + shoulder = tent.

Whenever Ingrid did arrive, I knew she was in for a surprise. I could just see it now: With all the innocence of Dorothy in *The Wizard of Oz*, she'd stroll into Laya — this oasis of spiritual progress and purity, where everyone is above the needs of the flesh — and Ryan and I would descend on her like a pack of wild dogs. Within moments, there'd be nothing left but the locals saying, "Poor girl, never knew what hit her." The funniest part was that not one of us had even seen Ingrid, yet already I'd placed her alongside some of the prettiest and most talented women today —Natalie Portman, Kate Winslet, and, of course, the German supermodel Heidi Klum. Whatever happened, I knew it wouldn't be boring.

As Norbu reminded us of our options for the day, a debate ensued about who should be the first in line for the hot-stone bath — should it be decided by age, sex, or picking straws.

"A woman has the right to go first," declared Kira.

We all laughed. "We thought you were a writer who believed in complete equality between the sexes."

"I'm all for equality," replied Kira. "Except when it comes to hot-stone baths."

As we went around the circle, it was agreed that Kira would get the first bath. Not only was she a woman, but we also didn't want her detailing in her article what protozoan and monstrous micro-organisms she found in the bath if she followed us. After Kira, "we" — which was to say, everyone except me and Ryan — agreed that we would go from oldest to youngest. This wasn't good for Ryan and me. Since the water in the wooden tub wouldn't be changed from one person to the next, it meant Ryan and I would be bathing in the dregs of seven people who hadn't showered for ten days. Collectively, that added up to *seventy* days of dirt, grime, sweat, bug spray, and suntan lotion. There was a good chance we'd be stepping out of the bath much dirtier than when we stepped in.

"Just look at the bright side of the bath," said Ryan, his breath steaming in the chill early morning air. "We might not be clean, but at least we'll be hot."

AFTER BREAKFAST I WAS ON MY WAY BACK TO MY TENT to shave when an arrow soared by my face. This happens a lot in Bhutan. You'll be strolling around, soaking in the scenery, and suddenly the feathers of an arrow will sweep so close to your nose, you almost start sneezing.

I lurched back to see a Bhutanese man standing with a bow near my tent. Bhutan has been called a living museum, and trekking through it, you always have the feeling that you're somewhere in the 1600s. That is until you stumble across an archery match, and then it's like you're catapulted into a futuristic movie like *Blade Runner*. The hi-tech compound bows the Bhutanese use are crazy—they have all kinds of sights, scopes, pulleys, asymmetric idler wheels, pivoting split limb pockets, stainless steel stabilizers, and a lot more accessories I can neither say nor spell.

"Kuzuzangbo la," I said, wandering over to a young man dressed in a maroon gho.

As with the sword-twirling park ranger on day three, once again, I was approaching a stranger wielding a weapon.

"Kuzuzangbo la," he said taking aim and firing.

As I watched the man shoot, I noticed the target was on the other side of a little ravine. The Bhutanese shoot at small wood-block targets more than 450 feet apart—about 300 feet farther than Olympic distance—and have no qualms about letting small details like a road, parking lot, or trail come between them and their targets. In other words, you might add a Kevlar vest and helmet to your packing list.

"What kind of bow is that?" I asked the man.

"A Ram," he said with a wad of doma bulging from his right cheek.

"A what?"

"A Rambo!" he replied with a sly grin.

As I remembered Sylvester Stallone's epic bow and arrow fight sequence in *Rambo* I had to laugh. Historically, the Bhutanese used long bamboo bows with nettle fibers for string, but those were gradually replaced, probably the year they first heard Stallone say, "They drew first blood, not me." While the two men that day were just practicing, archery matches typically consisted of two eleven-man teams, where every person is allowed to shoot two arrows and the first team to receive thirty-three points wins. Score is kept with multi-colored scarves that are worn on the back of their belts.

I watched them shoot for half an hour until Ryan, Peter, and Paul invited me to tour the village with them. "Sure thing," I said.

As we made our way up through Laya village, I relished the sights and sounds — wandering horses, yak hides drying on sunny balconies, the golden-roofed temple, and an old couple sitting together, spinning hand-held Tibetan prayer wheels.

When we passed a group of women threshing wheat, we stopped to watch. Six women, all wearing traditional Laya dress, threshed long stalks of barley on large bamboo mats with rotating sticks. The process of making barley flour involves harvesting the barley, drying it, separating it from the stalk, burning it, threshing it, sifting the grain from the chaff and then grinding the grain with mortar and pestle. The women that day took turns cutting the barley from the stalk, burning the awns, and threshing the wheat. Nearby, another woman sifted the grain from the chaff, whistling as she worked to summon the wind.

As I watched the women working together, I realized that when I arrived yesterday, I was defining Laya by what it didn't have — television, roads, electricity, or telephone service. Laya was a village that seemed to exist in a state of lack; however, after spending twenty-four hours in the midst of it, I was convinced the villagers of Laya lived a life of abundance and was far more impressed by what they did have. The people of Laya had a connection to the land, an intimacy with seasons, and a knowledge of the natural world that has more often than not been forgotten in the developed world. They also had a sense of community and participation in each other's lives that I could only describe as holy. They lived lives of authentic and human connection — with the land, with each other, and with themselves. Last and most important, they seemed eternally grateful for what they had. By their smiling faces, clean and well-kept homes, and by the way they sang when they walked and worked, they seemed truly happy. I decided Gross National Happiness was a fact, not fiction.

When Ryan nudged me with his elbow and said, "Let's help the ladies," I was quick to oblige. Within moments, Peter, Ryan, and I were working the rotating sticks threshing wheat. The ladies stood back and watched, pointing and giggling. The threshing sticks were quite amazing — a little hole was carved out of the end of one stick, through which another stick, curved at the end, was stuck and tied off at the end with a knot. The threshing motion was similar to chopping wood, and even though the rotating sticks weren't nearly as heavy as an ax, the work was immediately tiring. In the warm sun, our jackets quickly came off. As sweat freckled my shirt, Peter called out to me:

"Go easy, Kev. You're threshing the wheat — not beating the crap out of it."

As he said this, I realized I was beating the wheat as if it was some punk who had just insulted my mother. I relaxed. After our threshing episode, we took turns cutting the awns from the stalk with a little scythe and burning the awns by tending a little fire with a fork-shaped stick.

In the field below, Rob crept with his video camera behind a yak team plowing the field. Across Bhutan, plowing fields with yaks was quickly being replaced by the power tiller. The Bhutanese use power tillers for everything — plowing fields, pumping water, and hauling people. Power tillers can do a week's worth of work in a single day and have done a lot to solve Bhutan's labor shortage problem. Since the power tiller can do the work of twenty people, it has an unexpected benefit — it frees up children to go to school.

A peek at Ryan's watch revealed that it was almost 2:00 p.m., which meant the Hausers had either arrived or were about to. Naturally, we didn't explain our hasty departure to the Laya women, we simply handed them back their sacred tools and said, "*kadriche*," Dzongkha for "thank you." The women thanked us, and as we walked away, we heard them singing again to the rhythm of rotating sticks.

AS I RECALLED, INGRID JUST APPEARED. RYAN AND I WERE hanging laundry on the rope Peter had tied between two head-high wooden fence posts, and there she was, standing before us with a beautiful smile. It was as if Ingrid had just spontaneously materialized or, like one of Guru Rinpoche's female consorts, learned to travel by riding the light rays of the sun.

"Hi guys," she said with a gorgeous German accent. "I'm Ingrid."

Ingrid was a good-looking girl with dark shoulder-length hair, brown eyes, and an eager, available laugh. In the warm afternoon sun of that day, she wore a white t-shirt, black convertible trekking pants, hiking boots, and a white bandana to hold back her hair.

"Hi," said Ryan, extending his hand. "Ingrid, is it?"

"That's great, Ryan," I thought. "Pretend you don't know who Ingrid is, pretend you're surprised she's here — pretend we all haven't been fantasizing about her for the past six days!"

"Yes," she said, glancing over at me. "Ingrid."

"Ah, hey," I said, scratching my head. "They call me Kev . . ."

Talk about a stupid thing to say — no one calls me "Kev" and who was "they" anyway?

When a stare-at-my-shoes silence ensued, Ryan stepped in to save the day. "So how's your trip going, Ingrid?"

Ingrid informed us she was traveling with a group of nine Germans, of varying age and profession, and her trip was going great. And then somehow — I don't recall quite how — Ryan even got it out of her that yes, in fact, she was sharing a tent with her mother.

The Divine Madman's "flaming thunderbolt of wisdom" decorates a home. Photo by Peter McBride.

After twenty minutes, Ingrid told us she had to join her group, but before she left, I invited her to swing by our camp for tea later that night or the next morning.

"Oh, that'd be fun," Ingrid said, smiling. "Maybe I will."

We watched her go, tromping up a trail through a fresh-tilled barley field, and the moment she was out of earshot, Ryan turned to me. "Did you just hear the way she said 'Oh'?"

"Oh I heard the 'Oh,'" I said, still staring at the space she'd just left.

As Ryan and I congratulated each other for laying the groundwork and not being obvious about our intentions, we noticed a very disturbing sight—we were standing in front of a large painting of a phallus.

WE SHOULDN'T HAVE BEEN TOO SURPRISED TO SEE PHALLUS paintings because they are common in Bhutan, and when you encounter one, you're liable to start giggling the way you did when your sixth-grade teacher showed that video on puberty called *Changes*, complete with the David Bowie song. Not only were phalluses painted on the sides of houses, hanging as wood carvings from roofs, and used as key chain ornaments, but they were also detailed, very detailed.

Sure, I found it strange that such images appeared in a culture so refined and polite, but what was stranger was my reaction to the phalluses. The first time I saw one, I was shocked. The second time, I found it terribly funny, and by the third time, I was asking Ryan to take my picture in front of one.

"I will," said Ryan, as I handed him my camera that afternoon in Laya. "But why?"

Rather than being a symbol of fertility, the phalluses honor one of Bhutan's most famous saints, the Divine Madman. Drukpa Kunley, a monk who lived in the fifteenth century, believed that "whatever happens is the path of release," and thus, traveled throughout Bhutan and Tibet using humor, beer, foul language, flatulence, and yes, folks, his phallus to ward off evil spirits and teach Buddhism. For example, when a man asked the Divine Madman to bless a scroll he'd painted, the Divine Madman urinated on it. When the Divine Madman faced down a fierce demon with flying hair, he smashed it in the teeth with his "flaming thunderbolt of wisdom"; he also used it in other ways that, if written about, would put a "Parental Advisory" sticker on this book. However, Norbu later told me that the Divine Madman's teachings were a way of reaching his students and getting their attention so that he could teach them to find "purity in all forms." According to the Divine Madman, the divine wasn't limited to churches or sacred scriptures—it was everywhere, in everything, at all times. As for the scroll the Divine Madman urinated on, when the unfortunate owner presented it to a crowd of onlookers, he discovered it shining magnificently, gold-plated, pure, and precious.

When Ryan finished taking my picture, he handed back my camera. "So what are you going to use this picture for?"

"That's easy," I told him. "My Christmas card."

THAT NIGHT AT DINNER, THE CONSENSUS AROUND THE table was that Ingrid was most definitely a keeper. Over the course of the afternoon, everyone in our group had met her and shared my beliefs that she was smart, friendly, and cute. I especially liked her because already she'd passed the "camping litmus test," which is the test that all outdoor-minded guys give to new girlfriends to see if they can cut it in the woods. Like dipping litmus paper into a solution to test its chemical properties, in the camping litmus test, you "dip" a girl into the wild to see her true colors and test her high-maintenance properties. While it may seem a bit stupid, I think the test makes a lot of sense because camping demands the ability to be flexible, tolerate a few bumps and bruises, and go with the flow — skills necessary for life.

After the wonderful dinner of pasta with ketchup, squash, and meat sauce — which we all played some part in preparing — we slurped up Paul's guava crumble dessert, and Norbu and Joe debriefed us on the next part of the trek.

"We're going into the high country now," said Joe, growing serious. "In two nights we'll be camping at sixteen thousand feet, so like the beginning of the trek, we need to watch out for altitude sickness."

Norbu also informed us that we'd be trading our horses for yaks tomorrow because yaks do better at high altitude and snow. "However, we'll keep two horses to transport someone if they get sick or hurt and can't walk."

"What's wrong with a yak?" I asked.

Peter gave me a look. "Would you want to take a yak evac?"

"Good point," I said. "Horses it is!"

"We have a hard nine-mile hike with about 3,200 feet of uphill tomorrow," continued Joe. "So we'll have bed tea at 6:00 a.m., washing water at 6:15, breakfast at 7:00, and be on the trail by 7:30."

As we all stood up and flicked on our headlamps, a loud snore erupted from the end of the table.

"Is Larry continuing to Lunana?" asked Peter, gesturing in his sleeping direction.

"I think so," said Joe. "But his mind could change by morning."

When we woke him, Larry emitted a loud "Ha" as if he'd been awake the entire time and was in on some joke that had just been told. When he realized that none of us were laughing and that the joke may have been on him, he shuffled out of the dining room, embarrassed.

Exhausted, I assumed I'd fall right to sleep, but as I shut my eyes, I couldn't stop thinking about Larry. While everything within me wanted to say that the trek was going perfectly, without Larry, I couldn't. With the start of the Snowman Trek having disappeared from view and the end not yet in sight, I would hold onto the only flotation device I could — my trekking companions. However, I couldn't help but feel if Larry didn't continue, the "ship" of our trekking party would be terribly off-balance from missing its motor.

18

"WE'RE TAKING THOSE?" GASPED TOM, AS WE ALL STOOD watching a parade of yaks lumbering into camp at Laya the following morning.

"Yup," said Joe. "Although it might be more correct to say — they're taking us."

How would I describe the arrival of the yaks? They were like thirty, half-ton first-graders with sharp horns on a field trip. As they approached us in a long, not-so-single-file line, they were constantly head-butting each other, swerving anxiously, and making strange grunts.

Yaks are hulking animals that, with their shag coats and long horns, look a lot like mini wooly mammoths. They were domesticated by the Qiang people on the Quinghai-Tibetan Plateau thousands of years ago and are now found all across central Asia, from Nepal to Mongolia. These "snow camels" have many uses in Bhutan — along with being beasts of burden, they plow fields, thresh wheat with their feet, kick trails through the snow, and sniff out hidden crevasses. Their woven hair is used for tents, ropes, blankets, clothes, and to make an improvised pair of sunglasses to prevent snow blindness. Yak hides also make handy bags, warm blankets, and shoes.

In addition, yak butter helps light up homes and can be used as a skin cream and for yak butter tea. Yak dung provides a renewable energy source, and based upon the yak jerky Achula bought and boiled for us, yak meat is tender and tasty.

When I saw a yak bucking to avoid one of the yakmen placing a warm, wool saddle blanket on him, I turned to Joe. "If he's resisting a saddle blanket, what will he do to my duffel bag?"

Joe smiled. "Imagine dropping your bag from a thirty-story building and — "

"Just stop right there."

As we prepared for the day's hike by applying sunscreen and chapstick, as well as moleskin to blistered toes, Ingrid stopped by.

"Just wanted to wish you guys a safe journey," she said, bundled up in a North Face jacket and holding a cup of coffee.

Forget high heels and a fancy dress. For me, there is nothing more beautiful than a girl in outdoor gear. I smiled. "So we'll see you in a few days?"

Ingrid said she wasn't sure but she hoped so. "Your group is so fun. Mine is too, but a little bit more reserved."

"All right then," I said, "I'll look forward to it."

Ingrid then gave me and Ryan a friendly wave. "See you soon!"

When she'd left, Rob mock-punched me on the shoulder and told me I should've taken Ingrid back to my tent.

"Rob," I said, "my tent is packed on the back of a yak!"

Before we left, we met in front of the house where we'd been dining to thank our kind Bhutanese hosts and tip out the horsemen who would return to Paro. We also said farewell to the villagers who came to say good-bye. As Tshoyki ran up, I saw she was still chewing her bubble gum and wearing her traditional skirt, sweater, and conical hat. My guess was she probably slept in it like I used to do with my basketball jerseys growing up — I felt so proud in those jerseys I never wanted to take them off. As I crouched down next to Tshoyki, I got a little sad and a paternal instinct kicked in. I wanted to say, "Take care of yourself, Tshoyki. Go after your dreams. And if any guy ever takes you for granted, get rid of him." Instead I simply said good luck. "*Tashi delek*!"

"Tashi delek," she said with a giggle.

When Tshoyki extended her hand, I assumed she wanted to shake my hand. But when I presented mine, she handed me a piece of bubble gum and skipped out of sight. Touched, I thanked her by yelling, "kadriche" and put this never-to-be-chewed, good luck charm in the coat pocket, closest to my heart.

Tom walked over. "You ready to hit the trail again?"

I told him the only consolation I had for leaving the beautiful village of Laya was knowing we were hiking to Shangri-La. "To Thanza!"

As we threw on our backpacks and grabbed our trekking poles, I still didn't know what Larry was planning to do. However, from talking with Ingrid, I did know that a member of the Hauser group was dropping out. If Larry did want to leave, not only would he have a way to do it, but he'd also have company. To our left, Joe and Larry were finishing up talking.

Joe looked at Larry. "So what's it going to be?"

The moment of decision had arrived. With all our eyes on him, Larry gazed down at the trail leading out of Laya and then looked back at us. Then he turned back to the trail and tightened his fingers around his trekking poles. "I'm going for it!" he said, shrugging his shoulders.

"You are?" I blurted out.

"Why not," said Larry, starting off, "I like a good challenge."

His statement took a moment to register on us, then Ryan shouted out, "All right! Jersey is in the house!"

As I watched Larry trod off — this merry man in a bright orange hunting jacket — I realized, for him, the Snowman Trek had little to do with numbers, bragging rights, or completing the toughest trek in the world — it was simply about the joy of challenging himself. I couldn't help but smile and be immediately inspired by Larry, for he had introduced me to a new kind of heroism — one that is completely unconcerned with appearing heroic. Larry wasn't afraid of being honest with himself and with the rest of us. When he needed to rest, he rested. When he needed to take six hours to do a hike that took us four, he took six hours. And, when he was tired, he slept — even if it was at the dinner table. And while I was almost certain Larry had never meditated or touched his toes in a yoga pose, there was no doubt he was enlightened. When you encounter such people on the trail, people who are honest and unafraid, you connect to those traits within yourself, so I tightened my grip on my trekking poles and tromped off after him.

On our way out of Laya, we stopped at the little outpost that was one-stop shopping, Bhutanese style. There were necklaces of yak cheese, shoes, canned fruit, boxed drinks, hats, gloves, potato chips, knives, rice, soap, soda pop, batteries, whiskey, beer, prayer flags, and souvenir pins of the king. It was the kind of shop where everything was just stuffed somewhere on the shelves and the owner doesn't bother to ask if you need help finding something because he doesn't have a clue either. The rumpled bills the merchant received were tossed in the cash register, which was little more than a black wooden box sitting on the back counter.

As I walked in, I was reminded of the country store I used to go to as a boy. Growing up, we used to run down to Newfield's General Store near my grandparents' house to plunge our eager hands into jars of gummy worms, sour candies, bubblegum, chocolate kisses, peanut butter cups, and candy cigarettes and then spend the afternoon down at the river looking for eels.

The Laya store was a lot like Newfields, and I realized — as when I was a boy — my eyes were much bigger than my budget.

"Hey, Ryan," I said, "can I borrow a Bhutanese ngultrum?"

"You don't have one ngultrum?" he gasped. "How much candy did you buy?"

"Enough to keep us happy if we get stranded in Lunana."

Ryan handed me a ngultrum.

We all bought candy and boxes of a mango drink called Fruiti, not so much for the items themselves, but simply for the novelty of buying goods from a shop in Laya. When you travel in a place as magical as Bhutan, everything seems novel and, above all, an *experience.*

Moments later, as the trail entered the forest on the outskirts of the village, Paul and I stopped under a stone archway that greeted visitors to Laya from the south. According to local lore, the trees here turned into soldiers to repel Tibetan invaders. From there, we enjoyed a pleasant hike down the valley, past a grass-covered chorten, yak herders on their way up to Laya, and little homes hidden in wood thickets. However, the unfortunate truth on the Snowman Trek was that what goes down must also come up, and we learned this hard, blister-inducing fact quickly. After an hour of downhill, we crossed a bridge leading to another outpost of the Indian-Bhutanese Army, where our permit was checked and where, once again, the introduction of "Mera ghand phat gaya!" brought glorious laughter and slaps on the back for Joe and proclamations like, "You are a great man!"

The trail ascended steeply after the army camp, and we arrived at an important intersection — one trail headed east to Lunana and the other trail headed to the hot springs in Gasa and then down to the town of Punakha, three days away.

"Left to Lunana," I sang, excited.

My excitement, however, was short-lived. The trail following the turn-off was relentlessly steep, muddy, and riddled with slippery tree roots. Making matters worse, I felt terribly out of shape. My steps were hesitant and I was starting to wonder if Peter or Paul hadn't hidden a few cans of fruit cocktail in my daypack. While I hadn't mastered the art of swift walking before our rest day, I did feel as if I'd made progress. Based upon my labored breathing that morning, I had to seriously ask myself if I could have fallen out of shape in one day. Undeterred, I trudged on, up steep muddy sections, through impossible thickets, and over slippery root buttresses. As I did, my old worries about altitude sickness resurfaced. Over the next ten days, we'd be heading back up to high altitude and to one of the most dangerous parts of the trek. Not only would we be hiking over passes well above 16,000 feet, but we'd also be camping at that elevation — betraying the "hike high, sleep low" maxim. And while rescue is never quick on the Snowman Trek, few parts of the world are more remote than the Lunana Valley.

When I took an unusually big step, I tripped on a tree root and fell hard on my left hip. Curse words spewed in an angry torrent. Groaning, I rolled over to my right and hiked my shorts up my thigh to have a look. The skin wasn't broken, but I could tell there'd be a bad bruise. My hip ached immediately, but when I looked up, I noticed a spider web, fixed in the bent elbow of a branch. The web, still wet with morning dew, glistened like a string of diamonds in the sun, and I forgot all about my fall or hip pain. Entranced, it was a great reminder to me that, despite its unpredictability, grace always arrives when it's most needed.

I found these kinds of unexpected, but eternally welcomed, moments happened a lot on the Snowman Trek — I'd be trudging up some heartbreaking hill, cursing life, and then suddenly magic happened. I'd see a crashing waterfall, magical strands of moss dripping down from a tree, or just a single leaf floating down from the sky directly in front of me, as if for me. These moments made the slog worthwhile. And so it was back home — when I'd be having a bad day, at some point magic would undoubtedly always happen — a family member would call, a friend would stop by, or four of my favorite songs would play on the radio in sweet succession, as if God was spinning records in his DJ booth up above. Whether at home or on the trail, the effect was the same: I'd stand up, wipe off the dirt, shoulder my pack, and take a step. I'd walk on.

AFTER LUNCH, THE TRAIL SKIRTED THE RODOPHU CHHU up a narrowing forested valley, sliced by immense rockslides. Since the trail was composed of large rocks, it meant the size of my steps was decided for me — big rocks meant big steps. Sure, at first I felt strong walking with these big Paul Bunyan bounds, but after five minutes, I was exhausted and the prospect of a yak evac started to sound strangely appealing. I pressed on and decided to start dedicating miles. I learned this trick from my brother, who said when he was doing his Ironman triathlon and got tired, he'd just start dedicating each mile to someone special and take the race one step at a time. As I trudged over rotting tree trunks and tricky mud patches, I started dedicating tiny sections of the trail to family members and friends. I'd think about someone who had given me a great gift — like teaching me to read, to enjoy the outdoors, or to go after my dreams, and I'd think, "These next ten minutes of trail are for you!" When I'd exhausted that list, I started tossing out the names of people I didn't know personally but who had inspired me: Martin Luther King Jr., Gandhi, Aung San Suu Kyi. And then, to keep the game fun and my feet moving, I even started throwing out names of characters who, despite being fictional, had helped me discover important truths about myself and the world — Sal Paradise, Larry Darrell, the Little Prince, Tonio Kröger, Harold and Maude. It was a pure stream-of-consciousness shuffle step dedication and a kind of rap, set to the backing track of my trekking poles going tap, tap. After that, as the trail continued its relentless uphill and I found myself increasingly winded, I decided to try the Tibetan breathing meditation called *Tonglen* in which you pick someone, inhale their sufferings, and then exhale happiness, healing, and compassion to them. Naturally, I first thought of Kira, Ryan, and Paul and everything they'd mentioned on the second night of the trek. As I hiked, I brought each of them clearly and individually into mind and tried to inhale some of their grief. I inhaled Kira's and Ryan's sad expressions as they confessed to missing their brothers and Paul's vacant stare as he talked about the carnage of the ferry accident, and I exhaled innumerable wishes of lasting contentment to each and all of them. Of course, I knew they'd all reach that enlightened place on their own, but perhaps I could lend them support on their journey. To be honest, I felt a bit funny doing it and I wasn't sure if Tibetan Tonglen worked, but when Kira passed me on the trail, she just smiled and nodded which told me it did. By then, it was late afternoon and I was running on empty, so I decided to make one last hiking dedication of the day. I chose a dedication that had worked in the past and one that I was certain would work then.

"Dear Lunana," I thought, "Please let me in."

As I continued up through thinning trees and increasing wind, I expected an immediate thank you from Lunana, but it didn't come. Instead of the singing yak bells I heard on day eight, black ravens barked from the bare branches of dead trees, the sky darkened, and clouds like broken coal blew up the valley. I told myself that Lunana would thank me at the campsite called Rodophu, but when I arrived, it was a wet, rocky valley and the sun was gone. As I gazed out at the desolation, I wondered if I was even in Bhutan anymore.

AN HOUR LATER, WE HAD GATHERED IN THE RODOPHU'S tourist bungalow that had none of the woodfire warmth of the bungalow at Jhomolhari Base Camp. Instead, the wooden doors and wood windows had been ripped off for firewood and indecipherable graffiti-like scrawling adorned the walls.

"You must keep the foot pedal moving or the person inside will suffocate," Joe said, speaking slowly and gesturing to his feet.

We were all huddled around Joe who had Ryan zipped up in a portable altitude chamber, a long submarine-shaped nylon bag that is used to treat altitude sickness. Joe was prepping us on what to do if someone got severe altitude sickness. No one had gotten hurt, but based upon the mood in the room, it felt like someone had.

Joe peered at Ryan through a tiny plastic window in the red bag. "You alright in there?"

"Cooee," chirped Ryan, his voice muffled as if underwater. "I'm perfect!"

Ryan didn't look perfect to me — he looked as if he were lying in a bright red coffin and everything in me wanted to tear the zipper open and set him free.

Joe told us the reason he was showing us how to use the bag was that tomorrow we'd be hiking up to the Snowman Bottleneck.

"Bottleneck?" I uttered. "That doesn't sound good."

Norbu told us that we had to cross two passes over 16,000 feet to enter the Lunana District.

"But we've done that before," said Kira.

Joe said these passes were different. "After we cross the first pass, we don't descend. Instead, we traverse a high plateau and camp at 16,200 feet, directly below the next pass." Joe told us that since we ascend more than 2,375 feet in one day — nearly twice the suggested rate — and camp at high altitude, there was a renewed risk for AMS, HACE and HAPE tomorrow night.

"Can't we camp someplace else?" I asked.

Norbu explained that we were limited by the terrain and campsites. "If we wanted to avoid the high camp, we'd have to cross two passes in one day and do a three-thousand-foot descent at the end of the day on a muddy trail, overgrown with rhododendron roots."

"That's why we call it the bottleneck," said Joe. "Because you're stuck up high between two passes."

We learned the purpose of the portable altitude bag was to simulate low altitude if night, an injury, or a storm temporarily delayed descending. As the bag inflates, it increases air pressure around the person inside, improving the oxygen's carrying capacity, and could help treat altitude sickness.

"But the key word is help," Joe emphasized. "The bag provides temporary relief until descent is possible; it doesn't really cure altitude sickness."

I gazed around the room and for the first time, none of us were smiling.

"We're going to deflate the bag now," Joe said to Ryan, before releasing a small metal valve at the end of the bag. "You don't want to use the zippers to deflate the bag," he said, addressing all of us, "because it may blow out his ears."

When Ryan crawled out, the altitude chamber wheezed its last breath and I realized a small bit of my excitement about the hike to Lunana had deflated with it.

TEA AND DINNER IN THE WINDOWLESS BUNGALOW WERE quick and quiet affairs. The cold had us all silently shivering, and like snails, sinking into our down jackets. Gone was the dining tent and the laughter and impassioned discussion that always accompanied it. That night there was only silence, punctuated by the occasional sound of silverware tapping plastic plates. Despite the lantern light, there was a sense of impending doom and darkness pressing on all sides. A river of cold wind poured through the busted-out windows and seemed to settle somewhere in my soul. By 8:00 p.m., we were all hurrying to our tents through a hearse-black night with misting rain. There was no doubt now, we were heading for the high country.

LATER, AS I SLID INTO THE COLD SHELL OF MY SLEEPING bag, I had another "madeleine moment." As Sean, Kristine, and I got older, we graduated from our pillow forts and makeshift tents in the living room to camping in the backyard. It was always the same — we'd make our poor father drag the terribly heavy canvas family tent out into our backyard on a sweltering summer evening, swarming with black flies and mosquitoes, and ask him to set it up. When Dad would ask if we were certain we'd spend the full night out there, we'd swear we'd grown up a lot since our previous attempt the week prior and now had no fear of the woods at night.

"Alright," Dad would say. "I'll put the tent up."

Despite his feigned protests, my dad loved putting that tent up and it was great watching him — you could see a hundred nights of camping memories flood into him with each tent pole he set up. In no time at all, Dad would be chuckling to himself and smiling broadly with the memories. After our parents had tucked us in, inevitably, a pillow fight would erupt and we might pass around the can of soda that we smuggled into the tent with us. But at some point, we'd all suddenly fall silent and the night would begin to assert itself. In New Hampshire in the 1880s, the people who had lived in our old farmhouse had buried their deceased family members in the backyard. Gravestones stuck out of the earth a stone wall away from our tent. Everything seemed scarier at night, and it was easy to imagine those bodies waking up. In no time at all, usually when the shadow of a spider on the tent wall would look like the Lord of Death, one of us would scream, causing the other two to scream, the neighbor's dog would howl, and we'd sprint back inside to find my parents still awake in the living room, shaking their heads with amusement.

As with those nights, when I settled into my sleeping bag in Rodophu and shut my eyes, the forest woke up. Sticks snapped, wind whispered through the tent flaps, and I found myself sitting up and scanning my tent with my headlamp for an unwelcomed visitor. Why was I spooked? I was spooked because the Lunana Valley, for all its beauty, also happened to be one of the most haunted places on the planet. Instead of reading Rilke earlier that night, I read *Bhutan: A Trekker's Guide,* where I learned terrifying facts: The name Lunana translates to "The Dark Inner Region." Seven ghosts haunt the valley's ten villages. According to legend, these wicked demons were the spirits of seven Tibetans killed in battle who wandered over the wild frontier ranges into Bhutan. I had to wonder — why are the most beautiful places in the world also the most dangerous? Why does Tahiti's Teahupoo surf break — the

Roman Coliseum of waves — crash on a sharp and shallow reef? Why do hidden avalanches lurk in Utah's champagne powder ski slopes? Why do rivers in the Amazon hide the candiru fish, a nasty little guy that likes to swim up orifices, particularly the one endorsed by the Divine Madman? And, lastly, why does the Lunana Valley have to have ghosts? As if it didn't already have enough dangers!

As fate would have it, the most sinister ghosts were two brothers named Parep and Nidupgelzen. They lived around Chozo and Thanza, which of course, just happen to be the villages Marie Brown said were the two most beautiful. Parep lived in a cave near an alpine lake, and Nidupgelzen lived in the woods around Chozo Dzong. In fact, when passing through Chozo, you are not supposed to make any noise lest you wake Nidupgelzen and draw his wrath. Even the bells of pack animals are silenced as they pass Chozo Dzong. Along with this, the courtyard of Chozo Dzong is said to be especially haunted and forbidden — so forbidden that not even the King of Bhutan is allowed to walk through it.

Thus, I was to be found, shivering in my tent on the thirteenth night of the Snowman Trek, at thirty-three years of age, wishing I could sleep with the light on. When I heard something outside my tent around 3:00 a.m., the devil's hour, I unzipped the tent door and shined my light out. Swirling, ghost like columns of mist rose from the black earth, marching toward me, and I saw the red eyes of some beast I prayed was a yak.

19

AFTER A NIGHT OF FITFUL SLEEP, I AWOKE TO FIND SONAM at my tent door with bed tea.

"Morning, sir," he said

"Morning," I grumbled.

"Not happy, sir?"

It was an odd question first thing in the morning. "To be honest, Sonam, right now, I am a little apprehensive about the Snowman bottleneck and ghosts of Lunana."

"If you sad for one hour, sir," said Sonam, filling my cup, "you lose 3,600 seconds of happiness."

Before I could reply, Sonam lifted his tray and shuffled over to Kira's tent.

Like dinner, breakfast in Rodophu was a short, cold affair. Just outside the bungalow, exhales exploded from the nostrils of our yaks like car exhaust. We ate fast, washing mouthfuls of food down with slugs of coffee, and I suspected it was because we were all anxious to start hiking up to the infamous Snowman Bottleneck — better to get the adventure underway, letting the dangers come what may, than to loiter at the starting linc, wondering what might happen. On the bright side, it was a clear morning, and while it didn't do much to enamor me to Rodophu, I saw that the campsite was surrounded by some scenic alpine pastures and rocky peaks.

As always, the trail started by climbing the precipitous hillside directly behind the bungalow. Dark and light green rhododendron bushes covered the hillside like camouflage, and a little stream cascaded down shiny black rocks. Despite the dangers of camping at a high elevation, the camp at Narethang on the thirteenth night held the promise of sleeping under the glaciers of the 20,667-foot mountain known as Gangla Karchung. I was excited — how many people can say they've snuggled up next to a glacier?

As I fell in line with Tom and we reached the top of the ridge behind camp, black spires lined the valley and the place looked like the entrance to some fairytale land. "It all looks like something right out of *Lord of the Rings*," I proclaimed.

Tom told me many of Bhutan's grassy highlands reminded him of the movie *Braveheart*. "I keep waiting for Mel Gibson to come running over the hills, dressed as William Wallace."

Such conversations happened a few times on the trail, we'd be comparing the landscape we were hiking through in Bhutan to a movie. When I initially heard members of my group doing this, I was worried: Have we become so reliant on films and television that they are now our only basis of comparison? Was an experience only valuable if we could pin it down by a movie we've watched? Couldn't Bhutan exist on its own terms? However, I was to realize it wasn't about Hollywood but rather that Bhutan had, like the best movies, rooted itself firmly into our imaginations and made the world sparkle with magic and mystery. That we thought of Bhutan in the same context as places like Narnia and Middle Earth was a compliment to Bhutan — not a detraction. Apart from the world of fantasy, a number of places came to mind when I thought of Bhutan — the dripping green wonderland of its mossy forests hearkened the old-growth stands of America's Pacific Northwest. The grassy highlands were certainly reminiscent of Scotland, the icy peaks were — as Rob noted a few days earlier, "like Switzerland" — and parts of the trail that traversed flowering tundra plains could easily be found in Alaska. Discovering other places "in" Bhutan was great because it made Bhutan feel at once exotic and familiar. Plus, I hoped too that if I could find other countries here, then maybe I could discover a little of Bhutan back home.

The hike to the Tsemo La was full of broken rocks and a false pass, but it was also very scenic with thin ribbons of water plummeting down rocky cathedrals. After about three hours of hiking, we reached the pass at 16,090 feet. The Tsemo La consisted of two large cairns draped with player flags, leading up to the left side of a sloped valley. Seeing the rainbow banner of prayer flags strung up the side of the hill, I was reminded of the glorious spider web in the bent branch I passed yesterday.

Peter, Ryan, Rob, Kira, and Paul were seated up on the hillside fifty yards above the pass. As they waved from high on the hill, I realized they were the kind of hikers who typified the Zen koan that said, "When you reach the top of the mountain, keep climbing." At even the high passes, they were always scrambling up to some distant rocky outcrop for a better view.

"I'll be right up," I yelled back, scanning the ground for a rock that looked auspicious.

Along with prayer flags, rocky mounds called cairns sat atop the mountain passes. While cairns serve as trail markers in the United States, their prime purpose in the Himalayas is similar to that of prayer flags — they stop the traveler on his or her journey and remind them to give thanks for those that have gone before them, those that are there now, and those travelers that will pass by in the future. In short, on the highway of trails throughout the Himalayas, prayer flags and cairns are the sacred speed bumps.

When I found a smooth, softball-sized rock, I knelt down and picked it up. Little lichen patches covered the rock, and as I spun it in my hand, my mind painted seven continents and seven seas.

Next, I walked over to the shoulder-high cairn at the Tsemo La, set my rock down, and stepped back to admire my handiwork. Beside the trail, by itself, my rock had little appeal. Yet when placed on top of this magical mound pointing to the sky, the rock seemed to radiate like a precious gem.

As I gazed at the cairn, I was struck by its similarity in shape to the pyramids and the conical shape of the Laya hats. I also thought about Omphalos stones of Greece. According to legend, Zeus set two eagles loose and instructed them to fly across the planet and place Omphalos stones at the center of the world to mark the spot. The Omphalos stones were then draped with a woven net, meant to resemble a beehive, as bees symbolized death and resurrection during the Bronze Age. With the draped and knotted net, the Omphalos stones looked strangely like a cairn and vice versa. Was this a case of the kind of cross-cultural, collective unconscious and mythology Carl Jung and Joseph Campbell spoke of? It seemed so that morning.

As I pondered the knotted net below swirling gray skies, I thought of the Jeweled Net of Indra, a Buddhist metaphor for the ideas of universal interconnectedness and interdependence. Sir Charles Eliot, an eminent Buddhist scholar in the 1930s, interpreted Indra's Net and the Avatamsaka Sutra by saying, "In the heaven of Indra there is said to be a network of pearls so arranged that if you look at one you see all the others reflected in it."

Later, in the Avatamsaka Sutra, a Buddhist student asks his teacher how Indra's jeweled net is possible, and the teacher says if you put a dot on one jewel, there are dots on all the jewels. While this explanation was sufficient, I had trouble with the word "dot," which suggested a blemish or flaw. Instead, I preferred to think that the "shine" of one jewel was reflected in all the others. For as I looked up and saw Peter smiling as he told a joke, followed by all the others smiling with him, soon it was impossible to tell who started the joke. I only knew all were shining with laughter.

Suddenly fear shot across Rob's face. "Look out, Kev," he yelled, pointing behind me, "the yaks are coming."

I realized I was sitting in the middle of the yak track with a train chugging toward me. I hurried out of the way.

AFTER THE PASS, WE FOLLOWED THE YAKS DOWN A SHORT descent and had lunch on a desolate plateau surrounded by gray scree slopes and a shallow lake. Dark churning clouds reflecting in the still water made the lake like a gateway to some forbidden underworld. As I took a second helping of chicken and rice, I gazed around at the vastness surrounding us, and it dawned on me that we were remote — very remote.

"That's just dawning on you?" said Ryan. "Where have you been the last thirteen days?"

At that moment, we were two days past the village of Laya, which was in turn three days from the nearest road in Tashithang. And Thanza was still four days away. You can't get this kind of remoteness much anymore in the world and yet, the funny thing was, I didn't feel the least bit isolated. In the end, distance is not a measure of physical proximity between human beings, but emotional distance. I'd felt far more remote on a crowded anonymous street in New York City than I ever did on the Snowman Trek, where I had great companionship with each in my group, our support staff, and the villagers. Thus, despite being miles away from the road, I always felt close. Along with this, I couldn't help but think being in the presence of such open space was opening up something in me. Back home, that wonderful "Song of Myself" of which Walt Whitman spoke was a radio station of skipping songs and static. On the Snowman Trek, that song seemed to be always playing, sounding from every cell at a great volume.

Our lunch ended with the gloomy thought that we were now in the Snowman Bottleneck and at one of the most vulnerable points of our adventure.

"Cheers to that," said Peter, standing and raising a cup of tea.

That afternoon Peter drank alone.

HALF AN HOUR LATER, I WAS WALKING WITH PAUL THROUGH broken rocks, talking about the "normonology" of cookie names when a loud rumble sounded in the distance. It lasted a few seconds and sounded like a long growl. We froze.

"Please tell me that was an airplane," I said.

"That was no airplane."

"Then please tell me that was——,"

"Quiet!" said Paul, raising his hand.

When the rumble sounded again, it echoed across the rocky expanse and everything seemed to shutter. I was certain it was some mythic beast waking up.

"An avalanche," Paul said, peering around. "I suspect it came from the other side of those mountains."

There was no doubt about that — the plateau on which we found ourselves was snow free, as was the line of craggy peaks that lined like sharp granite fence posts. The avalanche must have either come from the Gangla Karchung's glacier — the glacier we'd be sleeping near — or from one of the other high peaks in the area. Either way, it was big and reminded me of the Nepal trekking tragedy in 1995, of Ron and Debbie Plotkin, and possibly exercising my option of an "emergency evacuation" on my travel insurance plan.

As we plotted on through thickening fog, into slicing wind, and by broken rocks, I couldn't shake my feeling of vulnerability. The trail to Narethang rose up and down like rolling waves of tundra and rock. And when Gangla Karchung's huge moraine appeared, it slithered up the valley in a tremendous pile of unsorted black rock, sand, and mud like a great *naga* serpent. Despite the frequency of encountering moraines on the Snowman Trek, their size and shape were always awe-inspiring. While I knew the geologic processes that made the moraine have been at work for thousands of years, it

Joe navigates through the fog on the infamous "Snowman Bottleneck." Photo by Peter McBride.

looked as if the moraine had been created moments ago. As I hiked over a small hill, Gangla Karchung rose up before me, a 20,667-foot razor-edged peak with splintering glaciers whose waving lines resembled fingerprints. In the distance, squeezed between rocks on a colorless tundra patch, our tents huddled together as if cold. High on the hillsides, yaks foraged unsuccessfully for food.

The camp at Narethang felt nothing like a beyul — it was a desolate plateau of shattered rocks and dead grasses that felt like the charnel grounds of Chakrasamvara, the blue Tibetan tantric deity with four faces who wore a crown of five dry human skulls, a necklace of fifty freshly severed heads, and whose hands held bone ornaments and blood-filled skull cups. I noticed my throat was terribly dry and I had a hard time swallowing. I hadn't planned on the entrance to the Lunana District to fill me with such dread. I told myself the scenery would improve, that these terrifying peaks were just the gargoyles guarding the gate. I told myself this and almost believed it too.

20

MY FIRST NIGHT SLEEPING NEAR A GLACIER WASN'T SOUND. Along with my internal critic shouting ceaseless worries, every sound from the campsite at Narethang was amplified in my mind and a lot more dangerous. Modest wind whipped into a hurricane. A chunk of ice falling from the glacier became an avalanche, and Larry's snoring became a life-threatening bout of altitude sickness from which I must rescue him. In fact, I turned my headlamp on and off so many times during the night I was certain the yakmen thought I was sending SOS light signals.

Despite this, when I woke on the fourteenth day, I was filled with Christmas morning–like giddiness, the kind of which I hadn't felt since I was eight and still believed in Santa Claus. With luck, we would enter the Lunana District that day and travel within her lovely embrace for the next eight days. Despite having four days until my empowered village of Thanza, I was excited knowing that after today's pass, we'd at least be in the Lunana District — kind of like the way you're excited just to be in the parking lot even though the concert or big game is hours away.

After bed tea and washing water, I packed up my bag and hurried to the dining tent. It was another cold, gray day, but I didn't care — I was hiking to Lunana. When I talked relentlessly in a too-cheerful chatter at breakfast, I was sure everyone in my trekking party thought I was crazy. But they didn't know all that was going on inside me — they didn't know how much I loved waking up each day on the Snowman Trek or how I felt like I could change again — that I was changing — and was on the cusp of great discoveries and revelations. They didn't know that for the first time in a long time I felt like anything was possible, for me, for them, for everyone.

As we enjoyed cornflakes and oatmeal, Norbu briefed us on our day. "Today's hike will take us ten miles, from Narethang to our camp in Tarina. After we cross the 16,465-foot Gangla Karchung pass, we have a 3,550-foot descent into Lunana on what many consider the worst trail in the world."

"Nah, mate, said Rob, "the worst trail in the world was me fleein' cannibals in Papua, New Guinea, with Kee-ra."

"But don't worry," said Norbu, "if you break both legs, you can take a yak evac."

"I'd rather try crawling out," said Ryan.

Shut off and snowbound from the rest of the world for four months each year, Lunana was not only the most remote district in Bhutan but also the world. It has 156 households — and seven ghosts — spread over roughly ten villages: Woche, Thega, Shanza, Lhedi, Tasho, Rilo, Chozo, Dyotta, Tajilancho, and Thanza. The Lunana District begins and ends with the high hurdle of mountain passes, all of them reaching more than three miles up into the sky. Coming from Laya, you enter Lunana via the Tsemo La and Gangla Karchung passes, and leaving from Thanza, you exit via the Jaze La, Loju La, and the towering 17,470-foot Rinchen Zoe La. There are a few other 16,000-foot passes along the way, but because they don't have names, the Bhutanese don't seem to think they count. Over the next three days, we'd trek through Lower Lunana until the village of Lhedi. From there, we'd ascend to the Upper Lunana villages of Chozo and Thanza. After leaving Thanza, we'd have three more days of hiking until we left the Lunana District on day twenty.

The hike to the pass was an hour-long scramble below the broken glaciers of Gangla Karchung. I hiked up a crumbling staircase of rock, wedged between peaks that had the color, shape, and sharpness of pencil lead, and then traversed a ridge overlooking two teardrop-shaped alpine lakes below. The morning was cool, but inside I was all sunny. "I'm going to Lunana!" From what I'd read in *The Life and Revelations of Pema Lingpa,* the story of one of Bhutan's most famous saints, I was certain my first sight of Lunana would induce a "great realization experience" and a "pure vision at dawn," where I'd gaze out over an infinite expanse under a "canopy of rainbow light," smell a fragrance of flowers, hear an "extremely sweet and continuous sound of horns and cymbals," and see "silk banners of dharma" flapping triumphantly from every peak. There I'd keep the good company of a glorious assemblage of joyful ones with "light rays emanating from their heart," who also went by the names of Kira, Pete, Ryan, Larry, Joe, Tom, Paul, Rob, Sonam, Sangey, Norbu, and Achula.

As I trod around a corner, a shaft of sunlight broke through the clouds and lit up the mountains. Up ahead the trail leveled, and around the corner, I could hear Peter, Paul, and Ryan chatting and the sound of prayer flags whipping in the breeze. "Thank you for letting me in," I prayed to Lunana. "Thank you." I slowed my stride, readied my camera, took a deep breath, and then stepped around a bend in the trail and up to the pass.

The pass was socked in, and there was nothing to see but swirling fog. There was no infinite vast expanse, no flower fragrance, no continuous sound of horns, no silk dharma banners, and my fellow trekkers, while still glorious, didn't look too joyful. Instead, they were all huddled together, shivering and silent. I dropped my pack and took a seat, disheartened. Okay, maybe it didn't have to be like one of the revelations by Pema Lingpa, but a little scenic view would have been nice. With the swirling fog and colorless rocks, I could hardly see a hundred feet in front of me. In fact, even the layout of Gangla Karchung pass itself paled in comparison to the other passes — instead of having multiple cairns and strings of prayer flags, the Gangla Karchung was but a brief shoulder section of a rocky crag. There was really no place to sit or celebrate. Without the prayer flags strewn about, I wouldn't even have known it was a pass. Evidently, the others thought so too, for less than five minutes after we arrived, everyone was shouldering their backpacks and hiking down.

I was gravely disappointed, but when I took my first step in the Lunana District, I was seized with a strange kind of kinetic energy that entered through my boot soles, traveled up my legs, and seemed to swirl in two crisscrossing currents up my spine to meet at the middle point of my forehead, exploding in a thousand points of diamond light. Not only that but as I plodded on I realized no one yelled, "Lha Gyalo" at the pass but instead talked in hushed and solemn voices, as if standing at the door of some immaculate cathedral. Were we? I wasn't sure, but it was worth taking a few steps down the trail to find out.

THE INITIAL HIKE DOWN FROM THE GANGLA KARCHUNG pass didn't feel like the worst trail in the world. The trail was a bit gravelly and slippery and boulders teetered precariously on high cliffs, but it also passed cool caves, snow leopard ledges, and a string of three magnificent glacial lakes. After an hour and a half of steady downhill, winding among the boulders, we found Norbu waiting at a ridge overlooking a fog-filled valley. "See those two beautiful lakes down below with that towering hanging glacier above them?" Norbu asked, pointing into the gloom.

"No," I said.

"I know," Norbu said with a smile. "But you could if it was sunny."

Norbu explained that we were about to enter a valley called Kephu. "This is a sacred valley where six glacial streams pour from the glacial moraines of the 23,000-foot mountains surrounding us."

"Let's go," I said, hurrying on.

Twenty steps down the trail, I quickly slowed and realized why it was called the worst trail in the world — it was full of rolling, leg-breaking stones, shin-deep mud puddles, and slippery rhododendron roots that grabbed at your boots like a bony hand. Yet little did I know as I was staring at my boots moaning and groaning, a sea change was going on in the sky up above — the cloud ceiling was lifting and suddenly I heard the glorious sound of streams and found myself in a sanctuary of radiant rhododendrons. "Wow," I uttered, suddenly awake. "Wow!" Gazing at a half dozen pure white streams pouring forth from the lifting fog, as if from heaven itself, I thought, "Maybe the rope hanging down from heaven in the Himalayas isn't cut; maybe we're just cut off from the rope." Suddenly I was filled with a burning desire to reach the bottom of that unconquerable valley, to that empowered point where six streams met, so I started sprinting, leaping logs, dodging boulders, dashing around bushes, and then when I saw an opening in the forest, I kicked it into high gear and, moments later, the trail delivered me out into the pure sunlight of the valley floor where the snowmelt streams poured into me like the spokes of a great, ever-rolling wheel, and I immediately threw my arms out to the side and started spinning, a *Sound of Music* moment, thinking, "Earth is amazing!" and "Anything is possible!" and "I hope no one is watching because I look really stupid right now."

AS WE LUNCHED AT THE CENTER OF THE VALLEY, SURROUNDED by high peaks, glorious streams, and hanging glaciers, the collective opinion was that the beauty of the Lunana District was worth every step.

Hanging glaciers and a sacred spot where six streams meet—Lunana. Photo by author.

"It's quite amazing," said Paul, professorially. "Even the birds seem friendlier."

When Joe told us he plans on making T-shirts to commemorate our trek, a number of names got thrown out — "Takin' our Time," "Yakety Yak," and "Operation Ingrid." Clearly with so many "good" choices, a decision that day would be impossible. We would decide on a T-shirt name at the end of the trek.

After lunch, we followed the river down the valley, crowned with sharp ridges that shot out of the earth like giant arrowheads. The trail meandered along, alternating between the open sunshine of the river and the shadowy enchantment of the mossy forest. It was as if whoever had cut the winding trail was so enthralled with the surroundings they couldn't decide which was prettier, woods or river, so they chose both. In the forest, birds sat unafraid on the branch and anytime my attention drifted inward and I'd get lost in thought, a waterfall crashing down sheer rocks would suddenly appear and catapult me back into the present moment. Waterfalls were the meditation bells of the Snowman Trek; they'd always suddenly sound and appear when you least expected it, pulling you out of your thoughts and waking you up to the wonder once again.

THAT NIGHT, I SLEPT PEACEFULLY IN THE PEACEABLE VALLEY of a peaceable kingdom.

21

THE ITINERARY FOR THE FIFTEENTH DAY CALLED FOR AN eight-mile hike from Tarnia to Woche, our first village in three days and the first in Lunana. From camp, the trail followed the Tarnia Chhu down the valley, passing frost-fringed bushes, colorful fallen leaves, and sunlit rainbows in the spray from the river. As I hiked, I found myself wishing for snow. My wish for snow wasn't unfounded, it just made sense. After all, I was on the Snowman Trek — to finish without hiking over at least a few inches of snow would have felt like cheating. Plus, I would love to see how the trail looked after a fresh storm. I would love to bound through the snow in my boots, see fluffy snow pillows hanging on the branches of pine trees, and catch frozen flakes on my tongue. Plus when I'd tell my friends back home that it snowed on the Snowman Trek, they'd assume I'd traversed vast glaciers and horrendous crevasses during a blinding whiteout and think I was extreme.

I used to love snowstorms as a boy. What kid doesn't? After all, with snowstorms arrived the possibility that school would be canceled. There was nothing like opening the window shade on school mornings to see my front yard transformed into a winter wonderland. The moment Sean, Kristine, and I heard on the radio that school was cancelled, we'd race outside to spend the day building caves, making snowmen, and having snowball fights. While I no longer wore a one-piece snowsuit or had my gloves on a string, I would love to have had such a morning on the Snowman Trek. Thus, as the trail passed a rockslide tumbling down to the river, I made a new wish: "Dear Lunana," I said, "please let it snow."

Well, I regretted this wish the moment I made it because if you believe the saying about the gods punishing us by answering our prayers, I'd just invited the gods to pummel us. Not only was snow the one thing that could stop our Snowman Trek, it was also the one thing that could kill us. Indeed, as the trail rose from the river, I imagined Lunana thinking, "You want snow, you got snow!"

After veering away from the river, the trail rose steeply through a juniper and larch forest, crossed a few more rockslides, and continued up and up. After forty-five minutes of intense uphill, stacks of fresh-cut wood decorated the trail in both sight and scent, yak tracks crisscrossed in every direction, and stone walls sectioned off little property plots — three signs on the Snowman Trek that a village was nearby. A line of prayer flag poles, standing triumphantly in the broken-cloud breeze, announced our arrival in Woche, a small village with ten traditional-style houses set behind fresh-cut barley fields, dotted with big rocks. The rocks had been purposely left there by the Woche residents, lest they move them and disrupt the resident deities.

Fortunately, rather than one of Lunana's many ghosts, we were greeted by twenty of Woche's villagers. They appeared silent and sudden, like deer, and the group of mostly women and small children stood together to receive us, as if at a wedding. The women wore their hair short and fine jewelry hung around their necks; they wore red sweaters or Western-style blazers over their kiras. The youngest children wore sweatpants and wind breakers and the adolescent kids — the ones who had danced around the fire with the women or grazed the yaks in the high pastures with the men — wore traditional kiras and ghos. Given the large number of women in this village, I was reminded of the role women have played in Buddhism throughout history.

Along with being one of the oldest religions in the world, Buddhism is one of the most progressive. In fact, more than twenty-five hundred years ago, Buddhism was progressive even by today's standards. The historical Buddha allowed women to be ordained and taught that enlightenment, the highest spiritual achievement, was available to everyone, regardless of race, age, or sex. In Tibetan Buddhism, women such as Yeshe Tshogyal, Princess Pemasal, the Great Bliss Queen, the Ever-Excellent Lady, and the Great Glacier Lady of Invincible Turquoise Mist were *dakinis,* or female tantric deities, who protected and served Buddhist doctrine, conducted rites, hid *terma* (or "treasures"), and helped Guru Rinpoche vanquish demons. Since I was curious how the vaulted place of women in Buddhism translated in Bhutanese society, I asked Norbu about it.

"Let's just put it this way," Norbu said. "Some *men* complain of discrimination in Bhutan."

"Really?"

Norbu smiled. "Sometimes!"

Norbu explained women often receive the inheritance of a family in Bhutan, and with the Marriage Act, all alimony payments fall squarely on the shoulders of the man, even if the wife initiates the divorce. Women are encouraged to vote and run for office and there is no limit on Parliament seats for men versus women. In addition, there are little to no gender gaps in basic education, and women are unafraid to be progressive in regards to their traditional dress — many women now wear half kiras and their hair is long and pulled back with a hairpiece. From reading *Kuensel,* it appeared the Fourth King's wife, Her Majesty the Queen Ashi Sangay Choden, was leading this movement. The queen often toured the country to educate people about women's health, and in the months following our trip, she would start the RENEW Center in Thimphu to "Respect,

Lunch in the hillside village of Woche. Photo by Peter McBride.

Educate, Nurture, Empower, Women," focusing on disadvantaged women, crisis support, and victims of domestic assault.

Despite this, Norbu informed me that women still have problems. There is a difference between the enlightened attitude of the government and public support. While some women had basic education, many did not go on to higher education. Only a few women were in public positions or civil service, and women in rural villages could be mistreated by truckers, tour guides, and civil servants, who occasionally took advantage of their transient profession to avoid responsibility. Norbu told me that even though many women can run for office, most don't because they're not encouraged to do so or don't have the confidence.

We toured the village of Woche after lunch, and the villagers graciously allowed us to peek inside their homes. The homes were modest and had few belongings — a woodstove, pots, pans, blankets, and Buddha statues. Bed mats and blankets were rolled up neatly and placed in corners, the wood floors had all been freshly swept with yak-hair brooms, and a few family pictures decorated the walls. Despite living subsistent lives with few material items, the villagers of Woche were rich in pride.

While trekkers used to camp in Woche, due to the lack of grazing land for the yaks, we would camp an hour up the trail. That, of course, would "make tomorrow's hike shorter," an explanation we'd heard from Norbu each and every day of the trek. We said good-bye to the children, took final pictures, and began to file out — but not before a woman pointed at Ryan with one finger, pointed at her daughter with the other, and started giggling.

"You want me to marry her?" Ryan asked.

The woman nodded, giggling.

Like most things in Bhutan, the rites and rituals surrounding marriage are flexible. Marriage can be an elaborate ceremony in the company of monks, friends, and family, who offer fruit, betel nuts, and sips of *chang* (a barley beer). Or a couple might just start living together and are then considered married. There are still arranged marriages in Bhutan, but the arrangement really just concerns the pairing of the couple, both the guy and girl in question must agree to it. In the past, rural communities have practiced polygamy, mainly out of economic convenience. One husband would be away tending the yaks, and the other husband would be at home with the family. Like water and sky burials, this practice is far less frequent today. In the past, most families had five to seven children, but with the falling infant mortality rate, families are today having three to five children, and the Bhutanese government would like to bring this number down to two by 2020.

Ryan politely declined the woman's joking gesture. "I must keep going." When the woman didn't understand, he pointed up the trail. "Snowman Trek," he said. "Thanza."

"Ah," the lady replied. "Thanza."

I expected to see the woman's face light up with the Lunana look when she said Thanza, but then I realized her face was already glowing because, after all, she lived in Lunana.

OUR CAMP THAT NIGHT WAS LOCATED ABOUT AN HOUR outside of Woche in a small clearing flanked by rhododendrons and autumn bushes drenched in immaculate greens, reds, and golds. As I marched into camp, I found Peter, petting one of the horses.

"How's it going," I said, wandering over to him.

"Not bad," he said, giving the horse's forehead a good scratch. The horse had a broad, brown forehead with white tuft of hair at the center.

When I reached to pet the second horse, it reared its head and stamped its feet, and I quickly pulled away. "That guy's mean!"

"You need to watch their ears," Peter explained, still petting. He told me I could tell what a horse was thinking by its ears. "If both ears are forward, the horse is happy. If one ear is forward and the other is back, the horse is thinking. And, if both ears are pointed backwards, watch out." As Peter told me that, I could imagine his Dad telling him the same thing on their Colorado cattle ranch and him one day passing it along if he had children.

"Give it a try," he said. "Extend your hand a little but also wait for him to come to you."

As I reached out my hand, both ears of the horse immediately shot back. "Awww, man," I lamented, pulling my hand away. "The horse is afraid of me."

"Just extend your hand halfway and leave it there," Peter coached. "You need to make the effort but also let the horse come to you."

"He's not going to bite me?" I asked, extending my hand.

"I promise he won't."

The horse looked at me for a few moments with wide teddy-bear brown eyes and then touched my hand with a quick kiss of his wet nose.

"Thatta boy," I said, reassuringly.

As the horse returned, sniffing my hand and shirt sleeve, one ear shot forward and the other pointed backward. "Don't worry, old boy," I said. "I'm not gonna hurt you."

A moment later, both ears pointed forward and the horse scratched his gray snout happily in my hand.

"I did it," I said, rejoicing. I couldn't help but think that there was some deeper lesson there, although, at the moment, I was at a loss for what it was.

"Nice," said Peter with a smile. "Now go try the same thing with a yak!"

22

IMAGINE YOU AND YOUR FAMILY LIVE IN A TWO-STORY home in the woods with a beautiful view of the river. It's a bright morning, you've just finished breakfast, and the kids are outside playing. Suddenly you hear a noise — a strange rhythmic whirling, shooting down the valley, growing louder. It sounds like a helicopter but you know it's not. You run out the door, and as you look up the valley, you see a dust storm rising strangely above the trees. Hoping for a better view, you sprint down to the river and what you see terrifies you — a wall of water, full of boulders, dead animals, and trees snapping like toothpicks, rages toward you. There isn't time to scream. Or grab the children. There is only time to run.

A situation like this occurred in the Lunana Valley in 1994 when a moraine dam burst and an entire lake, the Luggye Tsho, (*tsho* is "lake"), emptied into the Po Chhu valley, killing people and farm animals and destroying houses and crops. The flood was so strong it washed away part of the mighty Punakha Dzong, seven hours downstream, a dzong even the Tibetan Army couldn't overcome.

The science behind a glacial lake outburst flood (GLOF) is simple: as glaciers retreat, they leave bowl-shaped depressions framed by rocky moraines, which fill with glacial meltwater. When the meltwater penetrates the cracks and freezes, the moraine turns into an unstable dam, causing the water to pool into a glacial lake. As the lake grows bigger, hydrostatic pressure on the moraine increases until one day — triggered by its own weight, an avalanche, calving glacier, or earthquake — the dam bursts and an entire lake rages down the thin funnel of a river valley with the intensity of a tsunami. Glacial lake outburst floods have occurred periodically in the Himalayas throughout history, but the difference now is that their frequency seems to be increasing as well as the population within reach of their devastation. Much of Bhutan's population is concentrated in a few river valleys, and many rivers feed into one another — thus a GLOF in one river will affect others.

Bhutan has more than 677 glaciers and 2,674 glacial lakes, 24 of which hover on the verge of collapse. Of those 24 lakes, 14 are located in Lunana, including 2 that have the potential to create one of the biggest GLOFs in Bhutan's history. Just downstream from Ralfstreng Tsho, separated only by a 187-foot slab of unstable moraine, lies Thorthormi Tsho, the largest lake in Lunana. The glacier above Thorthormi Tsho is melting at an alarming rate, and in just ten years, Lunana's Ralphstreng Tsho deepened by more than eighty-nine feet. If Ralfstreng Tsho bursts its moraine dam, scientists fear it will pour into Thorthormi, creating a cascading effect and sending more than 53 million cubic meters of water charging down the valley. Since the river valley was widened significantly by the 1994 flood, this new flood would reach people much faster, primarily in the Punakha-Wangdue and Chamkha river valleys where about 10 percent of Bhutan's population lives. Scientists who say there is no "immediate danger" in one breath are quick to contradict themselves and say "we can't wait" in another. Day sixteen of the Snowman Trek would take us to a village called Lhedi in the Pho Chhu valley, the site of the 1994 GLOF, and as you can imagine, I found this a bit unnerving.

After breakfast, we started up the steep trail under overcast skies, bound for a 15,305-foot pass — the Keche La. As we hiked up into the cirque-like valley, flanked by dwarf rhododendrons, the village of Woche appeared nestled in the trees, far below in the distance. At the other end of the valley, black moraines poured forth from the towering mountains, Teri Kang (23,945 feet) and Jejekangphu-Kang (23,288 feet). Since so many of the peaks were ensconced in clouds, it felt as if I'd need to go back to Bhutan to see all the mountains I missed.

"No kidding," said Peter. "We could be in South Dakota and not even know it!"

As the trail made its final ascent to the pass, the rhododendrons yielded to rocks and gravel. When Sonam wandered up, twirling his red and white umbrella, I told him the gray-coated yak we'd recently named Scoobie was really a Buddha with big horns. Over the last few days, I'd noticed Scoobie always paused under the prayer flags of a pass. "He's giving thanks," I told Sonam. "Being a yak, he can't yell 'Lha Gyalo,' so he just pauses and says a prayer by chewing his cud."

"Maybe, sir," said Sonam, smirking.

"Scoobie only outwardly appears as a yak," I proclaimed. I knew, deep down, Scoobie was really Chenrezig, the Boddhisattva of Compassion who said he would not rest until he liberated everyone and everything from suffering, even the grass. But of course, grass never stops growing, just like Scoobie never stops working. He is the beast of our burden.

Sonam just shook his head and plodded on.

"Watch him today," I yelled. "He'll do it!"

I followed fifty yards behind Sonam toward the pass where, on the horizon, Tom, Rob, Norbu, and Joe were already celebrating — black silhouettes against a gray prayer-flag-colored sky. The trail wound around another lake — a lake that seemed never to have known a ripple — and then made its final, rocky push to the pass. When I arrived, the pass was shrouded in clouds that rose like smoke rings from the surrounding talus slopes.

As I sat down, I asked everyone if they knew what number pass that was. "Fifth? Sixth? Tenth?"

"I haven't a clue," said Paul.

Ryan, Peter, Rob, and Kira exchanged quizzical glances.

Before we started, the math of the trek seemed so important — twenty-four days, 216 miles, eleven passes, and a half million steps. But by day sixteen, instead of statistics, we cared about special moments with each other and the Bhutanese villagers. Using our collective wisdom, which took a few minutes of processing in the synapse-slowing high altitude, we concluded the Keche La was our seventh pass.

"And just think," said Paul, "in one day, we'll have one week of trekking left."

Kira laughed. "Is that supposed to make us feel better?"

Gradually, we heard whistles and saw our yak team thundering up toward the pass, their hooves echoing off the hard rocks. I looked over at Sonam and nodded. "Just watch Scoobie." The Keche La was the perfect pass for my little experiment — a string of prayer flags was stretched across two head-high cairns that stood like sentinels on both sides of the trail. It was impossible to follow the trail down and not go under the flags. If there was any pass Scoobie would genuflect under, the Keche La would be it. The yaks approached in a slow, side-to-side swaying gait, and I saw Scoobie at the end of the line. With his gray coat, big horns, elaborate red headdress, and fancy red rope "earrings," he was always easy to spot. As he approached, Scoobie dropped his head, lumbering reverently toward the pass as if in a communion line at church.

Wow," I thought to myself, "he's really going to do it!"

Scoobie slowed as he approached the pass and then, as he walked under the flags, stopped abruptly. I was just about to declare victory when Scoobie suddenly reared his head and caught the rope of prayer flags with his horns. As he did, his horns yanked the string of flags down, which, in turn, dislodged a few of the rocks of the cairn. When the stones fell, Scoobie bolted and the prayer flags were trampled and torn under his hooves.

Moments later, as we hiked down from the pass, I told Sonman the display was Scoobie's reminder to us that it wasn't the prayer flags that mattered but, rather, what they pointed to. "But that's how it is out here," I exclaimed, "dirt, divinity, and dung all in one luminous lump of love on the Snowman Trek!"

"Yes, sir," Sonam replied, knowing this all along.

WE HAD LUNCH AT THE LITTLE VILLAGE OF THEGA THAT appeared like an apparition two hours after the pass — wood-shingle roofs, a chorten, and yaks all suddenly right before us, floating in the fog. A village woman, wearing a blue coat over her kira, hurried out to say hello with her two little children who peeked out shyly from the space between her legs. Such interactions happened often, and when they did, I always pulled out my camera and took a few pictures. In doing so, a brief but beautiful exchange took place — the villagers gave me the gift of their picture and I gave them the gift of seeing their digital image on my camera. Critics may scoff at my "gift," but when I saw the villagers hunched over my camera, pointing and laughing, I realized it really was a gift. They'd thank me, I'd thank them, and as I continued down the trail, all of us were always left beaming. I also hoped that one day I might be able to do the Snowman Trek again and give them a heartfelt hard copy.

Our lunch spot was located in a freshly harvested barley field, and as we started eating, giggling sounded from the hillside directly across from us. We looked up to find two little girls in kiras with short cropped hair standing a hundred yards from us. As they giggled, it was clear both of the girls seemed to think that if they put their hands in front of their faces, the rest of their bodies were hidden. Thus, they peered at us through finger cracks, giggling.

"We see ya," yelled Rob.

The girls squeezed their fingers shut, suppressing laughter.

Rob presents his picture to some very interested villagers. Photo by Peter McBride.

Moments later, the fingers opened again like window shutters and the giggling continued. The girls were there not only to say hello but also to retrieve a large shaggy-haired yak that had wandered into the woods across from our table. Presently, the girls dropped their hands and set about catching their yak. But when they took their first step toward the yak, the yak took a step away. When the girls took a step away from the yak, he took a step closer. As a little dance began, I realized I was watching the Ten Bulls story enacted before my eyes. It was that delicate dance between human and animal, ease, effort, and enlightenment — much like my experience petting the horses with Peter or struggling to put the prayer flags at the first pass. I had to wonder, was it my reaching for the flags that led to their retreat? When I thought back on the scene, I realized Norbu didn't immediately chase the prayer flags but instead had waited patiently and faithfully for the wind.

The dance between the girls and the yak went on for ten minutes before an unspoken compromise seemed to have been struck. The girls wandered up the hill halfway toward the yak, he wandered halfway down the hill toward them, and they met somewhere in the middle. And how did these two featherweight, giggling girls respond to this sharp-horned yak when he arrived at their side? They gave him a good whack on the behind with a stick, sending him scuttling off like an adolescent sent to his room.

LEAVING THEGA, THE TRAIL TRAVERSED DOWN TERRACED farm fields and through yak pastures. The Pho Chhu Valley appeared, its trees glittering in magnificent fall colors. "There it is," I thought, "the start of my valley." The upper reaches of the valley were socked in, but behind that theater curtain of clouds, I knew a magical stage awaited — the villages of Lhedi, Chozo, and Thanza, and presiding over all like a jeweled crown, Table Mountain (22,960 feet). Naturally, I started sprinting to reach the valley floor. I expected another *Sound of Music* moment with further confirmation that "Earth is amazing" and "Anything is possible" and that time, I vowed I wouldn't be shy about spinning and would wear my happiness like a bright jacket of joy. But when I arrived at the river, my heart dropped.

The river was but a thin strip of whitewater surrounded by broken rocks and rubble — the remnants of the 1994 flood. Once again, Bhutan had defied my expectations, although not in a good way. I expected my entrance into this beautiful valley to be a time of song and celebration, but seeing the effects of the flood, I felt a little sick. And the saddest part of this tragic tattoo was that Bhutan, this country with the most enlightened conservation policies in the world, was being forced to pay the greenhouse tab of other countries, namely China, Bhutan's neighbor to the north. There are moments in life where all the effort seems pointless and you just feel like giving up. Standing there, gazing out at the rock and rubble, there seemed no point in trying to change anything. I was momentarily depressed but then I saw the river, threading its way through the rocks — still singing, still hopeful — and I decided, if the river wasn't giving up, well then, neither was I.

Minutes later I caught up with Peter and Paul as two traditional Bhutanese houses, framed by farm fields, appeared. The fields had all been tilled into fresh corduroy rows of dirt. From there, the trail alternated between skirting the river and wandering up above on a bluff, and soon, we saw three Bhutanese men walking toward us from the other direction.

"Kuzuzangbo la!" said Peter as we approached.

"Hello," the man said, shaking each of our hands with two hands. "I am Kuzang."

Kuzang was a Bhutanese man in his mid-twenties, wearing a winter coat over his gho and a worn pair of hiking boots. He introduced his two horsemen who didn't speak English.

"Where are you going?" Kuzang asked.

"We lads are doing the Snowman Trek," Paul proclaimed with his English accent and way of phrasing that always put a smile on our faces.

"Oh," said Kuzang, nodding. "A very long journey."

When Peter asked what Kuzang was doing, he informed us he was on a tour of northwestern Bhutan to document artifacts. "Scrolls, statues, thangka paintings, and ancient weapons," Kuzang explained. "Since Bhutan is the last Buddhist Kingdom in the Himalayas, there is a strong illegal market for these items. This is one of the reasons tourists are not allowed in some parts of dzongs."

Kuzang's job was to trek from village to village and from temple to temple, taking pictures and documenting exactly which artifacts were in each dzong and monastery. To do this, his tools were modest—a camera, pen, and pad. He was essentially doing the Snowman Trek in reverse—he had just come from Chozo Dzong and would travel to the temple in Laya, then onto Linshi Dzong, and eventually end up at Drukyel Dzong in Paro.

"How is it hiking the Snowman Trek in reverse?" I asked.

Kuzang smiled. "The same as you, my friend. Very difficult."

"Do people really steal artifacts?" inquired Peter.

Kuzang nodded sadly. "A few chortens have been ransacked. People steal precious artifacts and sometimes vandalize the statues themselves."

As I heard this, I realized Bhutan was at a precarious point in its development. With the majority of its population below the age of twenty-five and unemployment rising from 1.8 percent to 3.7 percent in the years between 2003 and 2007, new jobs and opportunities needed to be created to prevent further job loss and its dangerous side effects.

"Theft is not common," Kuzang stated. "But we must make every effort to prevent it."

As Peter snapped some pictures of Kuzang, I thought of Chaucer's *Canterbury Tales* and all the colorful characters I'd met over the last two weeks — the sword-twirling park ranger, the yak herder brothers, the monk near Lingshi, and sweet little Tshokyi on the night of her big dance. Along with these memories, I recalled all the other villagers I didn't speak with but whose brief images will forever be burned into my memory — the shepherdess rinsing laundry in the reeds before Robluthang, the little girl in Goyok sitting on the regal throne of Peter's lunch chair, the man plowing a field with a team of yaks in Laya, and countless little faces peeking from wood windows with wide-eyed amazement.

We took a few more pictures of Kuzang and his horsemen, and when we said good-bye, Paul, Peter, and I shook their hands with our two hands.

LHEDI WAS A SMALL RIVERSIDE VILLAGE OF TRADITIONAL stone homes, scattered around house-sized boulders that had crashed down from the high ridges above. That the homes of Lhedi were scattered throughout the rocks, I believe, said a lot about the Bhutanese relationship to the natural world. Rather than trying to control and conquer nature by dynamiting the rocks or putting up protective fences on the hillside up above, the Bhutanese simply live their lives in accord with nature and let the rocks fall where they may.

As I strolled through town, I happened upon three signs that announced in vertical succession: "Welcome to Lunana Community School"; "Basic Health Unit Lunana"; "Royal Government of Bhutan Livestock Extension Center, Lunana Gasa." I stopped and snapped a few pictures. Seeing the word "Lunana" in print seemed to affirm that I was actually standing there in my valley. "Awesome!" It was the manifestation of my multiyear dream. I enjoyed the moment at length, gazing up and down the river with a magnificent pride and watched freight trains of fog chugging up the valley. As I stood there, I again had the sense of Lunana as a snow-peaked princess and got the feeling I was standing in the presence of a lady. As such, I decided I would be a gentleman from then on. I would stop telling the guys jokes about sheep and Scotsmen. I wouldn't swear. I would throw my coat over a puddle for Lunana, and if we arrived at a door, I would gladly hold it open for her. But who was I kidding? It was she who was holding the door open for me!

I floated through the rest of the afternoon and evening, high on being in this valley, high on being with my group, high on being at high altitude. At dinner, as everyone laughed and conversed, I tilted back in my chair, savoring the scene, and tried to capture the moment by thinking up little *bantus* in my brain. A bantu is a two-line poem created by the Bantu tribe in Africa. The first line of the poem presents an image, and the second line "answers" that image. Traditionally, the poem is created by two people: one person throws out the first line, and another person riffs off it like a jazz improvisation. That night, I thought

Larry laughs.
Thunder claps.

Snow pigeons soar across the sky
The monk tosses rice.

A bank deposit.
The Snowman Trek.

Follow the yellow brick road.
The trail to Thanza.

Then, when I saw Sonam sitting in the corner of the dining tent, mumbling mantras from his well-worn, pocket-sized book of Buddhist prayers, I thought

Sonam reads Sutras.
A flower leans to the light.

23

FIFTEEN-YEAR-OLD MINDU WANGMO WAS MAKING HISTORY. Mindu, who grew up in Lunana, was the first girl to graduate from the community school in Lunana and go on to grade seven. In remote communities, girls finishing grade six usually graduate to a nomadic life of tending yaks and raising families. However Mindu, despite being short in stature, had big dreams, one of which was to earn her teaching degree and return to Lunana to teach at the community school in Lhedi. When I read about Mindu in *Kuensel* in the months following my trip, I was immediately inspired — for it's not the size of one's dream that matters but only that someone dares to, and all dreams inspire the world to spin again. Although Mindu wasn't at the Lunana Community School when we visited on the morning of the seventeenth day — she was studying at Bjeeshong Middle Secondary School a few days away in Damjee — I sensed some of her courage lingering like a fabulous fragrance in the classroom.

As we walked over to the single-story community school after breakfast, we found the students outside standing in rows in front of the white stone school, dressed in kiras, ghos, and blue boots, reciting Bhutan's national anthem.

Students at the community school in Lunana start their day with the national anthem. Photo by Peter McBride.

In the Kingdom of Druk, where cypresses grow,
Refuge of the glorious and monastic and civil traditions,
The King of Druk, precious sovereign.
His being is eternal, his reign prosperous,
The enlightenment teachings thrive and flourish,
May the people shine like the sun of peace and happiness.

Following the national anthem, the children recited prayers — stepping side to side and clapping — and stole glances of us snapping pictures from the hillside. When the students finished, we followed them inside, and before I entered, I saw a poster hanging outside the door: "Code of Conduct for Teachers: nurturing and guiding the development of each child in my school, promoting ethical and professional standards of the teaching profession, serving the king with loyalty, dedication, and integrity, and refraining from all kinds of defilement and unethical acts."

The thirty-five children at the community school in Lunana sat at knee-high tables with little chairs. Scattered solar lights cast a low, hushed glow, and colorful drawings of vegetables, fruit and animals decorated the walls with the English words written next to them: Tomato, Banana, Monkey, Gorilla. A lone woodstove radiated heat, and fresh-cut wood sat, neatly stacked, beside school books. "That's a lesson in itself," I told Joe, pointing. "True education doesn't just come from books but by being outside in nature, among the elements."

As the children worked on an assignment — with great vigor to impress their guests — we wandered through the room, introducing ourselves.

Like its counterparts in Lingshi and Laya, the community school in Lunana was open from late May through October. Most of the children were boarders and received at least two meals a day from the World Food Program. The WFP began in Bhutan in 1974 and currently serves more than forty thousand students in 197 schools. While a natural abundance of rice and potatoes guarantees children in Bhutan don't lack bulk, their diets are often short on fresh fruit and vegetables. Before the WFP came in, many students weren't getting enough iron or vitamin A.

Investing in the health and education of its children is a wise investment on behalf of Bhutan. Like America, there is a strong need for teachers in Bhutan, primarily in the fields of math and science. To combat the teaching shortages in rural areas, the government has mandated that all new college graduates with teaching degrees spend at least three years teaching in remote schools. In addition to more than seven hundred schools, there are six vocational technical institutes and two Zorig Chosum institutes, which teach traditional Bhutanese skills such as crafts, embroidery, mural painting, sculpture, silversmith, and wood carving.

"What's your name?" I said to a brown-eyed boy with a little cowlick of black hair cresting like a wave over his forehead.

The boy stood up. "My name is Rinzin Wangchuk, sir," he said before sitting back down.

"Nice to meet you," I replied, introducing myself. "What's your favorite subject?"

Rinzin stood up again. "My favorite subject is mathematics, sir," and then sat back down.

I thanked Rinzin for his politeness. "But please don't feel the need to stand on my account."

Rinzin stood up. "Thank you, sir," he said. "I will not stand."

Before Rinzin sat back down, he realized his mistake and we both busted up laughing.

EVER BEEN TO A NEW PLACE AND HAD THE SENSE YOU'D been there before? But along with the sense of having visited before, you also have the inexplicable feeling you are meant to be there now — at that exact moment in time — and a great destiny awaits? I had this feeling as we started up the rocky trail out of Lhedi, bound for Thanza. As I followed a thin trail out of the village, through small boulders and riverside bushes, the feeling increased with each step, and I was filled with an electric energy. Technically, each step was taking me farther from the United States, yet as I moved forward, I felt strangely like I was going home. It was a heavenly day of blue sky and crisp air, and the trail up the river was sandy and dry. With each step, I felt more connected, alive, and awake and as if I'd never truly touched, tasted, smelled, heard, or seen . . . until then. Certainly, Lunana looked nice when I first saw her after the Gangla Karchung pass, but the more I got to know her, the lovelier she became — the true sign of a good relationship. As the faint horizontal outline of Table Mountain slowly appeared from behind the clouds, I understood what the Tibetan saint Longchenpa meant when he said, "I would rather die here than be born elsewhere."

The day's hike would take us 10.5 miles — from Lhedi to the village of Chozo and then up to Thanza. At 13,470 feet above sea level and sealed off by snow for four months of the year, Thanza was not only one of the highest year-round settlements in the Himalayas, but also the world. After three hours, the river widened, great sand dunes rose up, and fluttering white prayer flags announced our arrival in Chozo, a lovely village at the start of a wide, windswept plain. I strolled into Chozo and found Sonam and Sangey setting up lunch between two archery targets, just above the river. When they informed me the rest of the group was at Chozo Dzong, I hurried through the stone homes of the village, waving to villagers threshing wheat and weaving colorful textiles from ancient, backstrap looms.

As I tore around a tall stone wall, Chozo Dzong appeared, large and looming. The dzong had that once-proud look of all houses that had fallen into ruin. The courtyard leading to the dzong was horribly overgrown and the dzong itself seemed on the verge of imminent collapse. Square, broken stones teetered precariously, black ravens with wood-splintered beaks cawed from empty windows, and a strange repelling energy hung in the air like a bad scent. I thought about Parep and Nidupgelzen, the ghost brothers who haunted the area, the curse on Chozo Dzong's overgrown courtyard, and then I got the heck out of there.

LATER AS WE LUNCHED BETWEEN THE TWO ARCHERY TARGETS, I saw a village boy watching us eat. He was holding a little bow in one hand and a single arrow in the other. He wore a green vest over his brown-checkered gho and, of course, blue rubber boots. Blue boots seemed to be on the feet of everyone under the age of twelve in Bhutan.

When I finished eating, I walked over to the boy. "Kuzuzangbo la," I said, "Nge meng Kevin."

"Nge meng Pema," he said, shyly shifting his weight from foot to foot.

With that, Pema smiled and gave me the greatest compliment a boy could give — he offered me his bow.

"You want me to shoot it?" I said.

Pema bit his lower lip, nodding enthusiastically.

The best moments on a trip are never the ones written about in an itinerary, the best moments just appear spontaneously like glittering rainbows of good luck.

"Yes," I proclaimed. "I'd love to shoot your bow."

Pema was not only one of the cutest kids I'd ever seen, but he was also one of the smartest, for he had insight enough to lead me far away from the group before I took my shot. Had he not done this, Ryan might have been the unwelcomed recipient of a Bhutanese souvenir stuck in his shoulder.

Pema's bow was made out of bamboo, bound with nettle string. As he handed me the arrow, I saw that his dad had dulled the arrowhead for safety — the Bhutanese equivalent of my dad letting me shave without a razor when I was five. As I crouched down on one knee, Pema helped me set the arrow on the bowstring and then gestured how to shoot.

"Got it," I said, standing up.

I set my sights on a little sandy bunker twenty feet away, tightened my grip, and pulled back. Closing one eye, I took aim and fired. My aim was good but my shot landed five feet short of the target. I did this purposely, for to break Pema's bow would break his heart. Based upon my shot, I expected him to be a little disappointed, but when I looked down, Pema's eyes beamed like two brown bull's-eyes. I handed him his bow, thanked him by saying "*kadriche*" and offered him the greatest compliment an adult could give. "Your bow is good!" I said, giving him a thumbs-up. "Good!"

With that, Pema scurried off to share his excitement with his friends.

AFTER CHOZO, MY IMMACULATE VALLEY REALLY BEGAN to open up. We followed a well-worn trail out of Chozo, passing a grass-roofed chorten (which I was certain had just exploded out of the earth), and emerged onto a sun-kissed plain with wandering

Pema and his buddy take aim in Chozo Village. Photo by Peter McBride.

yaks. With each step, everything felt more timeless and a kind of crystal dust seemed to hang in the air. "Wow," I thought, "this place really has been empowered by Guru Rinpoche!" Twenty minutes into my hike, Sonam and Sangey thundered up with the horses and before I even knew it, or thought to do it, I had a rock in my hand and was running alongside them.

"Yes, Mr. Kevin!" cheered Sonam.

"HAW!" I yelled when one horse slowed, giving him an encouraging slap on the side. When the other horse veered left, I instinctively hurled my stone. My shot was perfect, landing just to the left of the horse and he fell back in line.

"Yes," cried Sangey, slowing.

I didn't respond because the other horse, the one I just sped up, had veered wide to the right. Still running, not missing a stride, I grabbed another rock and threw it. As the horse veered back in line, I realized Sonam and Sangey were jogging, and I was running the horses entirely by myself. Naturally, there was a moment of panic — like when I rode my first two-wheeled bike and my parents let go — but I quickly refocused on the task at hand, running, shouting, and tossing my stones. Unlike my first attempt at running the horses, I didn't tire this time or feel the least bit hesitant. I was brimming with a strength and time-on-the-trail confidence, born of seventeen days of hard, Himalayan hiking. I ran the horses for another hundred yards and as the grassland transformed into a huge sandy plain, I slowed to a walk and tossed my stone to Sonam who had caught up with me.

"Okay, sir?" Sonam asked with a sweet concern.

I told him I was perfect but wanted to enjoy the walk. A towering hill had risen up in the distance and I had a hunch Thanza and Table Mountain lay in wait on the other side.

Sonam and Sangey thanked me and hurried on with the horses, their hooves tossing up sand like wedding rice.

Following my brief but beautiful stint as a Himalayan cowboy, the trail passed a lake so clear and shallow it seemed like Saran Wrap had been stretched across the sand. On my left, yaks loitered and locked horns. I waved. They grunted. I grunted back and they looked away, bored. As the trail rose up over a grassy hill, all expansive views were blotted out. I trod up the dirt trail through the bushes as little brooks trickled down each side. I walked slowly and purposefully, glancing side to side with a wide smile, not unlike a groom going up the aisle, glancing at his guests. At the altar up ahead, Table Mountain waited like a bride behind a thin white veil of clouds.

I hiked for twenty more minutes and when I ascended the ridge, everything suddenly opened up, and there it was — snowy peaks, Table Mountain, a triumphant river, and scattered stone homes — Thanza! "Wow," I said, stunned. "It's beautiful."

Thanza was everything Marie Brown and everyone else said it would be — breathtaking, awe-inspiring, and otherworldly. And again, I had to laugh at the notion of a supine ogress reclined across the mountains of Bhutan, for these valley walls joined together like two gentle hands, cupped together in a gesture of offering.

As I gazed out on this infinite expanse of mountains, I couldn't stop smiling. While many people have felt insignificant and small in the face of such immensity, right then, right there, I felt bigger than belief and felt humans mattered more to the planet now than ever before.

"Amazing!" I proclaimed, reaching for my camera.

From there, the trail descended to the river, crossed it on a wooden bridge, and wound up to the collection of homes whose children I could already see swarming around Joe, Kira, Rob, Ryan, and Tom. "I will hike down there," I thought, "but not before taking another sweet sip of this view." I inhaled deeply, gathering up all the majesty before me, and then I held my breath, allowing it to seep into me on a cellular level. We have landscapes living in us — particles of past trips, dancing in our DNA — Paul shines the magic of Mongolia, Ryan radiates with the enchantment of Easter Island, and in Peter swims all the splendorous colors of clear South Pacific reefs. I'd decided years ago that my goal would be to inhale as many landscapes of our beautiful world as I could. When I couldn't hold my breath any longer that day, I exhaled slowly. But I didn't exhale Thanza — I exhaled everything that wasn't Thanza, which is to say, everything that was not triumphant, joyous, alive, and everlasting. I exhaled everything that wasn't me.

Of course, I was reminded that the path to paradise is neither easy, nor safe, and has often been compared to the sharp edge of a razor. As I started down the bluff, the trail immediately thinned into a perilous and boot-wide path with a sheer drop-off to the river. One misstep and my head would've cracked on the rocks below like a crab claw. But I took my time and began synchronizing my breath to match my steps, right foot, left foot, inhale, exhale, right, left. A few stones got kicked over the edge as I descended, but minutes later, I found myself standing on the bridge leading to Thanza. While I still had eight days of trekking ahead of me, I couldn't help but feel a part of my journey was ending right there with that river crossing.

It was a journey that had really begun when I crossed that bridge on day six with the compassionate and wise-eyed monk near Lingshi and was seized with the feeling that everything was, and always would forever be, all good. Buddhism has often been referred to as a "vehicle" or "vessel" that carries the aspirant from one shore to another, from the littered city of samsara to enlightenment's island oasis. I knew great revelations, and perhaps the ultimate realization, awaited me in Thanza, so needless to say, I hurried across.

24

I DIDN'T GET A CLEAR VIEW OF TABLE MOUNTAIN THAT afternoon but it didn't matter. In the same way one word can stand for a thousand words in a secret Buddhist text, one glimpse of even a small section of Table Mountain was more dazzling than a thousand full views of lesser mountains. We spent the afternoon in Thanza, meeting the villagers, challenging the local kids to running races, and in Peter's case, purchasing an authentic "Lunap" hat from one of the local women. Like the women in Laya, the women in Lunana had a distinctive style of dress, namely the large wool hat they wore.

Later, as we tossed stones playing a game called *daygo* — the Bhutanese equivalent of bocce ball — Kira informed us she had made arrangements for a local shaman to visit us that night and bless our group. Kira was no stranger to shamans; she'd sipped *ayahuasca* — the "vine of the soul" — with Peruvian shamans in the Amazon and written a great article about her experiences.

"Where do you hear about these guys?" I gasped. "I can't imagine a shaman has a Web site."

Kira laughed. "Just be ready, it will be the experience of a lifetime."

Later, as we dug into butter dough Normans, we sipped tea, speculated about the shaman, and held high-brow intellectual discourse on the varied names for a mullet hairdo.

Wearing her large fur hat, a Thanza woman and her baby boy stop to say hello. Photo by Peter McBride.

Suddenly a man, trembling with terror, burst into our tent. He was a local man in his late twenties, wearing jeans and a brown jacket, with unruly black hair and wild eyes. He immediately began barking at Norbu in Dzongkha, and as the two talked in rapid-fire cadences, it was clear there was an emergency. Tragedy needs no translation.

"What is it?" asked Joe, standing.

Norbu told us this man, Chagay, had a sick mother. "She can't keep any food down. She has intense stomach pain and hasn't eaten in a week. His mom is dying."

Chagay held his hat in his hands and had the weary look of someone sleep-deprived and suffering. Norbu motioned for Chagay to follow him into the kitchen tent for tea while we talked things over.

When they were gone, Kira was quick to speak. "We have to do something!"

"Has he taken her to the Basic Health Unit in Lhedi?" asked Paul.

"The doctor at the Basic Health Unit isn't around," replied Joe. "He's in Gasa getting supplies."

"Then we have to call a helicopter," declared Kira.

"Wait," I said. "Let's think this over for a second."

Kira asked what there was to think about. "His mother is dying. We can pool our funds to pay for a helicopter."

"But who will go with her?" posed Ryan.

"Her family!"

"And how will they get back?" asked Larry.

Kira said we could help with that too. Such a response wasn't uncharacteristic from Kira — she'd once bought two female Bella slaves in Africa for $130 for the sole purpose of setting them free.

"How much are flights?" I asked.

"It's not about the money!" she exclaimed. "We can save a life."

"Look Kira," said Joe, "we don't like asking these tough questions any more than you like hearing them. But we have to do the right thing for all involved."

"Helicopter evacs cost around twenty-five thousand dollars per person," said Tom. "Most of us don't have that kind of money, and since we're not the ones being evacuated, our travel insurance won't cover the cost."

We all sat straight-spined, listening.

"If we get a helicopter this time," added Paul, "the villagers might expect trekkers to do the same thing anytime someone gets sick in the future."

"But we can save a life," said Kira, near tears. "Maybe they'll reduce the fees or waive them altogether."

We couldn't deny Kira's intentions, and I loved the fierce determination with which she was ready to drop everything to help someone. However, we also couldn't dismiss the reality of the situation.

Larry set down his cup of tea. "She's an old woman at the end of her life — there isn't much we can do."

Kira was silent, gazing down at her tea.

"If we really want to help Bhutan," Tom volunteered, "we should help the kids. We could set up a charity for the children, maybe at Lingshi school."

"I'd be up for that," said Larry.

"But that's in the future," protested Kira, looking up. "We can do something now!"

"Do we have anything in the first-aid kit?" I volunteered.

"It's not that we don't want to save her," tossed out Ryan, "We just want to make the best long-term decision considering all angles."

When Norbu returned, Joe asked him what he thought.

"There is nothing we can do," said Norbu. "These things happen."

Kira nodded sadly. "Can we at least give her some pills?"

"For sure," said Joe. "We have some anti-nausea pills to stop the vomiting and some oral rehydration solution to replace electrolytes."

We all immediately agreed on this treatment, and as we got the pills out of the expedition first-aid kit, Chagay returned. We instructed him about how to administer the medication and updated him on the new plan: we will give him the pills tonight to take home to his mother, and he'll return tomorrow to give us an update. Rob also reminded us the Hausers would be in Chozo tomorrow, and they had a doctor traveling with them.

Chagay took the pills, thanked us with a nod, and disappeared out of the tent, leaving us seated in a cold silence.

Moments later, as we staggered in a daze to our tents to wait for dinner, the sun dropped behind a western ridge, bathing that once-sunny valley with shadows. I didn't need my headlamp to navigate, but nonetheless, night had arrived.

THAT MY FIRST INTRODUCTION TO THANZA — THIS SHANGRI-LA — involved suffering felt like a kick in the stomach. As I lay down in my tent after tea, I shifted anxiously in my sleeping bag, but no matter what position I took, comfort eluded me. This wasn't supposed to happen. Thanza was supposed to be a spiritual oasis where nobody grew old or died. Why, then, did our first introduction involve great suffering? I felt shortchanged, as if I'd been spiritually slapped in the face, a victim of some elaborate beyul bait-and-switch scheme. Seeking relief, I scanned my memory for quotes from novels, movies, poems, and music lyrics — quotes that had always inspired me in the past. Normally, the quotes were quick to come but not that night. As I flipped through the pages of *Letters to a Young Poet*, even Rilke left me empty-handed. Desperate for my mind to be elsewhere, I tried singing Springsteen but the songs that came to mind — "Darkness on the Edge of Town," "Lonesome Day," and the "Devil's Arcade" — only reminded me of what I was trying to forget. And when I did have a clear thought, it was about the relationship between joy and pain that threatened the very sanctity of Shangri-La and had life-changing consequences. I wanted to be away from that thought immediately, so I was relieved when Peter knocked on my tent door and told me to come outside right away.

I peeked my head out. "What's up?"

"The shaman is here," said Peter. "And he's shit-faced!"

25

I FOLLOWED PETER THROUGH THE BLISTERY DARKNESS TO the dining tent and found Ryan, Rob, Joe, Kira, Larry, Tom, and Paul in the dining tent, but I hardly recognized them. As I peered around the table, not one person was smiling or talking. Everyone looked sad, defeated, and as if they might burst into tears. *Everyone cries on the Snowman Trek*—maybe this was why. There was no doubt the incident with Chagay's mom had changed the chemical composition of both the air and ourselves. For the first time on the trek, everyone looked helpless.

Across the table from us, a Bhutanese man held a double-headed drum. He was in his mid-fifties with uncombed graying hair and a chipped front tooth. He wore a red jacket, gray pants, and a string of *mala* beads circled around his right wrist a few times to form a bracelet.

I leaned over to Ryan. "Is that the shaman?"

Ryan informed me the shaman was on break.

"That's cool," I said. "I need a break, you need a break, shamans need breaks."

Norbu shook his head no. "I think his shaman has been hitting the Hit beer."

We sat in a depressed silence for a few minutes, then, moments later, the tent door opened and the shaman appeared. He wore a red robe, his head was shaved, and he looked very similar to the monk I met near Lingshi. That is, until he stumbled to his seat; there was no doubt that the shaman was totally blitzed. As he collapsed into his chair, I wanted to slap him on the back and say, "Been there, bro!" but I didn't because when the shaman gazed across the candles at us, he looked possessed. The monk in Lingshi had twinkling eyes, but the shaman had a pair of haunted black eyes, glazed over with milky cataracts. His eyes stabbed into me and through me. Not only did I have the sudden feeling he knew every bad thing I'd ever done in my life (i.e., teeing off on frogs) but I also had the disconcerting feeling that he could read my thoughts. That wasn't good because, right then, my thought was "Shit, get me outta here." There was no doubt the shaman had stared down some demons in his day, I just hoped he'd also kept the company of angels.

The shaman started into his mantra, which due to drink, was all mumbling and incoherent and sounded like, "Ommanipadmehu-mommanipadmehum." As the shaman slurred his words, his eyelids lifted and lowered and he appeared to pass in and out. I'd heard of a shaman visiting hidden spiritual realms and passing in and out of consciousness, but this wasn't what I had in mind. As the shaman continued, his head nodded up and down with sleep, I noticed his assistant was using the goat-skin drum as a sort of meditation bell — the moment the shaman's eyes dropped, his assistant banged the drum to wake him up. I bit my lip not to laugh.

Well, there is something about being in a situation where you know you shouldn't laugh that suddenly everything becomes funny. It used to happen to me at church as a boy — usually right after communion when the whole congregation was kneeling and you could hear a pin drop. On those occasions, the laughter from me and my siblings followed a typical pattern — one of us would chuckle and that chuckle would spread to the other two. Attempts to stop or hide these chuckles would lead to quiet giggling and then we'd all just suddenly burst out with loud laughter.

A similar scene happened with the shaman in the dining tent. As he continued mumbling mantras, passing in and out of consciousness, isolated chuckles began to erupt. Attempts to disguise these chuckles as coughs, bit lips, or cleared throats proved unsuccessful, and the chuckles quickly grew contagious and passed from me to Ryan to Tom to Paul to Peter and on down the line. When further attempts to suppress our chuckling led to quiet giggling, I knew we were doomed. Any moment, our chuckles would breach their banks and the laughter levee would break. Once this happened, the shaman would be terribly offended and would send us all to eternal damnation.

When the shaman stood, I assumed he was leaving, but instead, he reached into the pocket of his robe and started tossing rice to bless us. During our puja ceremony before the trek started, a monk tossing rice wasn't a cause for comedy, but it sure was that evening in Thanza. When a shaman can't see straight, he tends to not throw straight, and rice flew everywhere. When the rice hit its intended target — us — it stung like a bee. But it didn't hurt enough to stop that rising tide of chuckles. "We're doomed," I thought. And we would've been too, but just before everything went to hell (including us), the monk abruptly stopped. He quickly gathered his things and stumbled out of the tent.

The moment he was gone, we all lost it and even Achula, Sonam, and Sangey were in stitches. When the shaman didn't return, his assistant informed us that he was finished for the night. Suddenly worried, I asked Norbu if we had insulted the shaman by laughing.

Norbu laughed. "I don't think the shaman knew what was going on."

As we collected money to thank the shaman with a tip, I was about to make a joke — some dismissive comment questioning the shaman's authenticity — but when I looked around the tent, everyone's happy demeanor fully registered with me. What a change! Half an hour ago, after the incident with Chagay's mom and before the shaman stepped into the tent, everyone looked helpless and defeated. But not anymore, everyone looked . . . alive. In fact, if someone were to ask me now, I'd say that something had been exorcised that night. As I threw a few ngultrums in for the shaman's tip, I thought about the Divine Madman and his unorthodox way of teaching students and how Buddhist teachings, like water, often take the shape of their container. With our history of sipping Pabst Blue Ribbon and Hit beer at high altitude, the shaman probably knew that outwardly appearing drunk was the way to reach us and draw a laugh from a trekking party, momentarily languished with despair. Perhaps the shaman did sense our despair and tailor his teachings to his crowd, reminding us that although death may take us all tomorrow, in the present moment, it was important to eat, drink, and be merry. It couldn't have been a more perfect antidote to our uncharacteristic dark mood.

26

WHEN CHAGAY RETURNED THE NEXT MORNING, WE LEARNED his mother couldn't hold down the pills or the rehydration solution. However there was some good news, a yak herder had informed Norbu the doctor was back at the Basic Health Unit in Lhedi, and if Chagay hiked down with his mother, he should also cross paths with the doctor in the Hauser group. While this didn't solve the problem, it was the best case scenario of a worst case situation.

At breakfast we discussed further ideas on how we could help Bhutan, including contributing money to an organization that supports schools or, possibly, a charity that helps deliver food to the children since the World Food Program has plans to slowly pull out of Bhutan by 2015. As I heard Tom, Kira, Paul, and the others toss out ideas, I couldn't help but think that this was adventure tourism at its best—people visit a place, fall in love, and are motivated to protect it. It dawned on me that travel can, indeed, change the world. After all, it was a trip that prompted Greg Mortensen to build schools in Pakistan, a trip to the Amazon that inspired Sting and his wife to start the Rainforest Foundation, and a trip to Africa that prompted U2's Bono to help start the ONE Campaign. In a world where governments are increasingly interested in building barriers and insisting on our separateness, it is up to travelers to tear down the walls, reveal our shared humanity, and cause the good kind of global warming — the thawing of the human heart.

As we ate, Norbu updated us on our itinerary. "Today we will trade our yaks from Laya for some yaks from Sephu, the village we pass on the last day of the trek."

Joe also told us our route would be modified from the standard Snowman Trek itinerary. "Most groups make the trek from Thanza to Tsho Chena in one day, which is fine, but we are going to split the 9.9-mile hike up into two days since we're not taking a full rest day in Thanza." He explained we'd be gaining more than 2,822 feet of elevation, crossing the 16,890-foot Jaze La, and camping at 16,272 feet at Tsho Chena. "Instead of hiking to Tsho Chena, we will hike only 4.3 miles and ascend 1,640 feet to a campsite called Djundje, or Danji."

As Joe went into more detail about the next few days — about the high passes, high camps, and high likelihood for snow that awaited, I realized we were about to traverse another difficult and dangerous section of the Snowman.

While we waited for the new yaks to arrive, I dragged out one of the folding chairs to sit in the bright, early sunshine and take it all in — horses nuzzling their noses into feed bags, snow pigeons clapping across the sky, and blue cloud shadows on green mountains. Suddenly Table Mountain removed her veil of clouds and flashed an expansive summit smile of pure snow, rock, and ice. Naturally, I rose from my chair and faced this altar of ice and snow to receive this vow and then, like a groom, nodded. "I do!"

Moments later, as our new yak team approached in the distance, I saw Achula disassembling the gas cooking stove in the kitchen tent and decided to ask him about blossom rain. "Hey Achula," I said, peeking my head in. "How's it going?"

"Yes, sir," said Achula, hunched over in a Third-World squat.

I asked him what blossom rain meant. "You know, metok chharp?"

A yak wanders the grassy plain beneath Table Mountain (22,960 ft.). Photo by author.

"Yes."

"What do you mean, yes?"

Achula wiped his hands on his pants, cocked his head, and looked up at me. "Yes . . . Yes!"

I asked if he was telling me blossom rain meant "Yes."

"Yes, sir," Achula replied with doma-stained teeth. "Yes!"

"You have no idea what I'm saying do you?"

"Yes," Achula replied, going back to his stove. "Yes!"

Realizing it was hopeless, I thanked Achula with a pat on the back and left.

AN HOUR LATER, WE SAID GOOD-BYE TO THE VILLAGERS and began our hike out of Thanza. We passed scattered houses with barking mastiffs and started up the trail, which rose steeply out of the valley. As the trail zigzagged up, I fell in line with Sonam, who explained that every year villagers from all over northwestern Bhutan flocked to the mountains of Lunana, Lingshi, and Laya to search for *yartsa goenbub*, a caterpillar fungus highly sought-after for its medicinal qualities and which sells at a high price. According to ancient Tibetan and Chinese medicine, the fungus could treat everything from cancer to anxiety and also serve as an aphrodisiac.

"For Ingrid, sir," Sonam said, laughing wildly.

Since it was legalized in 2002, harvesting yartsa goenbub on a sustainable basis has become the number one source of income for many residents of Lunana, allowing them to buy clothes and food without having to slaughter a yak for money.

"Can we find some today?" I asked.

Sonam smiled. "No, sir. In summer."

The trail wove up through a pastoral slope of thin bushes and knee-high grasses and then arrived at a scenic ridge, overlooking the whole valley. Stepping forth to the edge of the ledge like a captain at the bow of his ship, my hands on my hips, I inhaled miles of saw-toothed mountains that extended infinitely into Tibet and beyond. Far down below, Thanza and Chozo looked like tiny train-set towns.

"Sonam, m'boy," I said, "this is the prettiest view I've ever seen!"

Sonam nodded.

I told Sonam that after that view I could go blind and would not mind.

"Yes, sir."

"I'm not saying I want to go blind, Sonam, m'boy," I said. "I'm just saying I could."

I had no idea why I kept saying, "m'boy," except that it seemed like something a Jimmy Stewart or Tom Hanks character would say at the end of the movie, when all the drama was over and they've realized once again it's a wonderful life.

As I gazed out over this mountain sanctuary that extended gloriously in all directions, I realized there was just one thing wrong — the trail stopped.

When I asked Sonam where the trail went, he pointed behind me where a new valley tumbled into Thanza. "That way, sir."

"What way?"

"South, sir," Sonam said quietly pointing.

"Why south?"

Sonam looked down and worked the dirt with his shoe. "South is home."

I laughed nervously. "You mean we have to leave this valley now?"

"Yes, sir."

With that, Sonam looked away, which is the polite thing to do after delivering heartbreaking news: you give someone the privacy of their own sadness. It dawned on me that I was then at a moment of departure, not arrival. Instead of an inspired hello, I would have to exhale a whispered good-bye to Thanza. And as strange as it sounds, I never saw it coming. Sure there were signs it was ending — the new yaks and Joe's and Norbu's very clear and explicit debriefing about the itinerary at breakfast. But sometimes, when you don't want something to end, you don't see the signs even though you see the signs. *The trip is ending and you still haven't found contentment,* my inner critic barked, *you're still searching!* As I heard this voice for the first time in five days, I suddenly grew worried that all my revelations since arriving in Lunana — that "earth is amazing" and "anything is possible" — would leave the moment I left Thanza. *You bet they will!* I wanted to argue with that voice but wasn't that the message of all the fairy tales and myths? Gold always turns to dust when descending from the mountain.

Sonam lifted my backpack from the ground. "We should go, sir."

I forced a smile, but inside I was dismayed with myself for not seeing the signs and letting myself think I could swing merrily on the branch of Buddhism and yet not learn its ultimate truth that everything ends — you, me, and my once-in-a-lifetime trip.

IT'S SAD WHEN YOU KNOW YOU'LL NEVER SEE SOME PLACE or someone again. You tend to extend the departure with meaningless conversation and then, as you walk away, you take good-bye glances every few feet, hoping to mold their memory into your mind. But inevitably, there comes a point where you tell yourself not to look back because it would be too hard if you did. There are two good-byes with every departure — you say good-bye to the person or place but also to that part of yourself that only that person or place brought alive. As I walked up the trail that day, hiking south into the new, slowly ascending side valley, I looked back toward Thanza every few steps, and strange as it sounds, had the sense the valley was looking back at me. How else could I explain the grass waving in the wind or the heartaching caw of a crow that flew right in line with me for a hundred yards? I didn't want it to end, but as the trail wound around undulating ridges, I told myself it was time. I had to take my good-bye glance. So I took a deep breath, stopped, and turned. But when I did, I discovered Thanza had already taken her last good-bye glance. There was nothing to see anymore, the theater curtains had closed, and my girl was gone.

WHILE THE NEW VALLEY I HIKED UP WAS ABUNDANTLY pretty with flower-freckled slopes, blue sheep grazing high on the hillside, and a river waterfalling over jagged rocks, it didn't matter. My whole psychology had changed — I was now hiking away from Thanza, whereas I'd spent the previous seventeen days hiking to it. I walked for another hour until I arrived at Danji, a small gift of grass in a valley of black rocks. Saddened, I drifted through the afternoon and evening. I was hungry yet couldn't bring myself to eat much. I was lonely yet didn't want to be around people, and as I crawled into my sleeping bag, I was exhausted but unable to sleep. A breakup will do that to you.

27

"DO YOU KNOW WHERE WE ARE?" PETER ASKED.

I looked around at the barren landscape surrounding us, and I wanted to say, "Yeah, we're lost and we're all going to freeze to death." But, instead, I opted for something more optimistic: "No."

Peter turned to Kira. "What about you?"

"I have no idea," Kira replied. "Our camp should be here, but it's not."

As negative as this sounded, Kira's comment was actually positive. If we accepted that we were lost, we might be able to save ourselves, for denial is often the underlying cause of death in the wilderness.

It was late afternoon on day nineteen and Peter, Kira, and I were wandering aimlessly on a rocky plateau above 16,000 feet with storm clouds assembling and night fast approaching. Already that day, we'd crossed two passes well over 16,000 feet and hiked nine miles. By then, our water bottles were empty and we'd long since put on the extra clothes we carried in our daypacks to keep warm.

Peter pointed to a distant ridge. "Shall we keep hiking that way?"

"I guess so," said Kira. "We don't have any better options."

Day nineteen had started beautifully. As we left Danji and hiked under sunny skies to the 16,890-foot pass at Jaze La, I decided to focus on the present, instead of on the past. Yes, I already missed Thanza terribly, but to focus on the past is to live in the past and great things would go unnoticed in the present. Once I changed my perception, the trail immediately came alive in both sight and sound. I saw air bubbles in frozen puddles wedged between rocks; snow-dusted peaks; and a string of dry, ancient lake beds, tucked in the folds of two false passes. This heart-thumping hike brought us to the majestic summit of the Jaze La, which was surrounded by 20,000-foot peaks whose tops were covered with billowing, shaving cream–like snow. From the other side of the pass, we descended slightly to a high plateau lined with majestic mountains and glacial lakes and stopped to have lunch in the warm afternoon sunshine.

Survival experts have said there's an element of human error in most every outdoor tragedy — a turnaround time was ignored while mountaineering, a dangerous shift in the tides wasn't recognized while surfing, or an avalanche beacon was left at home. This human error, when mixed with unruly elements — an injury, snowstorm, rogue wave, or avalanche — sets the scene for tragedy. As Peter, Kira, and I scrambled over the barren plateau, I realized that our mistake was a simple one: we didn't confirm our campsite with the yak herders at lunch. As we picnicked in the sun and the yak train thundered by, we simply waved and watched them disappear around the bend. After all, on most days, there was only really one place to camp on the trail.

Well, no sooner did the yaks disappear around the bend, than an armada of moody clouds rolled in and blotted out the sun, a cold wind kicked up, and the temperature dropped. The cold caused everyone to throw on all available clothing and start off down the trail to get warm. Already tragedy had scored a major point; instead of hiking as one group, we and our collective resources were spread out on the trail.

Searching for camp on a desolate plateau above 16,000 feet. Photo by Peter McBride.

As Peter, Kira, and I walked closer to the high ridge, we realized it was a pass we should've been scaling the following day — the 16,875-foot Loju La. By then, I was shivering and my inner critic was using every opportunity to break me down. *Humans are built to live in warm environments.* What's your point? *You are going to die.* No, I'm generating heat by shivering. *That's bad, instead of blood being pumped to the core vital organs of the body, it's being directed to the skin surface.* But I feel warm. *For now. Shivering burns energy and soon the shivering will stop and the downward spiral will begin.* I'll keep hiking. *No, you'll lose mental and muscular function, your heart rate will skyrocket and you'll be off to the snowy land of no return.* No, I won't. *Yes, you will!*

Instead of thinking about the many negatives, I decided to focus on the positive — I was with Kira and Peter. I couldn't have picked two better people to be lost with. Together, they probably spend more days in the wild each year than I had in my entire life. While I wanted to attach my carabiner to this thin rope of hope, my critic reminded me that we were still in serious trouble. *Peter's strength can't hold back the night.* But Kira's here too! *Ha! Kira may be able to escape kidnappers in Mozambique, but she can't outrun the approaching cold!*

"The Loju La before us," I thought to myself. "A barren plateau and two passes behind us — talk about the Snowman bottleneck!"

"Shall we hike up?" said Peter, pointing to a wall of rock standing before us.

Kira looked up. "What other choice do we have?"

"What if we get to the top of the pass and our camp isn't there?" I mused. "We'd be stuck at 17,000 feet with no shelter and night approaching."

Peter asked if I have a better idea.

I pointed to faint boot prints on weathered rocks. "How do we even know this is the right trail?"

Kira thought we should keep hiking. "Let's hike to the top of the pass to see what's beyond."

Peter nodded. "Good call. We can always hike back down here if we need to."

As we started up the pass that afternoon, I couldn't help but wonder if we did offend the deities by making noise near Chozo Dzong. I knew from reading that gods and goddesses in the Himalayas always had two manifestations — maybe that night it was Lunana in her wrathful aspect. Maybe instead of appearing, the ghosts of Lunana make things disappear — friends, food, shelter, warmth. No longer did I feel bigger than belief, I felt like an insignificant speck of life in an inhospitable universe.

During every bad trip, there comes a point when a gamble must be made, the kind that can only be judged in hindsight. If you succeed, the gamble makes you look smart. However, if you don't and you die, the gamble looks utterly ridiculous. As we clambered up the final hundred feet to the top of the pass, using our arms as much as our legs and every last ounce of energy, I knew this was our gamble. If successful, people would champion our risk and trail wisdom. If we didn't find our camp or one of us fell and got seriously injured going back down the pass, our gamble would be declared ridiculous.

When we scrambled up, there was no cairn at the Loju La, only two softball-sized rocks with one badly frayed string of prayer flags stretched between them. There was also no sign of our camp, and it appeared as if no one had passed that way in many years. Beyond the pass, another barren, rocky expanse with a shallow gray lake taunted us. We quickly fell silent, for hopelessness has no sound.

As Kira and I collapsed onto rocks to collect our breath, Peter staggered down the other side of the pass.

"It's pointless," I called out to him.

Peter waved me off and kept walking.

"We should turn around now and make it down from here before night falls," I said to Kira.

Suddenly Peter yelled. "I see tents."

"Are they ours?" I asked.

"Who cares?" said Kira, grabbing her bag. "Let's go!"

I hurried after her, and as the trail skirted the lake, I spotted our gray dome tents, far up on the right side of the rocky hill. When I arrived, I discovered our tents scattered and wedged between patches of uneven tundra. Worse, I heard yelling, yelling, and more yelling — the yak herders, our kitchen staff, and my trekking companions — everyone yelling.

I had no energy to take sides or inquire what went wrong or who was responsible. I had only energy enough to drag my bag over the rocks to an empty tent and collapse into my sleeping bag.

"The yak herders weren't trying to find a good campsite," yelled someone. "They were trying to get home early so they could get an extra day of wages!"

"No, sir," hollered Achula in response.

"That's crap!"

When a litany of expletives followed, Achula started tossing pots and pans in protest.

"The yak herders may get home early," Paul called out, joining the fray, "but they're going to kill an old man!"

Suddenly, I realized Joe and Larry had yet to arrive in camp . . . and may not. Given Larry had so much trouble early on in the trek, I could only imagine how tired he must have been that day — a nine-mile death march with three passes well over 16,000 feet. I threw on my shoes and hurried under darkening skies to the dining tent. There, I found Peter, Rob, and Norbu seated around the dining table. Norbu was trying to talk to Joe on the radio. "Hello, Joe," he said into the static. "Can you hear me?"

No response.

"It won't work," replied Peter. "They are only line-of-sight radios."

I felt my stomach drop. That night felt like one of those times where everything that could go wrong would. The black dominoes of bad luck had already begun to fall, and I wondered where and when they'd stop. At the other end of the table, Peter threw some cookies into his backpack. To his left, Rob poured hot tea into his water bottle, sending up smoke-like columns of steam into the frigid air.

"You guys going somewhere?" I asked.

"We're bringin' food and hot tea to Larry," said Rob as he packed furiously.

I asked if they knew where Larry and Joe were.

"Probably at the pass" said Peter. "But if not, we'll find them."

I reminded them night was approaching.

"Larry might not make it without us," said Rob.

"Need any help?"

"No," said Peter, "the less people out there, the better."

I took a seat, warming my hands with my breath, and watched them finish assembling gear. As I saw them throw the last items into their backpacks, I realized something special was happening before my eyes. That night I was witnessing a noble example of heroism. Even though both Peter and Rob knew that the first rule of emergency medicine is that one should never attempt a rescue unless the scene is safe; that night, they would leave behind the warm security of our camp and rush out into the cold to find Joe and Larry. Heroism isn't born in the hour of convenience — but when you're cold and tired and want nothing more than to go to sleep — and yet, you still go. Sure, I'd shake the hands of people who have summited the world's tallest mountains and congratulate them on their achievement, but show me the one man who turns back short of the summit to save the life of a stranger, and that is the man who I will invite into my living room and say, "Let me learn from you." As Peter and Rob clicked on their headlamps and shouldered their packs, I was moved to the extent that if ever the goodness of the human spirit were put on trial, I could now raise my right hand on the witness stand and tell the jury that I've seen living proof. I could testify that one dreadful night on the Snowman Trek, I saw the lamp of the human spirit burning bright.

As Peter and Rob hurried out of the tent, I called out to them. "Be safe, guys!"

They didn't answer, for they had left long ago. Already, Peter and Rob were mentally hiking with Joe and Larry.

IT WAS DARK WHEN PETER, ROB, JOE, AND LARRY ARRIVED back in camp. We were all seated in the dining tent when they staggered in and collapsed into their chairs. We didn't talk about the incident initially, but rather, tended to the most important task at hand — rehydrating and eating. Like a family who waited to eat until everyone was present, Kira, Ryan, Tom, Paul, and I had held off on having dinner until Rob, Larry, Joe, and Peter had returned. As we ate noisily, everyone seemed to gain more energy — breath deepened, skin color returned, and notched forehead creases relaxed. That was, except for Larry, who looked terribly pale, had glazed eyes, and couldn't seem to catch his breath. Despite this, when Kira asked how he was doing, Larry didn't lash out at the yak herders, he simply said to her, "Slow but steady recovery."

"Everyone is safe," noted Ryan. "All is good."

I wanted to agree, but all was not good. While we were seated in our dining tent complaining about the yakmen, the kitchen crew was in their tent complaining about us, and the yakmen were under their tarp complaining about everyone. In fact, all had gone to absolute hell. We had managed to anger those people responsible for the two most important elements of our trek — the guys who made our meals and the guys who hauled our gear. Angering the ghosts of Chozo Dzong probably would've been a better idea! Being unfairly blamed, I wouldn't be surprised if Achula refused to cook for us again. With the prospect of not getting tipped, I wouldn't blame the yak herders if they took off tonight and left us high and dry. Gone was the unity and sense of a cohesive team working toward a common goal. We had assumed a hierarchical structure and it really couldn't have happened at a worse time. We were stuck on a desolate plateau at the highest camp on the trek; we were supposed to attempt the tallest pass on the trek in two days time, and if there was any place on the trek where we were most likely to get snowbound, that was it. I remembered the wish I made for snow leaving Tarina on day five. Why did I make that wish? Stupid!

Joe looked out across the table. "What do you guys want to do?" he asked. "Do you want the yakmen to apologize to us?"

"Indeed, I do," said Paul. "They screwed us royally!"

Ryan nodded. "I think they wanted to get home a day early."

"I don't," said Peter. "They thought we instructed them to set up camp by the third lake."

"I agree," said Kira. "There was no place for the yaks to graze at the second lake."

"It's not any better here," chimed Tom. "Unless we make the yak herders accountable, they'll do the same thing to the next group."

I agreed. "They should apologize."

Peter reminded us it wasn't about who was right, it was about finishing the trek.

"Yes, but we could've had a major problem," I said.

"We could've," added Kira, "but we didn't."

Ryan consented. "Yeah, we need these guys on our side."

Joe turned to Larry. "What do you think?"

Since he was the one most affected, Larry would decide for us. If he didn't have any lingering ill feelings, then we probably shouldn't either. Larry set his tea cup down and fell silent for a few moments. "We should apologize to the yak herders. But if we discover they did try to get home a day early, then they should apologize to us."

When the yakmen filed in, it was immediately obvious it was an honest mistake. It was clear from their eyes and shame-bent heads that they were just trying to find the best camp for us. As Norbu translated, we apologized to the yakmen, Sonam, Sangey, and Achula. Then they, in turn, apologized to us. The truth was, not only did we need each other, we also liked each other.

By eight o'clock, we were all exhausted and ready for bed. "Before you guys leave," said Joe, standing, "we should figure out tomorrow's itinerary."

"What are the options?" asked Tom.

Joe laughed. "Since we've done most of tomorrow's hike today, we could cross the highest pass tomorrow, the Rinchen Zoe La, and camp beyond it. The good part of that is it would guarantee we don't get snowed in. Or we could do a very short hike to a campsite called Jichu Dramo, essentially having a rest day, and hike the Rinchen Zoe La the following day."

"But we'd still have the risk of snow," added Paul.

"It's up to you guys," said Joe.

As Joe said this, I was reminded that a good leader doesn't call all the shots but uses the collective wisdom of the group to make the best informed decision.

"If we stay at Jichu Dramo tomorrow night," said Norbu with a sly smile, "Kev could see Ingrid again."

I told them I was on this trek for purely spiritual matters. "I am above the needs of the flesh."

Tom laughed. "Wasn't it you hitting on Ingrid in Laya?"

Peter suggested, once again, the decision should be Larry's. I was happy to hear this. Less than ten days ago, we debated whether or not Larry should even be on the trek, and there he was, our elder statesman, making all decisions.

Larry finished blowing his nose at the head of the table and tucked his handkerchief in his pocket. "I know some people want to clear the pass tomorrow and be done with it. But, to be honest, I need a rest day."

The truth was, we all needed a rest day, and in speaking for himself, Larry had spoken for all of us.

"Then it's decided," said Joe. "Tomorrow will be a short day hike to Jichu Dramo . . . and another chapter of Operation Ingrid."

28

WE STARTED EARLY FROM CAMP — IF IT COULD BE CALLED that — the next morning and trudged across the expansive plateau, which rose and fell in succession like rocky sea swells. The two-hour hike up the U-shaped valley to Jichu Dramo was amazing with singing streams, curving glaciers, and a line of snowy peaks stretching up into the forever horizon. It was great knowing it was a short day — I didn't feel the least bit rushed or guilty about stopping to take a break or a flurry of pictures. After two hours, we arrived at Jichu Dramo, a little patch of golf-green grass nestled among the rocks.

Sonam and Sangey placed blankets on the soft grass and unveiled steaming, silver bowls of chicken, vegetables, tuna, rice, and mackerel — Achula's tasty apology for throwing the pots and pans. As we all dove in, Tom informed us he'd forgo lunch and hike up to a rocky spire overlooking camp.

"But you need to eat," I said like an overprotective mother.

Tom pulled three pancakes from his pockets. "I grabbed these at breakfast," he said. "They'll hold me till dinner."

I had to smile. Like the Bhutanese, Tom knew there was joy to be found in embracing difficulty and building your monastery on the side of a rocky cliff even though the flat valley floor sat easily accessible below. As I sat with my warm plate of food and watched Tom picking his way through the rocks, I couldn't help but smile and feel proud. Right then, I made a vow: When I got older, I would travel like Tom. I would not limit my travel experiences to what was comfortable or convenient, for to do so is to shrink the planet. Certainly, I found camping on the Snowman Trek to be a drag at times, my lower back hurt most every morning and having to trek to the toilet tent at night was never fun. But when I found myself standing under the stars at 2:00 a.m. in Thanza, I felt an inexpressible kind of companionship and realized I never would have had that experience if I'd been in a hotel. The backache of camping was a blessing; it gave me a key to the city of stars.

FOUR HOURS AND ONE WONDERFUL NAP IN THE SUN LATER, I was to be found getting kicked out of our dining tent, and it wasn't just because I'd eaten the last chocolate Norman.

"What are you doing sitting here?" gasped Tom. "Go!"

"Yeah," added Paul, giving me a nudge on the shoulder. "We don't want you."

"I'll drag you out of here if I have to," warned Joe.

Where did they want me to go? To go see Ingrid, of course. The Hausers had hiked into Jichu Dramo around two that afternoon and were camping ten minutes up the valley.

Ryan started pounding the table with his fists. "Do it! Do it!"

As I heard this, I felt like Chandler Bing from the TV show *Friends*, and instead of the dining tent, I was sitting in Central Perk coffee shop, with Monica (Kira), Joey (Ryan), and Ross (Rob).

"Aw Kev," cried Rob. "Give us one good reason why ya' wouldn't visit Ingrid?"

I told him I'd give him a few. "I've gone almost three weeks without a shower. I have twenty days of bed head, and despite brushing daily, my teeth feel like they're wearing wool sweaters."

Rob reminded me that the "Sheilas love a rugged bloke."

I also reminded the group that Ingrid was sharing a tent with her mother. "And let's face it, despite being in the middle of nowhere, our camp ain't exactly the most private place on the planet."

"Who cares?" said Peter. "It would be fun."

"Do it, do it, do it," Ryan began chanting again.

Paul suggested getting a female's opinion. "Kira?"

"He should go," said Kira without a second thought. "Plus we need to find out what time the Hausers are leaving for the pass tomorrow. We have to beat them!"

With that, everyone — including Sonam, Norbu, and Sangey — erupted, "Do it, do it, do it."

There was nothing I could do but accept my fate. Thus, at 3:30 p.m. on the afternoon of the twentieth day of the Snowman Trek, I wandered up to the Hauser camp to gather intelligence and embark on another chapter in the ongoing opus, "Operation Ingrid." As I started up the trail, I was filled with the knowledge that instead of my best interests, my "friends" had sent me on a crazy journey purely for their own entertainment; "Kevin-Ingrid" was a game they played just like all the others. It would have been a fun game too if I wasn't the pawn. But to be honest, I wanted to go. Everything felt predestined about the Snowman Trek — hearing about Bhutan, finding the group I was traveling with, and meeting Ingrid. While I'd only spoken with Ingrid briefly and only in a group setting, I sensed a connection between us and there seemed to be some kind of unspoken agreement when our eyes met.

As I followed the dirt trail through the rocks, I felt like I was in seventh grade again, sauntering across the cafeteria to ask Anne Fowler if she'd dance the final dance of the night with me. The final song at all of our junior high dances was always Led Zeppelin's "Stairway to Heaven." Depending on your luck with the ladies that evening, the "Stairway" meant either ten minutes of pure dancing pleasure or ten minutes of arm wrestling with the dweebs and dorks in the back. How did I fare that year? Let's just say, my right bicep got very big. You'd think approaching a girl would get easier with age, but it doesn't. With the right girl, my heart always races, my tongue trips on words, and I'm filled with the knowledge that if turned down, I'll be listening to Bob Marley's "No Woman, No Cry" nonstop for months.

It was one thing approaching Anne Fowler at a junior high school dance as Robert Plant sang about a lady who was sure all that glittered was gold, but it was quite another to stroll into a remote outpost occupied by Germans. It was crazy and, perhaps, life threatening. I had no idea how to start the conversation with Ingrid. I couldn't say, "Hey baby, come here much?" — that question didn't really work on the Snowman Trek. Nor could I pretend to "just be in the area" or feign surprise and say, "Wow, fancy meeting you here!" Borrowing an egg was out, as was buying her a drink, and lastly, there was the whole issue of her mother. How would Ingrid's mom take my barging into camp to meet her daughter? No Peter, going to the Hauser camp wasn't going to be "fun," it was going to be suicide. My trekking companions had sent me to my death and all for what — so they could have their fun!

"Forget it," I thought, stopping. "I'm turning around."

Before I could, I noticed a very disturbing sight — I'd stopped in full view of the Hauser camp. Six of them sat on blue folding chairs in front of their dining tent, waving to me. As I waved back and my feet shuffled forward on their own volition, I felt myself being drawn irresistibly forward, not unlike that scene in *Star Wars* where the Death Star's tractor beam pulls in the Millennium Falcon, and Luke and Han Solo know they are totally screwed. Only this time, instead of Stormtroopers, I'd meet a squad of Germans, and sitting in for Darth Vader with a light saber would be Ingrid's mother wielding a trekking pole. As I approached, I prayed, "May the force be with me. May the force be with me!"

The Germans were camped in a little hilly patch of grass, set among quiet streams and infinite rocks. As I approached, I noticed a very disconcerting sight: Ingrid was missing, and I'd be meeting the six other adults who comprised her trekking party. Not good. That would be like having that awkward pre-date living room conversation with three sets of parents. I was always great in high school, I'd take a seat, fold my hands politely in my lap and say something like, "Why yes, Mr. and Mrs. Fowler, I plan on attending an institution of higher education after graduation and really hitting the books so I can make something out of my life." However, with the Hausers, I had no idea what to say — the only German words I knew were *bier* and *die toilette,* and until then, I thought that's all I needed to know in any language. As I stepped over a small stream announcing my arrival into their camp, I realized I was in trouble because, if accused, I could not defend myself because I did have eyes for Ingrid.

I would have been doomed too if the Bhutanese guides weren't the best on the planet. Sure, they're experts on Buddhism and Bhutan's culture, and they do us all a favor by wearing long underwear under their knee-length robes, but they also know how to help a brother out. The moment I entered camp and said a quick hello to the group sitting outside, the Hausers' Bhutanese guide ran up to my side and shook my hand.

"Welcome, sir," he said. "I am Dawa. So happy to make your acquaintance." Then he turned and informed the rest of the Hausers that tea was ready and that they should proceed to the dining tent. The six of them chatted with me for a few moments — all very friendly and personable — and then they filed into the dining tent.

A moment later, Dawa returned. "I will go get Ingrid, sir," he said with a wink.

When I realized that it would be Ingrid and me sitting alone before a panorama of snowy mountains, I decided Dawa would get my vote for Best Guide in Bhutan.

When Ingrid appeared, she looked great. She wore wool socks

under her camp sandals, black leggings, and a red sporty vest over a wickable, white shirt. Her hair was tucked back in a cute European-style cap and her rosy cheeks perfectly framed her wide, white smile.

"Hello there!" she said, lighting up.

"Hey," I said, "I just came by to say hello."

"Great!" she said with a hug, "Have a seat."

As Ingrid and I took a seat overlooking vast mountains, Dawa hurried up with a cup of hot tea. "To keep you warm while you are visiting, sir."

Forget Best Guide, Dawa would now get my vote to be the new Prime Minister of Bhutan.

As we settled in, I asked Ingrid how she liked Thanza.

Ingrid informed me they camped in Chozo. "But I did a day hike to Thanza. Amazing!"

"Did you notice a little boy in Chozo with a bow and arrow named Pema?"

"Oh god," Ingrid exclaimed, "he was the cutest kid I've ever seen!"

When I asked if the doctor in the Hauser group had looked at Chagay's mom, Ingrid shook her head. "She didn't have to. She could tell by her symptoms that it was the end."

I felt a twinge of sadness, so I changed the subject and asked Ingrid how she heard about the Snowman Trek. However, before she could answer, a woman in her late fifties appeared.

"Uh oh," I thought. "The mother."

"You must be Kevin," she said with a smile. "I'm Gerti."

I stood up and shook her hand. "Nice to meet you."

Gerti was a sweet, soft-spoken woman in her mid-fifties with reddish hair and a delightful demeanor. As we sat, I was about to start into the whole "do something good with my life" bit from high school, but then I realized I didn't have to. If you're on the Snowman Trek, you're already doing something good with your life.

As Dawa brought another drink for Ingrid's mom, I realized this was a Snowman Trek memory in the making—sitting here with Ingrid and her mother, the hot tea, the mountains, and everything glowing with that luminous late-afternoon light.

"How cool is it that your Mom is doing the Snowman Trek," I said, glancing at Ingrid and her Mom. "How did you convince her to do that?"

"I convinced her," Gerti piped in.

Ingrid laughed. "Yes, but you didn't tell me anything about the mileage or the duration."

"You didn't ask!" Gerti said to Ingrid, grinning.

I turned to Ingrid to get the story straight. "Your mom invited you, and you had no idea about the Snowman Trek when you signed up?"

"Pretty much," Ingrid declared. "But I'd always wanted to visit Bhutan."

I told Ingrid I liked her style. "Well, at least you were in great shape."

Ingrid shook her head no. "I've been stuck in a library working on school papers. And then I caught a terrible cold a month before the trip."

"That's crazy," I said. "I trained like a madman. Well, except for the mandatory 'board meetings' my brother called any time the waves were head high and glassy."

"I'd love to learn how to surf," Ingrid mused.

"Well, you've got a teacher now!"

The conversation was immediately scary, but not because it was strained and awkward, but because it was so easy and effortless. As we exchanged travel stories, Gerti told us about trekking in Nepal, Ingrid talked about Switzerland, and I mentioned hiking in New Hampshire's White Mountains while growing up. Then we talked about our families, Germany, the United States, our guides, and of course, how we heard about Bhutan. People always had amazing stories about how they first discovered Bhutan and spoke about the experience with a kind of blushing pride reserved for a romance which, indeed, it was.

When the sun dropped behind the western ridge, Dawa appeared once again.

"It is getting cold," he said. "We should move into the dining tent."

I expected the tent to be filled with the rest of the Hausers, followed by a military-style interrogation about my true intentions for infiltrating their camp, but once again, Dawa had come to the rescue. The tent was empty.

"Where is everyone?" I asked.

"I advised them to get some rest before the big pass tomorrow," he said, chuckling.

By then, I was convinced Dawa should win a Nobel Peace Prize on account of his many gifts to humanity.

As we sat, Gerti brought us each a blanket and informed us that she too would be taking a brief nap. "It was great meeting you," I said, "See you on top of the Rinchen Zoe La tomorrow!"

As Gerti disappeared, Ingrid and I continued our conversation in the cozy tent. She told me about school and her upcoming graduate thesis, and when she asked about screenwriting, I didn't feel the least bit uncomfortable about telling her that if I didn't get the Disney Fellowship, I was dropping the dream.

"Yeah," she said. "There's a fine line between working at something and having something not work out."

"If Disney turns me down," I confessed, "I'll just take it as the universe telling me I should do something else."

Ingrid agreed, and I realized the best people in the world are those you can tell your dreams to and who don't chuckle when you say an esoteric phrase like "the universe."

"Sometimes you can be so focused on a goal, you miss other options," Ingrid replied.

I nodded and then we both looked out the tent window and fell silent watching the alpenglow paint the mountains pink. The most important thing in a relationship is a shared sense of awe, and there was no doubt Ingrid and I had it.

Suddenly Ingrid sat up in her chair and looked at me. "Oh dear, it's almost dark."

"Huh?" I said, snapping out of my reverie.

Dusk was descending on the valley, and Ingrid asked if I had a flashlight.

I told her I didn't.

She stood, wiping cookie crumbs off her lap. "Then you must leave right now."

"Well, I don't think I have to leave right . . . "

"Yes, now!"

I'd never disliked the arrival of night so much. "I guess you're right," I said softly, my voice trailing off.

We left the dining tent, and I stopped by the kitchen tent to thank Dawa for his hospitality. Then, as Ingrid walked me to the trail, I again felt like I was in junior high, wondering if I should put on the moves or not. As we stepped over a trickling stream, already icing up, I was plagued with similar seventh-grade feelings of inaction. Certainly, I hadn't planned on kissing Ingrid goodnight, but after our conversation, a kiss kind of felt right. In fact, I felt closer to Ingrid after only two hours of talking in the tent than I had to girls I'd dated for two months. Plus, she was walking me to the trail—that was a good sign. I decided it was worth a shot, and if she turned her cheek or got offended, I'd defend my action by informing her that science has shown that a passionate kiss uses all thirty-four muscles of the face, improves skin tone and circulation, and emits the same neurotransmitters as parachuting. "No I can't kiss her," I suddenly thought. Trying to kiss a girl on the Snowman Trek was just so cheesy. I went to Bhutan to trek, not to tongue wrestle. In that context, a kiss seemed ridiculous. Forget that, I will kiss her.

No I won't. Yes I will. *No I won't.* I will. *I won't.* Will. *Won't.* Will. *Won't.* Will. *Won't.*

When we arrived at the trail leading to my camp and I still wasn't sure, I stalled by asking if her group was leaving early for the pass.

"I think so," said Ingrid. "We always leave early."

"That's cool," I said, half listening. "Early departures are good."

When an awkward silence ensued, I didn't know what to do so I asked her the first question that popped into my head. "How do you say good-bye in German?"

Ingrid laughed. "Formally you might say, *Auf Wiedersehen,* but most people where I live use the Bavarian phrase, *Servus.*"

"Servus," I repeated.

Ingrid zipped up her coat all the way, until her chin was half hidden. "Servus."

"Wait," I said, putting up a hand. "I didn't mean we had to say good-bye right now."

Ingrid reminded me it was getting dark and I needed to get back.

"Okay," I said, certain that was a sign not to kiss her.

But then she looked deep into my eyes, and I thought, "That's a good sign!" But a moment later she took a step backward, and I thought, "No wait, that's a bad sign."

"Servus, Ingrid," I said, taking a step back myself.

With that, Ingrid bit her lip, tilted her head as if trying to figure me out, shrugged with a smile, and then spun around to start back to her camp.

That spin will haunt me for the rest of my life because (a) it was the coolest spin I'd ever seen, and (b) with it, I realized I should have kissed her. *You idiot!* my inner critic howled. I did the right thing! *Are you kidding me?* I was being a gentleman. *You were being an idiot!* As I started back toward my camp, I tried to convince my critic I did the polite thing by not kissing her, but to be honest, I couldn't even convince myself. As I stumbled back through cold rocks and dark swirling skies, I was filled with remorse. I wanted to forget the visit with Ingrid ever occurred, but as I arrived at our dining tent, I realized there were eight reasons why I couldn't and they went by the names of Tom, Ryan, Joe, Peter, Paul, Rob, Kira, and Larry.

29

"DON'T WORRY," SAID RYAN, THE FOLLOWING MORNING AT breakfast, "It's happened to all of us."

Norbu reminded me we'd be traveling close to the Hausers for the remainder of the trip. "You will get another chance."

"And if things don't work out with her," added Joe, "there are always sheep."

Just then, the tent flaps flew open and Rob and Kira burst in. "Cooee, comrades," shouted Rob with a mock accent, "Ve must hurry! Operation Squash Bratwurst haz begun. Ve must beat ze Germans to ze pass!"

Beating the Germans to the pass was another game we'd invented to keep our feet moving. And as a result, on the morning of the twenty-first day, breakfast was a fast affair.

As I drank my oatmeal from the bowl and swallowed half-chewed pieces of toast, I was reminded of my rushed life back in California, where I was perpetually doing two things at once. One of the joys of the trek had been that it had reminded me to be mindful and take joy in the pure engagement of only doing one thing at a time, be it hiking, conversing, or reading. That morning, I was reminded how awful stress felt in the body: the shallow breath, the tight muscles, and the vice-grip jaw.

Moments later, we were racing up the trail under cloudless morning skies. Rob and Kira led the way followed by Tom, Ryan, Norbu, Paul, and myself. As we ran, Ryan yelled back to me. "Where were the Hausers camped?"

"Should be right around the corner!" I yelped.

To be honest, I had no clue. I was too nervous going to the Hauser camp and too remorseful coming home to remember anything about the trail.

"Hurry," hollered Peter as he ran, his camera gear clinking in his bag.

"I bet the Hausers are already at the pass," cried Tom.

Well, the Hausers weren't at the pass. In fact, they were not even hiking. When we raced around the next corner, we saw them sitting at a table in front of their dining tent. The Hausers were having breakfast outside, savoring the sun and a slow start to the day as only the Europeans seem to know how to do.

As we rushed by, Ingrid waved. "Join us!" she called, and my feet slowed.

"Don't!" yelled Tom. "It's a trap!"

I declined Ingrid's invitation with a wave and hurried on, rushing up the valley and leaping from rock to rock in great hurdles. I felt strong at the start, but twenty minutes up the trail, everything just gave out and I had to stop.

"You alright, Kev?" said Paul, running over.

"Keep . . . going," I managed, hunched over with my hands on my knees. "I'll . . . catch . . . up."

"You sure?"

"Go!"

As Paul scampered on, there was no question that running above 16,000 feet was hard on the heart. But as my breath slowly returned, I began to think my heart gave out for different reasons. As I gazed out at the scenic valley, I was filled with remorse for rushing through breakfast, missing a visit with Ingrid, and not stopping to take pictures. They were moments that couldn't be repeated, even if I did retrace my steps and walk back down the hill. Remembering my pledge from the first day of the trek to slow down everything, I decided to walk the rest of the way to Rinchen Zoe La.

After crossing a little stream, the trail started its direct ascent toward the pass, climbing up steeply through the rocks. Immense snowbound mountains exploded from scree slopes and a string of glacial lakes appeared. When I saw a large flat rock, perfect for sitting, I sat. As I did and my breath slowed, a sense of peace and calm abiding arrived. Despite seeing Rob, Kira, Tom, and Ryan celebrating at the pass and hearing their triumphant cries in the distance, I had no desire to move. From my little seat, I could see the 17,470-foot summit of Rinchen Zoe La, and gazing in the other direction, the bottom of the valley far down below. As I sat there, I thought about the nature of my contentment. Was that seat giving me a lesson about the Middle Way? In Buddhist texts, I'd read about the paths of life being compared to the strings of a lute. As the Buddha taught, "When the strings of the lute are loose, its sound won't carry. When the strings are too tight, it breaks. Only the Middle Way, not too tight and not too loose, will produce harmonious sound." I thought of the prayer flags on day five and that rope hanging down from heaven. Maybe the lesson of my seat was that true contentment wouldn't be found at the highest or the lowest point on the horizon but at the immovable, middle spot where I could behold each equally and completely.

Suddenly I noticed Larry plodding along below, mindfully and reverently in his orange hunting jacket — ever aware of his breath, ever in the moment. I couldn't help but smile to myself. "Oh, Larry," I thought. "Soon you will return to Jersey to hang up your victorious coat in the closet, and at the supermarket some distracted teenager, text-messaging, will cut in front of you in line and never even notice.

Front (*from left*): Sangey, Peter, Nema (horseman); back (*from left*): Sonam, Larry, Rob, Joe, the author, Ryan, Tom, Paul, Kira. Photo courtesy of the author.

He will not know that before him stands a great and accomplished man, a hero and a yogi who has completed the Snowman Trek at age sixty-six on courage and guts alone. He won't know, Larry, but we do!" That there were Larrys and others like him strolling the streets of the world — plainclothes superheroes — inspired me that day and made me feel ever hopeful.

I waited for Larry, and fifteen minutes later, he came plodding up.

"What happened to the race?" he asked.

"I dropped out," I said. "Shall we walk to the pass together?"

"Slowly but surely."

The great irony was that the highest pass of the Snowman Trek was also the easiest. We camped less than a thousand feet below the Rinchen Zoe La. There were no false passes and no unruly rocks, and the trail was dry and smooth. Larry and I made it to the top quite comfortably, and as we crossed the finish line of cairns, we yelled "Lha Gyalo!" together, triumphantly.

We had a great celebration at Rinchen Zoe La, the tenth and highest pass of the trek. The view was breathtaking — prayer flags, snowy peaks, scattered glacial lakes, and mighty Gangkhar Puensum. At 24,734 feet, Gangkhar is not only the tallest mountain in Bhutan but also the world's highest unclimbed peak. And though the Zen koan said, "When you reach the top of the mountain, keep climbing," I had no desire to hike higher — my cup runneth over right there.

When Norbu suggested we take a group picture, we all assembled and huddled in close.

"On the count of three," he said, holding my camera. "Say 'yak cheese.'"

At the start of the trek, I swore I'd never take a picture like this. In the back of every adventure travel magazine, you see the same trekking picture in the classified section — a group of travelers standing atop a snowy mountain pass with arms raised triumphantly under perfectly blue skies. Prior to the Snowman Trek, I thought such moments were few and far between. I was certain those pictures were false advertising that hid the real truths of diarrhea, altitude sickness, and rainy skies. Before that moment at Rinchen Zoe La, I thought such joyous pictures were fake, but know what? They're not.

BEFORE WE STARTED DOWN, NORBU TOLD US THAT RINCHEN Zoe La marked the end of the Lunana District. "From here we will be traveling in the Wangdue Phodrang Dzongkhag," he said. "This will be our final sight of Lunana and her mountains, so take a last look now."

I waited for the others to start down from the pass so I could have a quiet moment alone with Lunana. I assumed I'd be sad at that moment, but to be honest, as I gazed back over vast peaks extending in all directions, I couldn't stop smiling. Hidden somewhere in those great mountainous folds was the village of Thanza, where Lunana's pretty hands were still, and forever would be, cupped together in a gesture of offering. "Thank you for letting me in, Lunana," I said with my eyes closed and head bowed. "Thank you for gracing me with your presence." Then I blinked my eyes open and gave her a great wave. "Don't be a stranger!"

A glance good-bye at Lunana. Photo by author.

30

OUR ITINERARY FOR THE TWENTY-SECOND DAY CALLED FOR a 9.5-mile hike from our riverside camp at Chhu Karpo to a lakeside camp at Tampoe Tsho. The trail continued down the valley from our camp, and as it did, I found myself uncharacteristically apathetic to both the scenery and my experience. Certainly part of the reason was that the Hausers had camped across the river from us after the Rinchen Zoe La, and I didn't get to see Ingrid again, but the main reason was that I'd been in Bhutan for more than three weeks and had seen twenty-two days of stunning mountains, dazzling rhododendrons, and rivers. Regardless, such apathy frightened me, so when I saw Joe hiking up ahead, I told him what was on my mind and asked a very pressing question. "Am I normal?"

Joe said that that kind of thing happened a lot on trips. "When I took clients to Africa," he began, "they were begging me to stop the van anytime they saw a lion for the first two days. But by the time the third day arrived, they only wanted me to stop the van on two occasions: if the lions were fighting or getting *very* friendly—if ya know what I mean."

I didn't like the thought of taking Bhutan for granted. "How do you prevent it from happening?"

Joe told me to find new things to look at or new ways of looking at the old things. "Like a river, you can't hike the same trail twice. Not only is it changing, but you are too."

I asked Joe if he really believed that.

"For sure," Joe said, his feet dancing over mossy rocks. "I've done the Everest Base Camp trek in Nepal for years. Yet every time I go, I discover something new about the trail."

From there, we talked about the importance of finding one moment each day that reminds you why you're doing what you're doing. "Ideally, you'll have a lot of moments each day," said Joe. "But on the days you don't, just find one good moment."

As he said this, I realized that in the past, I'd thought something was broken if it wasn't perfect all the time. And yet, this trek—this amazing experience—had been a wonderful combination of rain, sun, sleet, and snow. Maybe Sangey was right on day three, maybe my definition of perfection was wrong.

As Joe hiked in front of me, I realized his job wasn't so much being a trekking guide but rather a moment maker. His job, which he did exceedingly well, was to take care of all the logistical and safety concerns so people could literally and emotionally have peak experiences.

To make the hike more exciting, I decided to challenge myself to see what I could find new about that valley. Instead of following mud footprints, I hopped up above the trail a few steps where there was an untracked line of rocks. The results were immediate. I discovered hidden fire rings, a sun-bleached yak skull, colorful red and black birds, and a rock that appeared to have a body impression on it—certainly Guru Rinpoche. Suddenly the trail, which moments earlier had felt routine, cracked with novelty and newness. I thought, "Everything is alive and electric if you're patient and give yourself permission to look."

Now wearing contact lenses of curiosity, it was a wonderful walk. As I followed the river down, there was a sense of going with the flow and changing seasons. It was autumn, yet descending from the icy highlands, I felt like I was hiking into spring. The air warmed. Pine trees shot up out of the earth, color dripped back into the leaves, and I heard the sound of melting snow. Everything felt like it was thawing that morning, including me.

After three and a half hours of steady downhill, we arrived at a small clearing beside the river, our lunch spot. Across the river, yaks wandered on high ridges. At the far end of the clearing, a Bhutanese family sat on a blanket around a small fire. Their black pots were propped up over the fire on a circle of rocks and they were cooking lunch. As in Laya, it appeared there were three generations — grandparents, parents, and children traveling together. When I asked Norbu their destination, he told me they were heading back to Lunana for the winter. "They've gone to town to get supplies and are returning."

The family sat among rice bags, neatly folded yak-hair blankets, and canvas bags and bamboo baskets stocked with supplies. Like an American family, they'd all piled into the car to go shopping. Only in that case, their SUV was a yak, and their grocery store was a six-day journey away. I would imagine such a journey makes you double-check your shopping list.

"Can I go over and say hello?" I asked.

Norbu smiled. "Please do. I'm sure they'd like to share some yak butter tea."

I walked over, and before I even asked, the woman poured me a cup of butter tea. Rather than kiras and ghos, this family wore winter jackets, sweaters, long pants, and hiking boots. When I pointed up the trail and said, "Thanza," they nodded. But when I told them their village is beautiful — "*Choe kie yue na me sami laysham dhu*" — they positively beamed.

Yak butter tea is like a thick soup, and thanks to the oxidation process, a bit rancid. Made with butter, salt, and tea leaves, it is also very salty, but it grew on me quickly. Used to provide warmth and calories in cold climates, the butter also acts as a lip moisturizer.

I took a few pictures of the family and then showed them the pictures I'd taken.

"Chozo!" they exclaimed, when I showed them a picture of stone homes with a backdrop of sandy river dunes.

"Laya," they sang when they saw a woman in a colorful, conical hat.

Gradually, everyone else from my group wandered over to try some butter tea, and Peter and Paul, ever the gentlemen, brought some of our food to share with them. It all ended as one great shared picnic in the sun.

31

THAT NIGHT WE STAYED AT TAMPOE TSHO, A BEAUTIFUL lakefront campsite surrounded by green mountains that rose fjord-like from the still, reflective waters. A terrible rainstorm blew in that afternoon, lasting through the evening, and I found my mood similarly soggy and cynical. When I woke on the morning of the twenty-third day, I discovered my tent uncharacteristically dark and the walls frozen. I cinched my sleeping bag to the front of the tent, yanked down the frozen zipper, and threw open the tent door to find everything bathed in white. "It snowed!" I declared with glee. The snow was a mere dusting that morning, but it didn't matter. Whether two inches or two feet, with snow there is always the same diamond silence, the same sense of a pure white world, and the same opportunity to nail a fellow trekker with a snowball. Naturally there was a rush to be out in the snow — which is no different than the excitement of a surfer sprinting to the sea — so I hurried out of my tent and stomped down to the lakeshore.

A perfect and still mirror that morning, the lake reflected the crystal mountains, wisping clouds, and my own image, peering down. As I saw my reflection, I became immediately entranced,

Snow-dusted mountains reflect in the morning mirror of an alpine lake. Photo by author.

but this wasn't Narcissus in love with his own image. Instead, I was only looking at my eyes — eyes which, no matter how old I got, would never age. There, I saw someone gazing back that was, at once, me and not me. It was a beautiful moment of connection but also twinged with sadness, for I suddenly mourned all the years of separation. However, no sooner was I convinced of humankind being created in divinity's own image than a soft breeze rolled through the valley. The surface of the lake shivered, as if laughing, and my reflection was rippled into a thousand tiny fragments. Three weeks ago, standing atop the first pass of the Snowman Trek, I might have gotten anxious and frustrated, but now I had a patient faith, born of watching Norbu work with my prayer flags, Peter petting the horses, and the two giggle-filled girls taming their "bull" in Thega. As I watched my image distort and reappear that morning, I realized blessings were always present in my life. Sometimes I didn't see grace, sometimes I didn't feel it — sometimes the water rippled and the wind whipped the prayer flags out of my hand — but it was there, eternally reflective and radiant. And who was I to judge what constituted "good" and "bad" for me on my path? I had only to look at the last twelve hours to realize that the rain I'd cursed last night had transformed into the snow I rejoiced in this morning. And this snow, made to melt, would one day summon the flowers I'd celebrate in spring.

At my tent, I discovered Sonam, standing there with a steaming cup of tea. "To keep hands warm, sir."

I thanked Sonam, and together we gazed out over the dawn lake in silent awe. Sonam always seemed to be at my side during the biggest moments of the Snowman Trek — teaching me to take it one step at a time on the first day, running with the horses, and my bittersweet last look at Thanza. I used to think Sonam was simply present for these moments, but that morning it dawned on me that he may very well have been the cause of those moments — that perhaps something in the consciousness of this farm boy, who at the end of a hard day of trekking still poured over his Buddhist Sutras, woke something up in my own.

"One day I hope I can take you trekking in America, Sonam," I said, gazing out.

Sonam smiled. "Is America pretty, sir?"

I told Sonam that America was beautiful and also had beyuls, only instead of Laya and Lunana, they went by such names as Yosemite, Grand Canyon, Yellowstone, and Glacier.

The truth is you discover two places when you travel: the place you departed to and the place you departed from. I had not expected the beauty of Bhutan to make me so keenly aware of the beauty back home, but it did. Along with that, over the last few days, I'd come to believe that the jeweled net of Indra not only referred to people but also to places — that one pristine part of the planet reflected all the others. How else could I explain Bhutan looking like, by turns, the Pacific Northwest, Scotland, and Switzerland? Certainly

America was my promised land, but I knew it was but one of many promised lands spread out across one promised planet.

"America," said Sonam, "I would like to go."

I knew there were sacred beyuls hidden in the Rockies, White Mountains, Tetons, North Cascades, and Sierras. "We will find those valleys, Sonam," I said, "And we will go."

"Yes, sir."

Ryan strolled up and slapped me on the back. "Hey man, stop holding up the coffee cart!" He then gave me a good whiff. "Man, you stink."

"Yes, I do," I said, proudly. But I knew there was purity in that dirt — that dirt had made me clean.

When Rob wandered over, I asked him if the snowy mountains looked like Switzerland.

"Nah, mate," he said, "looks betta' than Switzerland."

NATURALLY IT WAS A GREAT MORNING AND THERE WAS MUCH to celebrate — fresh snow, the last pass, our last night camping, and as Sangey removed the lids at breakfast, our last serving of hairy bacon. As we ate, Joe told us about the last two days of the trek. "Today we will be going up to the Tempe La — the eleventh and last pass of the trek. And from there, we have twenty-seven miles and about 6,500 feet of descent before we arrive back at the road."

At breakfast we asked Norbu if we could have a fire that evening to celebrate the final night on the trek.

"Fires aren't allowed on the trail," he explained. "Because it encourages cutting down trees."

But Norbu explained we could still have a party. "Two hours after the pass, there is a family who runs a little shop," he said. "You can buy soda pop, candy, and beer there."

"Sounds great," said Ryan, "and Kev can have his final, big night with Ingrid."

"Great," said Larry, throwing on his white Jansport cap. "Let's do it!"

The trail rose steeply from behind camp, and rather than two groups in friendly competition, our group hiked with the Hausers. Gradually the view of Tampoe Tsho was replaced by snow-dusted mountainy folds, and up ahead I saw Ingrid's mom standing motionless on the trail, holding both trekking poles in one hand.

"What are you doing?" I asked, sauntering up.

"Just looking," she replied, which I thought was very wise.

As I continued on, a worry rose up that I had not lived as much of life as I could have on the Snowman Trek — that I had rushed past sections of trail where I should've walked, missed miles of jaw-dropping scenery because I'd been lost in thought, and generally not had the kind of trip that a more experienced traveler like Peter or Kira had. Kira really seemed to make her trip a twenty-four-day meditation, always working her *mala* beads, journaling, and sitting with the villagers to meditate and pray when she could. As for Peter, well, he threw himself into the experience like a method actor researching a role — sleeping under the tarp tent with the yak herders, spending countless hours in the kitchen tent with Achula, and always offering to help the villagers with their chores in exchange for a picture.

Fortunately, my concern didn't last long, for I realized we were all on our own trip, and as such, I would embrace all the aspects of my trip — the irrational worries, the inner critical voice, and, laughingly so, Ingrid aspirations. Each had their appointed place because they'd made me who I was at that very moment, and you know what, I liked that guy. Doubtless, I was a work in progress, but I would try to stay open during construction.

Suddenly I rounded a corner and the wind blasted me — a definite sign the last pass was close. I increased my pace and sure enough the pass appeared up ahead, wedged between rocky ridges. Peter, Ryan, Tom, Kira, Rob, and Paul were there, celebrating in a prayer flag swirl.

"Kevin!" they yelled triumphantly as I approached.

"Lha Gyal-o-o-o-o," I yelled, tossing my baseball hat in the air like a graduation cap and deciding there is no better sound than your own voice bouncing off beautiful mountains.

When the celebration quieted down, I wandered off to a cairn, knelt down, and pulled the prayer flags from my backpack. Despite twenty-three days on the trail, this set of final flags was still delicately and devoutly folded, carried at the top of my day pack. As with the first pass, when I went to tie my prayer flags, there were complications. The first knot was effortless, but with the second came the wind, one of the large branches wedged between the rocks toppling over, and Ryan shaking my shoulders, saying, "Hurry up and let's celebrate!" But I took my time, waiting patiently for the right moment. And when I finally tied the second knot — with the string lute-like, neither too loose nor too tight — my prayer flags whipped triumphantly in the wind and made sweet music.

"Nice job," said Norbu, giving me a high five. "Congratulations!"

Suddenly Paul yelled. "Here comes, Larry!"

We all turned — Larry and Joe were plodding up the trail a hundred yards down from the pass.

"Let's bring him in," Peter cried.

We ran back down the trail to bring Larry in the way the Marines at Camp Pendleton will run the last few miles with the exhausted athletes during the Southern California Ironman. The only difference was that when we reached Larry, we didn't jog in front of him or beside him, we jogged behind him, for it has been him leading us for twenty-four days.

"Lha Gyalo!" Larry cried, extending his arms, and it was a glorious, fist-pumping, peal of joy.

AFTER CELEBRATING AT THE PASS WITH THE HAUSERS FOR an hour, we started down a steep, rocky trail. By then, the sun had risen high into the sky and already the little ice rinks between rocks were cracking and the snow was melting. And then, from high up on the pass, came the sound of Dawa singing and belting traditional Bhutanese songs as loud as his lungs allowed. As I looked up, Dawa came hurtling down the trail, leaping tall rock buildings with a single bound, wearing a cowboy hat, and carrying a large staff-like walking stick. As he approached, I was just about to ask him about blossom rain, but before I could, Dawa threw his head back, belted his song louder, and did a little jig down the trail. For some reason, it felt strangely like his answer.

When he was gone, I looked back up at the trail to make sure no one else was coming and saw a parade of yaks marching down from the pass high above. From where I stood, it looked as if the yaks were stepping right out of the sky, and I thought, "The rope from heaven isn't cut, and we are never cut off from the rope — sometimes we just forget to hold on."

Feeling happy and healthy, I hiked on, and when I fell in line with Paul, I told him about the Tertön tradition. Before my trip to Bhutan, I read a book on Pema Lingpa and Buddhist *tertöns*, or "saintly treasure revealers." Knowing spiritual teachings tended to dilute over time, Guru Rinpoche hid treasures and sacred texts all over the Himalayas in special power places. There were two types of treasures: earth treasures were hidden in high cliffs, under rocks, and in lakes; mind treasures were hidden in, you guessed it, the minds of the tertön. Since Buddhism is entirely concerned with thoughts, every treasure was ultimately a mind treasure — the earth treasures simply triggered a latent treasure locked in the mind.

The treasure cycle followed a similar pattern: Guru Rinpoche (along with the help of his female consort, Yeshe Tshogyal, and innumerable protectors and deities) would hide a treasure and then soar off on his flying tigress to fight demons, build monasteries, and leave a few body prints in rocks. Then the tertön, a past disciple of Guru Rinpoche who had been reincarnated, would start receiving clues about the treasure in dreams and visions. Gradually, the tertön pieces together the clues and has a pure vision at dawn, falling into a trance, and discovering the treasure. The tertöns were usually normal people, who would one day out of the blue just start having visions or dreams. Many times the treasure scroll was written in an undecipherable script, but fortunately for the tertön, there'd be a *dakini*, or female Buddhist saint, who would appear to assist with the translation. The tertön would then retreat to some hidden hermitage and, after soaking in the essence of the treasure, take it public. The treasures that were revealed had all kinds of great names like "The Lamp That Illuminates the Darkness," "The Clear Mirror," and "The Supreme Intention."

"There were five great tertön kings," I told Paul as we walked, "but Pema Lingpa is the most celebrated in Bhutan, because he was born and raised in Bhutan. Pema found treasures, texts, and artifacts and promoted dance and the arts. If you can believe it, he had no clue he was a saint until age twenty-five."

"What happened then?"

"He had a dream telling him to take five friends to the Tang Valley in Bumthang on the night of a full moon and a treasure would be waiting for him in a section of the river that pools into a little lake."

"Did he go?"

"You bet, Norman!" I said, doing a little ski jump off a rock with my trekking poles. "Pema dove underwater where he saw a temple with many doors. All of the doors were closed but one, and when he swam through it, he saw a life-sized statue of the Buddha and a woman with one eye."

"Dear god!" said Paul. "What happened with her?"

"She handed him a box and the next thing he knew he was standing beside the river with his friends, holding a treasure. The only problem was the local people didn't believe Pema was a saint, so they gave him a different challenge."

"Why didn't they believe him?"

I told Paul if people can't see the divine nature in themselves, they can't see it in another. "So they told him to swim to the bottom of the lake with a lamp, find a treasure, and return to the surface with the lamp still lit."

"Did he do it?"

"Pema disappeared into the river and was underwater for so long, everyone assumed he was dead."

"Was he?"

"Does the hero ever die?" I mused. "Not only did Pema burst out of the lake with the lamp still lit, but he also had found a treasure. The site of that discovery is called Lake Mebartso."

Paul smiled. "Can we go there?"

"Not on the Snowman Trek," I said. "But just ahead of us on the trail is another lake where Pema found a treasure, Om Tsho."

"Cool bananas!"

Paul and I hiked on, swift-stepping over mossy rocks and around ice puddles, and our boots made squishy sounds in the spongy tundra. As we plodded on merrily, I told Paul that Pema found more than thirty-four statues, scrolls, and sacred relics in Bhutan. "Not only that, but he also visited Guru Rinpoche's celestial paradise — Zangto Pelri — and brought back some of the dances to Bhutan that are still being performed today."

Paul laughed. "At Space 34 disco?"

"Who knows?" I said, "But we'll find out in a few days!"

When Om Tsho appeared, it was exactly the kind of lake where you'd expect to find a sacred treasure. The lake sparkled with a magnificent blue, its surface as still and clear as the Buddha's mind.

"I imagine there are a few more treasures down there," said Paul, snapping a photo.

The trail skirted around Om Tsho, ducked under some prayer flags, and descended steeply to another scenic lake. There we found our group picnicking on the grassy banks. As I took a seat on a blanket and shoveled myself a plateful of warm food, Larry informed me we had a name for the trek.

Guru Rinpoche hid treasures in sacred spots such as Lake Om Tsho. Photo by Peter McBride.

"Yakkety yak," I said. "In honor of Scoobie."

"Nope."

"Operation Squash Bratwurst?" I asked.

"Guess again!"

"The Legend of Larry!"

"Nope," said Larry with a smile, "We're calling it 'Pimp my Yak'!"

FOLLOWING LUNCH, THE TRAIL TRAVERSED ALONGSIDE the river, descending through mossy boulders and forested slopes fragrant with tiny blue flowers. As the trail crept below treeline, I gave a final wave to the soaring peaks. A few days ago, I might have wished to stay, but as the trek was drawing to a close, I was comfortable that the mountains had worked their magic on me. Already all the struggles I faced — the sleepless nights, thigh-crying climbs, and cold rain — were becoming polished with the passage of time, leaving only the shining essence of the Snowman. Up ahead, the trail crossed the river on a wooden bridge, and we discovered a little cabin nestled in the woods, our first sign of human habitation after four days of hard walking.

"Welcome to the Snowman Shop," Norbu said as I sauntered up.

As he said this, the father of the house, a middle-aged man in a brown gho, threw open a wooden window, revealing candies, chips, sodas, and bottles of beer. Ryan bought two beers to share, and as we passed the bottle, we all took great victory swigs. As I looked around, I couldn't help but think that this little happy homestead in the middle of the immaculate woods was a beyul. The thing about beyuls is that once you spot one, you begin to see them everywhere.

Suddenly, a horrible scream shattered our celebration, and a young girl sprinted from the home with blood gushing from her hand. Joe, Kira, and Norbu immediately sprung into action, applying gauze and direct pressure to the girl's hand and elevating it to stop the bleeding. As the white gauze quickly became soaked in red, it was impossible to tell where the girl was hurt. I couldn't tell if it was on top of her hand, a finger, or her whole hand. Her mother ran out from behind the counter and stood behind her, stroking her hair, comforting her in Dzongkha.

When the bleeding slowed, Joe and Kira removed the gauze and I saw the girl had cut off the tip of her forefinger, just below the nail. With the bandage removed, her finger began to bleed again so Kira, Norbu, and Joe quickly rewrapped it. Tears poured from the girl's eyes and her sobs elicited sympathetic tears from nearly everyone.

As in Thanza, this was, yet again, another instance of suffering in Shangri-La. Indeed, every time I'd thought of Bhutan as a paradise, there had been some painful intrusion — the blue sheep skull at Jhomolhari, Chagay's dying mother, and now this little girl. The thought I didn't want to think that night at Thanza arrived again

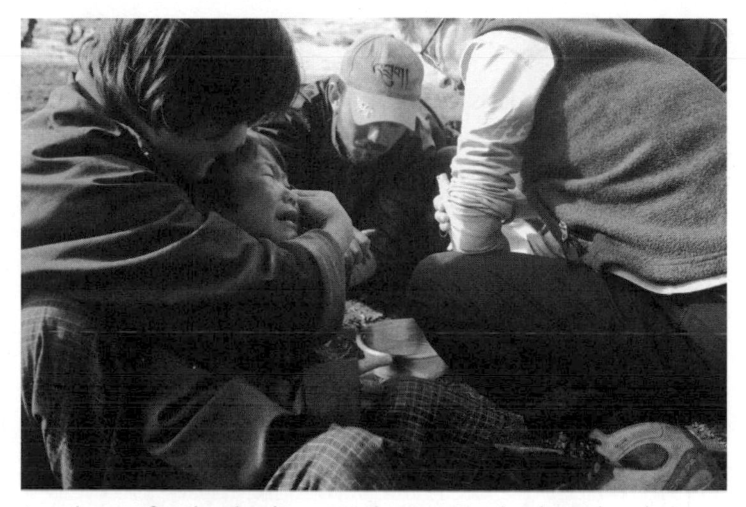

A mother comforts her daughter as Norbu prepares a bandage. Photo by Peter McBride.

and this time with more force. Were joy and pain two parts of one beyul braid? Before my trip, I thought paradise was the absence of pain, but what Bhutan — this country where nothing is black or white — seemed to be insisting was that pain wasn't separate from joy but was inexorably wound up within it and enlightenment waited like a welcoming shore somewhere beyond both. If this was true, if accepting pain — in order to let it go — was the secret door into paradise, did my inability to cry mean I was stuck in purgatory?

I looked up at the sky, hoping blossom rain would fall and give me my answer, but it was only dark and moody and the sun was missing in action.

WHEN I WALKED BACK TO THE TRAIL, NORBU POINTED TO the river tumbling down the valley. "This is the last river we'll hike next to," he said. "The Nikka Chhu."

As he said this, it truly dawned on me the trek was ending. Instead of speaking of firsts like we did at the beginning of the trek, we'd now be speaking of lasts. But the one good thing about lasts is they make everything once again feel like a first. As I arrived at our camp at Maurothang, the usual routine of hauling my duffel bag to a tent, unpacking my belongings, and meeting for tea rang with a first-day flair. After tea and cookies, we all threw Joe's Frisbee around camp, all tossing the disc of friendship back and forth between us. Hard to believe that days ago we were camped on a desolate cold ridge at each other's throats! We played until the sun set, filling the forest with shadows, and when I nearly caught the Frisbee between my teeth, I called it quits. I could just see the headline now: "American Man Killed on the Toughest Trek in the World . . . By a Frisbee!"

At dinner, Joe brought the yakmen and kitchen crew into the dining tent to be thanked for all their hard work. When Joe handed the yakmen their tip, they accepted it with a head-lowered humility and two-handed gratitude. I had the sense that they'd be as thankful for two hundred dollars as they would have been for two dollars.

As the yakmen filed out and Ryan uncapped our last bottle of beer, which was split between the nine of us, it started to rain. The rain began with isolated scattered drops, but then the storm quickly blew in. One by one, everyone shot discreet glances in my direction, for they knew what high hopes I had for that night. We were camped ten minutes down the trail from the Hausers, and I'd invited Ingrid to celebrate the final night on the trek with us. The rain was making any prospect of another meeting with Ingrid a distant possibility. Finally Rob addressed it directly: "Doncha' worry, Kev. I'm sure she'll come."

I expected the storm to pass quickly but it grew heavier, falling in a relentless wet torrent, and I accepted my fate. Like blossom rain, love would have to be another question answered in the future. I thought of Ingrid that night with a sad but thankful smile. Granted, I hadn't officially asked her to be my girlfriend, but sometimes you don't have to ask. Instead of focusing on what Ingrid and I wouldn't share, I would remember what we did — the laughter that accompanied our introduction at Laya and that great afternoon tea we had with her mom at Jichu Dramo. Instead of focusing on the life I was missing, I would have faith in the yet-to-be-life waiting for me. I took a deep breath and with it reconnected to the present moment and my friends around me. We laughed and joked for another hour but gradually the raindrops penetrated the ceiling seams and began falling inside the tent.

By eight o'clock, we were snug in our tents, and I read and underlined a sentence from Rilke that seemed to sum up the Snowman Trek perfectly: Being "among conditions that work at us, that set us before big natural things from time to time, is all we need." Then I put the book away, clicked off my headlamp, and just laid there looking up at my tent ceiling, thinking about all the amazing moments I'd had on the Snowman Trek. The three weeks of the trek really had been, without a doubt, the best of my life. Around ten, it dawned on me the rain had stopped and the only drops left falling were wind-rattled leaves teaching me a lesson about letting go. I unzipped my tent and crawled out to have my good-bye glance at the Bhutanese night. When I stood up and looked around, I noticed Peter standing outside his tent a few feet away. We didn't speak, we both just gazed up at the night sky, which said it all. As we did, first stars blinked in the black space between white, moonlit clouds, and I decided the twilight was just as beautiful as the dawn of day. But when I thought about returning to the tumult of the city and all my unanswered questions, I suddenly got worried. What do you hold onto when nothing is certain and everything is changing? I decided to make another wish to Lunana, but before I could, a wish was made for me.

A shooting star blazed brilliantly and briefly across the sky.

32

OUR LAST BREAKFAST ON THE TWENTY-FOURTH MORNING was a feast. Sure, Achula wanted to make sure we were all well fed, but he also wanted to get rid of as much food as he could. Hence, we gorged on pancakes, cornflakes, oatmeal, toast, chapatti, and sausage links.

"Hey Joe," said Peter with a mouthful. "I don't think the Snowman Trek is a guaranteed weight loss program after all."

"I think I've gained weight," remarked Tom. "Achula's cooking rules!"

Of course the Snowman Trek didn't let us off easy because, if it did, it wouldn't be the Snowman. The twenty-fourth and last day of the trek, also happened to be the longest mileage-wise. As we ate, Norbu briefed us about the day's itinerary. "Today we will do a 14.5-mile hike and descend 3,510 feet from Maurothang to the roadhead at Nikka Chhu. We will hike down from broadleaf forests into dense bamboo forests and ferns. And if you get lost, just follow the river."

Twenty minutes later, we shouldered our packs, threaded our hands through the leather straps of our trekking poles one last time, and started down the trail. As I did, I took a good-bye glance at our camp. Sonam, Sangey, and the yakmen were busy taking down our tents, which deflated like gray and green balloons. The carnival was really coming to a close. As my head started to pound and a nausea pit developed in my stomach, I had to wonder: Could there be another kind of altitude sickness that affects you coming down a mountain? When you have to leave such great heights and hang your heroism up like a coat in the closet? I believed so that morning, and there was a physiological truth to it — your heart gets bigger at high altitude because it needs to pump more blood — but I knew people got bigger in other ways too. When the scene became too sad, I fixed my gaze on the trail in front of me, and I hiked on.

DESPITE A FOREVER-DESCENDING TRAIL AND AN EXHAUSTED set of leg muscles that had long since lost their ability to resist, I had no wish to hurry that day. Not only was the bouldery trail quite slippery in places, but more important, I wanted to stretch out my Snowman experience as long as possible. It was a beautiful day with morning mist rising from open fields, sunlight streaming through lime green bamboo stalks, and the river playing hide-and-seek with the shadows. When a village woman hurried up behind me with a train of yaks, I stepped aside to let them thunder past. As they did, one of the yaks veered off, and before I knew it, I'd already yelled "Haw!" and thrown my stone. It was a perfect shot, landing to the left of the yak, causing him to veer back in line and speed up. But no sooner did that yak fall back in line than another yak bolted out. I grabbed another rock, shouted "Haw" and for the third time on the Snowman Trek, I was running the pack animals.

Running yaks is exactly the same as running horses, except if you hit a sharp-horned yak with a stone by accident, you apologize profusely. As we thundered over mossy rocks and plowed through tremendous mud sections, I felt wild, supremely happy, and thought of staying in Bhutan forever and living the simple life. But as the trail entered a shady, woodsy section and the yaks fell in line of their

A village woman steers her yak train down the trail. Photo by Peter McBride.

own accord, I slowed to a walk and dropped my stone. There was a great life running pack animals in Bhutan, but I knew it was not mine. When the village woman looked back, she smiled but did not wave thank you. I didn't expect her to — on the trail it was a given that everyone helps out. That was just the way it was.

So I hiked on, ducking under silvery spiderwebs and admiring birds singing in the shade. Crazy to think a few days ago, I stood on top of the world at Rinchen Zoe La and now I was running yaks through a bamboo jungle, keeping my eyes peeled for monkeys and royal Bengal tigers.

I found my trekking team a few hours down the trail, sitting in an open field of golden grasses, surrounded by lofty meadows. Over the last hour, the trail had left behind the dense bamboo jungle and widened into rolling farm fields. Down the valley, two-story, traditional-style Bhutanese homes once again dotted the hillsides.

"This is my village Sephu," Sangey said with great pride.

"You live here?" I remarked.

"Yes, sir," he said, as if standing before the Taj Mahal.

When I told Sangey his village was beautiful in Dzongkha, he looked so proud.

We spent an hour there, picnicking in the bright sun, napping, and smoking tobacco from the pipe Achula made by cutting out a potato and attaching a bamboo shaft. As I exhaled with a cough and handed the pipe to Ryan, Norbu pointed down the valley. "There she is."

When I heard the word "she," I assumed he meant Lunana and leapt to my feet. I expected to see Thanza and Table Mountain. "Where?"

Norbu pointed to a thin strip between the rolling hill folds. "There she is — the road."

Not only had I not seen a road for twenty-four days, I also hadn't even heard the word.

"Oh" I said, "The road . . . "

I thought the sight of the road would fill me with dread, but that day, I felt content. The road was right for me then in the same way the trail was right for me twenty-four days ago. And after all, that road will lead back to family who will want to see pictures, to Boston Celtics games, to Bruce Springsteen and the E Street Band, and to friends who will have a burger, beer, and a barstool waiting — that road leads home.

"Let's do it!" I said, grabbing my trekking pole straps one last time.

Then, as with the first day of the trek, Peter cracked a joke. "Anyone up for a short meander?"

"A Sunday stroll perhaps?" added Paul, busting up.

Laughing, we marched merrily down the hill.

THE SNOWMAN TREK EASES YOU OUT OF THE EXPERIENCE as slowly as it eases you in, only instead of a dirt road gradually thinning into a trail, as it did in Paro, houses appear and the trail gradually widens into a dirt road. I didn't even know the dirt road was approaching, I just looked down and suddenly it was underfoot. Still nothing prepared me for the sight and sound of my first car.

The car totally surprised me. I heard something coming up behind me, the ground shook, and my first thought was, "The yaks!" When I turned and saw metal, my second thought was disbelief: "An electric yak?" And by the time I stepped aside to let it pass, I realized it was a Toyota truck with two stone-faced men sitting in the front. I waved as they drove past, but neither responded — both stared steely eyed at the road without smiles. As they drove by and I coughed from the dust kicked up by their tires, I realized life would be different off the trail. Instead of everyone saying hello and helping each other, I'd be returning to silent city buses filled with adults who were once excited children who couldn't be kept quiet. Life can make you lose things along the way, certainly I understood that — sometimes the wick gets caught in the wax and you need to flee to the white snow peaks to light the flame again.

As I spat the dry dust from my mouth and the trail entered Sephu village, I saw a little boy in a gho standing in his yard, his tiny fingers wrapped around the wood fence. I scrambled to get my camera out of my bag to take a picture, but when I turned the camera on, the battery died.

"Stay there," I told the boy, fumbling in my backpack for another battery. "Don't move."

When I put my second battery in, it too was dead.

"Cute kid," said Peter, ambling up.

"Quick," I said, "Take his picture!"

Peter smiled but shook his head no. "I've put my camera away for the rest of the trip."

I was nearly frantic by then. "Are you kidding me? That shot will make you famous!"

With a calm authority, Peter told me some moments aren't supposed to be captured.

As he said that, I suddenly understood the reluctance of the Bhutanese to talk about blossom rain — some moments should be left alone and simply lived. "You're right," I said, putting away my camera.

As we left, the boy suddenly became animated, waving with tiny fingers and calling after us: "Bye bye!"

From there, the dirt road undulated through the river valley for another half an hour and then the concrete road appeared, cutting our trail off like the top of the letter *T*.

"You ready for this?" Peter asked, gesturing to the road lined with small shops.

"Ready as I'll ever be," I said, marching on.

I tripped slightly when my feet touched the road, which was no different than the lurch of a small boat hitting the beach. The journey was over. As with all the passes on the Snowman Trek, my trekking companions were there to greet me, along with the champagne and tasty lemon cake Joe had arranged. Before Sonam, Sangey, and Achula left for Thimphu to get paid, we tipped them out, took final pictures, and gave them some of our gear as a gift.

"Thanks for a great trip," I said to Sonam, handing him my headlamp. "This is for you."

Sonam looked at the headlamp and then back up at me. "I have flashlight, sir."

I started to protest but quickly stopped myself. "Is there something else you want?"

Sonam pointed to my shades and said, "Sunglasses, very cool!"

"Here you go, my friend."

Moments later, Achula, Sangey, and Sonam hopped aboard the pickup truck, and as they drove off, we waved and shouted goodbye. The last thing I heard was Achula yelling "Yes!" which trailed the departing truck like a white jet stream of joy.

When they were gone, Pete, Rob, Joe, Ryan, Tom, Kira, Larry, Paul, and I all stood around silently, gazing forlornly at our tourist bus. Now there would be barriers like hotel walls and bus windows between us and our open air experience of Bhutan.

"Aw cheer up, guys," Rob suddenly announced, slapping me on the back. "The trek is over, ye'. But that doesn't mean our advencha is too!"

"A very good point!" Larry remarked.

With that, I climbed aboard the bus — but not before turning to the trail once more and yelling, "Lha Gyalo!"

33

A POLICEMAN DIRECTING TRAFFIC WITH WHITE GLOVES, HIS hands fluttering like doves, was our introduction to Thimphu. With around one hundred thousand residents, Thimphu is Bhutan's largest town and the only capital in the world without a single traffic light.

We drove through the town's winding streets — bustling by Bhutanese standards — and checked into our guest house. As I keyed into my cozy room, I delighted in electricity, a bed, a wood floor under my feet and a roof over my head — things I once took for granted now sparkled like modern miracles. My twenty-minute shower was warm and wonderful and sent an exodus of mud marching down the drain. Then, like James Bond in his bathrobe, I gave myself the smoothest shave of my whole life. But once I threw on the blue jeans and a sweater I'd left behind, combed my hair, and saw myself, I froze. Suddenly I looked like everyone else in the world, and it appeared as if something hard-won and holy had departed with the dirt. But when I looked closer, there it was — that Snowman stamp of approval and Thanza twinkle. My eyes had the Lunana look, and now when anyone asked me about the trek, my face too

Prayer flags keep a devoted eye on Bhutan's capital city of Thimphu. Photo by Peter McBride.

would light up as if standing over a heap of jewels, and I could say, "It is the most otherworldly place . . . "

"Let's go, Bro," yelled Ryan, peeking his head in the door, "Space 34 awaits!"

Normally the nights with the biggest buildup have the biggest letdown, and if you don't believe me, I have three words for you: New Year's Eve. But as we followed up a huge gluttonous feast at a Western-style pizzeria with karaoke at a local bar, and a hilarious game Joe taught us called "Are You There, Moriarty?" I could tell that night would surpass all my expectations. Granted, I was a little disappointed when Kira, Paul, Larry, Tom, and Norbu bowed out early on account of early morning obligations; but when I found myself with Ryan, Rob, Peter, and Joe, I knew all was good, for there's no better feeling than marching down the streets with your buddies, knowing a fun night awaits.

Space 34 occupied the second floor of a nondescript yellow building, next to a hip lounge called the Om Bar. You forget that when a country modernizes, it must do so on every level. Prior to our arrival, the Royal Bhutan Police had just finished training twenty-four bouncers, including eight females, and 2007 would be the first year that discotheques in Bhutan had security watching the door. While Space 34 didn't have a bouncer at the front door, it did have all the pillars of a great party — flashing lights, Michael Jackson's "Thriller" blasting through the speakers, and a dance floor that was perfect for my much-hyped moonwalk and backspin maneuvers. However, the disco was missing one key element: people.

"We walked 216 miles for this?" exclaimed Peter.

"The club was packed last time," declared Ryan.

I decided that once again Bhutan had defied my expectations but, sadly, by not meeting them. Like many a New Year's Eve, that night might not happen. On our way out, we peeked into the Om Bar, which was full of cozy couches and standing lamps and had an impressive array of beer and liquor. A hip-looking Bhutanese man shuffled out and introduced himself as Thinley. With his dark features, goatee, jean jacket, and white T-shirt, Thinley looked like a Bhutanese version of Johnny Depp.

"You guys from the U.S.?" he said, with a cigarette dangling from his lips

"You bet," I said. "California."

"I know California," Thinley said. "Hotel California."

Thinley was a DJ at one of Bhutan's only radio stations, and we became fast friends based on a shared affinity for Bob Dylan, Springsteen, and U2.

"Where is everyone," I asked.

"At the graduation party," he replied, gesturing with his cigarette. "It's the biggest party of the year! You guys want to come?"

Moments later, Ryan, Joe, Rob, Peter, and I had piled into a small sedan that belonged to someone like Thinley's brother's wife's second cousin's roommate and were hurtling through the Saturday night streets of Thimphu. During the day Thimphu's streets were alive with shoppers, school kids, and monks spinning prayer wheels. In the bright sunshine, the town felt warm, alive, and active. But that night, the town felt empty and abandoned.

"Don't worry, the party will be packed," cried Thinley, clapping his hands above the steering wheel and driving with his knee.

Personally, I didn't believe the party would be packed, but then again, Bhutan is a land of myth and magic and a place where saints ride on winged tigresses, so who was I to say it couldn't also summon some dancing bodies and booming bass? As we screeched to a halt in a great cloud of dust in front of Thimphu's Youth Center, stray dogs scurried for shadows.

"Hey, Thinley," I said. "We were hoping for an older crowd."

"It's cool, man," he said just like Johnny Depp. "The youth center has been rented out — no kids!"

As we walked in, a sign greeted us at the door.

Once Again . . . It's Party Time
All the Centennial Graduates
Welcome One and All
Let's Make the Sweetest Memory and Enjoy
Time: 9 p.m.–2 a.m.
Day: Saturday
Date: 18/10/2007
Even Others Are Cordially Invited!!!!

We hurried into a crowded lobby that looked like the lobby of every recreation center in the history of the world — peeling paint, a trophy case smudged with dirty fingerprints, and a wall mural of a rainbow from the '70s. There was also a sign that said: *No Smoking, Drugs or Alcohol,* below which, I should note, were three kids smoking cigarettes and five garbage cans filled with ice-cold beer.

Thinley tossed us beers, and as the door to the gymnasium opened and closed, disco lights bounced off the walls and pulsing rap music poured out.

"Let's get in there!" cried Ryan, taking a sip.

"Welcome to the underground of Bhutan," Peter announced. "Perhaps never glimpsed by Western eyes before."

The gym was packed with Bhutanese kids in their twenties wearing blue jeans, cocktail dresses, fashionable tops, T-shirts, kiras, ghos, khaki pants, and sneakers. A DJ wearing a knit cap was spinning records from a little booth on the balcony, and everyone was jumping and bouncing to the beat.

Until the coronation of the Fourth King in 1974, Bhutan kept itself cut-off from the rest of the world, and when it did open its doors, it did so slowly and cautiously. The only way into the country — until Druk Air made its first landing in 1983 — was via the border town of Phuentsholing. As is the case with border towns, some items make it past international customs over the years, some items don't, and there is little apparent science to the sorting. Nowhere was this more evident than with the music at that party that night. The first three songs we heard were Bryan Adams's "Summer of '69" set to techno music, Billy Ray Cyrus's "Achy Breaky Heart," and Peter, Paul and Mary's "Puff, the Magic Dragon."

We finished our beers and immediately rushed into the mix, spinning and bouncing wildly. We were energetic dancers, we were creative and inspired dancers; we were absolutely dreadful dancers. Not only were we uncoordinated, but we were also trying to dance in thick, lug-soled hiking boots. But here's the thing — the Bhutanese kids loved us and welcomed us on the dance floor with a Saturday night fever, as if we were a team of trekking John Travoltas.

As I gazed out at the dance floor, I realized the scene was a perfect representation of Bhutan at this exact moment in time — there was the daytime street solemnity of Buddhist belief and tradition and there was also this strobe-lit new world of youthful energy, freedom, and frantic dance. All I could do was to raise my glass to toast it all and say, "Cheers."

The night wore on and it was great. All we wanted was to dance and have a good time, so we didn't feel the least bit shy about dancing with any Bhutanese girl or guy and they didn't feel the least bit shy about dancing with us. As Dr. Dre and Tupac's "California Love" began, the DJ started working the crowd by sending shout-outs: "Yo, we got Thimphu in tha house! Paro definitely in tha house! Samtse definitely in the house! We got Haa up in here! Merak way up back! What up, Trongsa? What up, Mongar? Punakha! Aw yeah, Punakha gonna rock ya!" When the DJ said the name of the town, the kids who lived there yelled, threw up their hands, and it was nuts. Let's just say, the roof of the world was being raised a little bit higher.

"And yo," the DJ continued, "we even got some Westerners up in here. Some mad trekkers in tha back who know Thimphu's where it's at! What up, y'all? So jes' throw your hands in the air and wave 'em like ya jes don't care." Naturally, we went crazy. I had no idea how the DJ knew about us until I saw Thinley standing in the booth next to him, smoking his cig, and nodding to us with a smile.

Whenever I'm at a party that's just completely off the hook, I love nothing more than to wander off by myself, gaze out on the scene, and take a moment to rejoice. That night, I wandered back to the far corner of the gym, leaned against the wall with my beer, and gazed out over hundreds of dancing people filled with Gross National Happiness. I knew right then that 2008 would be Bhutan's year. Not only would Bhutan hold its first-ever elections and crown a new king, but also, like a rock 'n' roll band, the country would go on tour. During the summer of 2008, Bhutan would travel to the Smithsonian Folklife Festival at the National Mall in Washington DC and introduce America to its temples, artists, musicians, masked dancers, cuisine, traditional arts, and love of archery. While a part of me wanted to see Bhutan stay small (so I could always get a front-row seat), another part of me — the larger part — knew the good word of this small country with big ideas needed to be heard. The world needed to get hooked on Gross National Happiness and environmental conservation. These were ideas that could change the world and, more important, were needed to save it.

"Take care, Bhutan," I said, gazing out and raising my drink. "Trust in your tradition. Stay grounded but never stop reaching for the stars."

When a Bhutanese girl invited me to dance, I dashed back into the mix and the party didn't let up until 2:15 a.m., at which point the DJ suddenly cut the music, hit the house lights, and dropped his gangster swagger to say very politely, "Ladies and gentlemen. I am sorry, but we must go now. Good luck to all the new graduates."

With that, Rob, Pete, Ryan, Joe, and I poured into the parking lot and thanked Thinley profusely for his hospitality.

"No problem, man," he said. "Come back soon!"

Then we sauntered under the stars to the hotel, where we tried our best to be quiet. But the moment anyone who's had a few drinks tries to be quiet is the moment they get very loud. Thus hiking boots echoed through the hallways, room keys crashed to the floor, and doors inadvertently slammed. However, in hindsight, those sounds were fairly quiet compared to our laughter.

34

OUR TOURIST BUS PULLED UP TO THE PARO AIRPORT THE following morning at 7:30 a.m.

"Man," said Ryan as we stepped off. "It feels like we just got here."

I find all trips are like this, the first few days are slow rolling and then, blink, it's all over. However, not all of us were leaving Bhutan on Druk Air that day. Paul, Joe, and Larry planned to stay for a few extra days of sightseeing, and Rob, of course, would roar off on his Royal Enfield motorbike to start revolutions and tame tigers. We said good-bye to Norbu, Joe, Larry, and Rob at the airport and exchanged e-mail addresses along with hugs. When the inbound flight from Bangkok arrived, we watched the tourists step off the plane into Paro's bright sunshine with the same sense of wonder we had had twenty-six days ago — and still had. An hour later, the plane sped down the runway with us in it, lifted into the sky, and like a dream, the Dragon Kingdom disappeared.

THE TRIP TO BANGKOK WAS SMOOTH, AND UNLIKE MY inbound flight, I didn't sweat or feel the least bit anxious because I had faith in the success of airplane landings, and by then, a few other things. However, as we landed in the Bangkok smog and made our way to the chaos of international customs, Kira, Tom, Peter, and Ryan dispersed into different customs lines, and I realized with heartbreaking suddenness we were departing for separate lives. Along with Sonam, Sangey, Norbu, and Achula, there was a good chance I'd never see them again. The tragedy of adventure group travel is that you meet all these amazing people, live a hunk of life together, and then scatter like rose petals across the planet.

"Next person!" barked the customs agent, like a trip-ending executioner.

I hustled forward and presented my passport. When he directed me to look into the camera, I tried to make myself smile by saying "Yak Cheese," but no smile came.

I expected to find everyone waiting for me immediately after customs, but as I exited, all I saw were strange faces and the chaotic swirl of the Bangkok airport hit me like a fist. As I staggered toward baggage claim under the too-bright lights, I couldn't believe my trekking companions didn't wait. Had they forgotten me already? Did the Snowman Trek mean so little to them? But as I learned on my initial descent into the Lunana District eleven days earlier, when you're staring at your shoes, you're not in the present moment and you tend to miss things like four of your best friends waiting at the baggage claim with handshakes and big hugs. "You waited!" I proclaimed. "You guys are the best!"

We exchanged e-mails, gave second hugs, and reconfirmed what we all already knew — it was a great trip. Then, after a few pictures, they left for different departure terminals, radiating out like spokes from the centerpiece of our shared Snowman Trek. I gave a good-bye glance to Kira, Peter, Tom, and Ryan and then, like the Dragon Kingdom, my friends were gone.

WHEN I BOARDED MY CONNECTING FLIGHT TO LOS ANGELES, I felt sick to my stomach. As the plane sped down the runway, I thought about the magnificent trail, the mountains, my trekking companions, the villagers, and all the sweet children with their side-splitting laughter. By the time the plane took to the sky, I was crying. The tears arrived like lightning, as sudden as a storm in the mountains, and poured down my cheeks in great salty torrents. I tried to stop the tears by shutting my eyes, but then they just squeezed out the sides.

It stinks crying in an airplane, especially during take-off. There is no way to hide the fact that you're crying, everyone can hear you, and because the seatbelt sign is illuminated, you can't hide in the bathroom. Not only was mine a sudden cry, but it was also a messy one, complete with a horribly runny nose. It was as if all the tears from the dry-eyed years suddenly said, "He's open! Get out while you can!"

It would've really been bad if it wasn't for the sweet lady in the seat next to me who handed me a tissue.

"Thanks," I managed.

She touched my arm tenderly. "You lost someone, didn't you?"

I wanted to tell her I lost eight friends, a trekking staff of four, countless horsemen, and a yak named Scoobie, but before I could, my words were swallowed in sobs.

The woman told me to have a good cry. "And when you're done we'll have a drink to celebrate the life you lived with the ones you lost."

"Okay," I said, blowing my nose loudly.

When I looked past the woman, there was a shaft of golden sunlight shooting through the clouds outside the plane window. "Maybe this is what blossom rain means," I thought. "Seeing the sunshine through the tears."

Suddenly, I just started laughing uncontrollably.

"What's so funny." the woman asked with a sideways glance.

As I wiped my eyes, I told her Peter was wrong. "Not everyone cries on the Snowman Trek, I said. "Some cry immediately after."

35

WHEN I RETURNED TO THE UNITED STATES, I GOT A SERIOUS case of post-vacation blues. How could I not? I went from the solitary mountains of Thanza, Bhutan, to the crowded coastline of Huntington Beach, California. I knew it would take some time to readjust to rush hour traffic, supermarkets the size of city blocks, and the sight of small dogs prancing down the sidewalk, but nothing prepared me for not being able to sleep without the sound of horse bells, feeling a reverse form of claustrophobia because my room felt too big, and at times, not even wanting to talk about my trip. It was like coming home from war — how could anyone understand what we experienced?

Anxious to relieve the feelings of loss, I tried to bring Bhutan back. I made a photo album. I watched YouTube videos of Bhutan — even of the scary Druk Air landing in Paro. I bought Bhutanese red rice at the local specialty foods store. I flew through parts of the Snowman Trek on Google Earth. Nothing worked. I even went so far as to try sleeping in my four-season sleeping bag, which, given the balmy SoCal nights, was a horrible failure. There was nothing I could do. My trip was over, and I had to grieve this loss like any other.

I was down — real down — and just when I thought it couldn't get any worse, everything fell apart. Disney rejected me for the screenwriting fellowship, and my old spiritual unrest returned. That I couldn't find lasting contentment in the Himalayas — the abode of the gods — only made me feel more disappointed. As for blossom rain, I was convinced it had no meaning. After all, Norbu hadn't even heard about it. Sonam had laughed at me, Achula didn't understand my question, and Sangey seemed more interested in listening to Peter's iPod than giving me a definite answer.

One night in late December, when I told Sean how I felt, he sympathized like any good brother would and said he had just one request.

"What," I replied, certain he was going to suggest I see a therapist.

Sean cracked a smile. "A 6:00 a.m. surf?"

Some rituals will always remain.

AFTER A NIGHT OF TOSSING AND TURNING, I WOKE TO rain and the wind rattling my bedroom screen. I didn't even have to look at the surf report to know waves would be windblown and terrible. As I walked downstairs, I called Sean to cancel, but there was no answer. Knowing my brother will surf in all conditions and not wanting to stand him up, I reluctantly squeezed into my wetsuit, grabbed my surfboard, and hopped on my bike to ride to the beach.

Normally, riding my beach cruiser always put me in the best mood. I think it's because on the regal seat of a beach cruiser, you never feel the desire to make your pedaling more difficult or the disappointment in needing to make it easier. Instead, there is only one speed — the perfect speed. However, riding my beach cruiser that morning brought me no joy. The beach was empty, a dead seagull lay half-covered in sand, and the marine layer was so thick I couldn't even see the water. When I arrived at the Huntington Pier and hopped off my bike, Sean was nowhere to be found. I parked my bike at a rack decorated with the skeletal remains of bikes that resembled me — punctured, broken, and missing pieces. With my surfboard under my arm, I wandered to a bench overlooking the beach and took a seat to wait. As if it couldn't get any worse, rain began to fall, pattering on the bench and pooling in the sand at my feet.

I knew it wasn't the good kind of rain, it was the kind that only accompanies an ending. This rain was telling me to let go. "The Snowman Trek is over," I thought. "I'm finished with screenwriting and there is no such thing as blossom rain." As if to confirm those facts, the sky opened up and it poured. I was too depressed to seek shelter, so I just sat there on the bench in my wetsuit and let the rain wash away the parts of myself that no longer fit. Naturally, there was a lot to let go of — the misguided hopes, the futile efforts, and the deep disappointments of both blossom rain and my botched screenwriting career. It took me some time. When I spotted a gray stone beside my feet, I picked it up. "Good-bye screenwriting," I said, holding the rock up to my face as if addressing an enemy. "Good-bye Bhutan." Then, like the running pack animals in Bhutan, I reared back, yelled "Haw!" and threw my rock into the fog. No sooner had it landed with a splash than I was seized with a sweet and profound feeling of presence. I was having another "madeleine moment," only that time I was right back standing atop the Gangla Karchung pass, the gateway to Lunana. Suddenly in the swirling fog, I swear I smelled a flower fragrance and heard a continuous sound of cymbals and horns, and the flags on the Huntington Pier became dancing silk banners of Dharma. The best trips never end, they go on forever and expand and keep you healthy like a wonderful time-release vitamin of moments and views. While I'd left Bhutan, I knew Bhutan would never leave me — somewhere I'd always be laughing with the children of Lingshi and shooting the bow with that blessed boy from Chozo.

"Forget screenwriting," I said into the salty air. "I will write about the Snowman Trek."

I knew I couldn't truly capture the luminous beauty of Lunana in words, but I also knew I didn't have to — all my words had to do was point beyond themselves — to Thanza! — like scribbled hymns on the white prayer flag of a page. As the clouds began to break up, I knew I was done searching for my blessing because the search *was* my blessing. My salvation wasn't going to be found in the parking space of a single faith but would be a colorful quilt of different cultures, pieced together over a lifetime of traveling to new countries. I brought my hands together in *Namaste* and said a new prayer to Lunana, this one from the book of Psalms, "That I may publish with the voice of thanksgiving and tell of all thy wondrous works!" And then, as is her habit, Lunana immediately thanked me, this time with a brilliant sunbeam pouring down through the purple, punctured clouds.

I immediately leapt to my feet the way a congregation stands when the priest appears. As I stood there, gazing at the sun sending a thousand golden ships of itself through the falling rain, it dawned on me: "I'm standing beneath blossom rain." I felt a boundless joy and knew immediately what blossom rain meant, but in keeping with the Bhutanese tradition of brevity, all I can say is that to me it had something to do with saying "Yes!" to everything like Achula and receiving both the sun and rain of my life with open, equal, and ever-thankful arms. But don't take it from me, stand beneath blossom rain and you'll know too — all the gifts in your life will suddenly unwrap themselves — and you'll just know. But if you don't, simply start singing and dancing like the ladies in Laya, which is the highest wisdom anyway.

Just then, a man walked up with his Chihuahua. Both were sporting matching yellow raincoats.

"It's raining and sunny at the same time!" I exclaimed.

"So what?" he huffed with his head down.

"It's blossom rain!"

"Who cares?" he said, shuffling on.

As I watched him go — this man completely unaware of the requiem going on around him — I exhaled a wish for his future understanding and awakening. No, this man didn't care. But I knew others would, a whole happy assemblage of others, beginning with Sean, who I suddenly saw on his surfboard, far out in the silver sea. Seeing him sitting out there, waiting for waves in the calming ocean, I felt such pride. Like the Tibetan guru Marpa who sent Milarepa on his quest, Sean was the one who championed my trip to the Himalayas and told me to "live it all." And now there he was to welcome me on that immaculate morning of wet-sun surf. "That's my brother," I said proudly, "with his eyes always on the horizon!" I had a lot to tell him — about Bhutan, Gross National Happiness, and blossom rain. I grabbed my surfboard, yelled "Lha Gyalo," and splashed into the sea.

Blossom rain glitters above the Huntington Beach Pier. Photo by Kris Sundberg.

ACKNOWLEDGMENTS

I have been lucky enough to publish my first book with University of Nebraska Press and feel honored to have my book on its distinguished list. Robert Taylor, the sports acquisitions editor, has worked with me from the beginning and his support, guidance, encouragement, and friendship have been amazing. I also wish to thank Courtney Ochsner, the acquisitions assistant, for her help in assembling all the materials that go into a book. Yet more gratitude is owed to Joeth Zucco for her superb copyediting, Nathan Putens for the design, and Darrel Stevens for the cartography, as well as Cara Pesek and Acacia Gentrup for their tremendous publicity work.

I owe great thanks to professional photographer Peter McBride for letting me use his images of Bhutan, which really capture the beauty and heart of the country. Further thanks is owed to Ryan Goebel for his shot of prayer flags in the first chapter, Mukesh Gupta for permission to use Bhutan Travel's dragon graphic on the map, and Kris Sundberg for his beautiful photo of the Huntington Pier that ends the book.

Mike Leonard, Randy Sue Coburn, and Tony D'Souza, thank you for reading the book and providing advance promotional quotes. If you're unfamiliar with the work of these three immensely talented authors, I highly recommended their books.

I am very grateful for the excellent freelance writer and editor Kate Siber, who read a first draft of the manuscript and offered great encouragement, expertise, and insight. Not only did Kate's x-ray eyes find the bones of my memoir, but she also helped fix a few of the fractures.

Laura Slavik, thank you for giving me my first assignment and encouraging my foray into freelance journalism. I would also like to thank my mentor and dear friend Stewart Stern, as well as poet Sam Green and the English Department at Seattle University for providing great insight, support, and inspiration on the writing path. Family friend Bill Burrows educated me about the publishing business, and his tales about Sasquatch instilled in me a love of stories at a very early age.

I would like to send a big *kadriche* to everyone involved who helped in getting me to and through Bhutan over the years: Marie Brown, Joe Pilaar and Michael at Canadian Himalayan Expeditions, World Expeditions, Tenzin Phuentsho, Yeshi Tenzin, Sonam Dorji, Khandu Wangchuk, Ugyen Wangdi, Norbu, Sangey, Nema, Kesang Wangdi, the Tourism Council of Bhutan, Namsay Tours and Resort (Paro), and Yeedzin Guest House (Thimphu). And, of course, I can't forget my fellow "Normans" — Rob, Tom, Kira, Paul, Larry, Joe, Pete, Ryan, and Ingrid (our honorary member) — thanks for giving me the trip of a lifetime.

Thank you to all my amazing friends and to the extended Grange and Morse Families, which branch out like a flow chart of good, gracious and friendly people.

Last but not least, my biggest thanks goes to my immediate family: Mom, Dad, Kristine, Sean, Ola, Corie, nephews Bjorn, Hunter, Finn, Taylor, and my beautiful niece Lauren — words cannot express how much your support has meant to me over the years. Thank you for encouraging my dreams, for dreaming with me, and, of course, for all of our amazing family camping trips. I love you!

SELECTED BIBLIOGRAPHY

Two books were especially invaluable for my research and are highly recommended for any traveler venturing to the Dragon Kingdom: *Bhutan: A Trekker's Guide* (Cumbria, UK: Cicerone, 2005) is a wonderful book by Bart Jordans that is full of colorful route descriptions, local mountain lore, and detailed trekking maps. *Bhutan*, 2nd edition, (Victoria, Australia: Lonely Planet, 2002) by Stan Armington widens the lense beyond the trekking trail and offers an enlightening and entertaining look at Bhutan's many regions, as well as its unique history, religion, and culture.

Baker, Ian. *The Heart of the World: A Journey to Tibet's Lost Paradise*. New York: The Penguin Press, 2004.

Bell, Diane. "3 disasters now lead to thanks." *San Diego Tribune*. November 15, 2005.

Bernstein, Jeremy. *In the Himalayas: Journeys Through Nepal, Tibet and Bhutan*. New York: Lyons & Burford Publishers, 1996.

Buckley, Michael. *Shangri-La: A Travel Guide to the Himalayan Dream*. Guilford CT: The Globe Pequot Press Inc, 2008.

Campbell, Joseph. *The Hero with a Thousand Faces*. New York: Bollingen Foundation/Pantheon Books, 1949.

———. *The Masks of God: Occidental Mythology*. New York: Penguin, 1964.

———. *The Masks of God: Primitive Mythology*. New York: Penguin, 1970.

Cohen, Elizabeth. "CDC: Antidepressants most prescribed drugs in U.S." CNN. July 9, 2007. www.cnn.com.

Corbin, Amy. "Beyul of the Himalaya." *Sacred Land Film Project*. August 11, 2009. www.sacredland.org/beyul.

Crossette, Barbara. *So Close to Heaven: The Vanishing Buddhist Kingdoms of the Himalayas*. New York: Alfred A. Knopf, 1995.

Dondrup, Rinpoche Khamtrul Jamyang. "The Lama's heart advice which dispels all obstacles." *Rigdzin Publications*. www.khandro.net.

Dowman, Keith, and Sonam Paljor. *The Divine Madman: The Sublime Life and Songs of Drukpa Kunley*. Kathmandu, Nepal: Pilgrims Publishing, 2000.

Eliot, Sir Charles. *Japanese Buddhism*. London: Routledge & Kegan Paul, 1935.

Ganguly, Dilip. "Hikers in Nepal spared from deadly avalanche." *The Detroit News/Associated Press*. November 16, 1995.

Grewal, Bikram, and Otto Pfister. *Birds of the Himalayas*. London: New Holland Publishers, 2004.

Harding, Sarah. *The Life and Revelations of Pema Lingpa*. Ithaca NY: Snow Lion Publications, 2003.

Mierow, Dorothy, and Tirtha Bahadur Shrestha. *Himalayan Flowers and Trees*. Kathmandu, Nepal: Sahayogi Prakashan, 1987.

Pelden, Sonam. "Poverty alleviation: Key to 10th Plan." *Bhutan Observer*. April 19, 2008. www.bhutanobserver.bt.

Pommaret, Francoise. *Bhutan: Himalayan Mountain Kingdom*. New York: W. W. Norton & Company, Inc, 1998.

Rilke, Rainier Maria. *Letters to a Young Poet*. New York: W. W. Norton & Company, Inc, 1937.

Ronaldshay, Lord. *Lands of the Thunderbolt: Sikhim, Chumbi and Bhutan*. Berkeley CA: Snow Lion Graphics, 1987.

Smith, Huston. *The World's Religions: Our Great Wisdom Traditions*. New York: Harper Collins, 1955.

Stevenson, Richard. "Investigators Cite Bow Door in Estonian Ferry's Sinking." *The New York Times*. October 1, 1994.

Tsogyal, Yeshe. *The Lotus Born: The Life Story of Padmasambhava*. Hong Kong: Rangjung Yeshe Publications, 2004.

Vyas, Karishma. "The lure of TV irks Bhutan's authorities." Asia Media Archives. June 20, 2007. www.asiamedia.ucla.edu.

ARTICLES FROM *KUENSEL* NEWSPAPER
(www.kuenselonline.com)

Chiramal, John Michael. "Dragon Kingdom's Date with Democracy." April 22, 2008. Choden, Phuntsho. "Bhutan Bags 21 New Birds." April 29, 2008.

Choki, Kunzang. "Second Best but 'Scariest.'" March 16, 2009.

Dema, Kinga. "Bhutan Observes World Environment Day." June 6, 2007.
———. "Sakten's Unique Burial." August 22, 2007.
Dorji, Kinley. "Paro Airstrip Long Enough: Druk Air." January 3, 2005.
———. "A New Level of Friendship and Cooperation." July 19, 2008.
Kusago, Takayoshi, interview. "Good Social Relationship: A Key to Happiness." June 15, 2007.
Lamsang, Tenzing. "Medical Profession in Poor Health." 23 April 2008.
———. "Flying against the Wind." March 28, 2008.
———. "A Decade of Crime in Bhutan." April 12, 2008.
Layard, Lord Professor Richard, interview. "Can Development be Reconciled with Happiness?" April 24, 2007
Norbu, Passang. "From Phuentsholing to Paro, by Prostration." February 28, 2008.
Pelden, Sonam. "The Full Story behind the Half Kira." April 21, 2008.
———. "Bouncers for Discotheques." May 21, 2007.
———. "Police Crackdown on Chorten Robbers." May 26, 2008.
———. "Layaps Await Electricity." June 14, 2007.
Palden, Tshering. "Unemployment in the Era of Imported Labor." April 25, 2008
Penjore, Ugyen. "Glaciers Are Retreating." December 3, 2006.
———. "Forests Falling Fast." April 22, 2008.
———. "On the Winds of Prayer." May 4, 2008.
———. "Yartsa Goenbub Collection Legalised in Lunana." May 4, 2008
———. "The Power Tiller: An Agent of Change in Agriculture." February 22, 2008.
———. "Helping Difficult Schools." May 4, 2008.
Wangchuk, Samten. "Tourist Arrivals Continue to Increase." March 24, 2007.
———. "Financial Security for Happiness." June 6, 2007.
———. "More Tourists but Less Trekkers." January 25, 2008.
———. "Global Warming Guarantees GLOF." April 11, 2008.
———. "Not Too Late nor Early Either." April 26, 2008.
———. "Education Moves Forward." May 4, 2008.
———. "Cordyceps Harvesting Legalized." May 4, 2008.
Wangchuk, Tandin. "Book of Bhutanese Birds." April 28, 2008.
Wangdi, Kencho. "A Yak Herder and a Yak Song." December 29, 2003.
———. "Subtropical Royal Bengal Tigers Move above 3000m." September 8, 2004.

———. "Bhutanese Documentary Wins Award." May 31, 2005.
Wangdi, Nima. "Holy Water Gets Bottled." April 24, 2008.
Wangdi, Phuntsho. "A book on Bhutanese Cuisine." May 5, 2008.
Wangmo, Kinley. "Trekking: A Long Way to Go." April 17, 2006.
———. "Burden on Government after WFP Exit." July 11, 2007.
"India Commits Nu 100 billion to Bhutan." May 22, 2008.

WEB SITES

Tourism Council of Bhutan: www.tourism.gov.bt
RENEW: Respect, Educate, Nurture & Empower Women in Bhutan www.renew.org.bt
World Wildlife Fund: www.worldwildlife.org
World Food Program: www.wfp.org

IN THE OUTDOOR LIVES SERIES

Kayaking Alone
Nine Hundred Miles from Idaho's Mountains to the Pacific Ocean
by Mike Barenti

Bicycling beyond the Divide
Two Journeys into the West
by Daryl Farmer

The Hard Way Home
Alaska Stories of Adventure, Friendship, and the Hunt
by Steve Kahn

Pacific Lady
The First Woman to Sail Solo across the World's Largest Ocean
by Sharon Sites Adams with Karen J. Coates

Beneath Blossom Rain
Discovering Bhutan on the Toughest Trek in the World
by Kevin Grange

To order or obtain more information on these or other University of Nebraska Press titles, visit www.nebraskapress.unl.edu.